LIVING LANGUAGE®

COMPLETE
RUSSIAN
THE BASICS

Written by
Constantine Muravnik

Edited by
Suzanne McQuade

Published in the United States by Living Language, an imprint of Random House, Inc.

www.livinglanguage.com

Editor: Suzanne McQuade
Production Editor: Carolyn Roth
Production Manager: Tom Marshall
Interior Design: Sophie Chin

First Edition

ISBN: 978-1-4000-2421-6

Library of Congress Cataloging-in-Publication Data available upon request.

This book is available at special discounts for bulk purchases for sales promotions or premiums. Special editions, including personalized covers, excerpts of existing books, and corporate imprints, can be created in large quantities for special needs. For more information, write to Special Markets/Premium Sales, 1745 Broadway, MD 6-2, New York, New York 10019 or e-mail specialmarkets@randomhouse.com.

PRINTED IN THE UNITED STATES OF AMERICA

10 9 8 7 6 5 4 3 2 1

To my son, Matthew

ACKNOWLEDGMENTS

Thanks to the Living Language team: Tom Russell, Nicole Benhabib, Christopher Warnasch, Zviezdana Verzich, Suzanne McQuade, Shaina Malkin, Elham Shabahat, Sophie Chin, Denise De Gennaro, Linda Schmidt, Alison Skrabek, Lisbeth Dyer, Carolyn Roth, and Tom Marshall. Special thanks to Rita Safariants.

COURSE OUTLINE

Welcome to *Living Language Complete Russian: The Basics!* We know you're ready to jump right in and start learning Russian, but before you do, you may want to spend some time familiarizing yourself with the structure of this course. This segment will make it easier for you to find your way around, and will really help you get the most out of your studies.

UNITS AND LESSONS

Living Language Complete Russian: The Basics includes ten *Units,* each of which focuses on a certain practical topic, from talking about yourself and making introductions, to asking directions and going shopping. Each Unit is divided into *Lessons* that follow four simple steps:

1. *Words,* featuring the essential vocabulary you need to talk about the topic of the Unit;

2. *Phrases,* bringing words together into more complex structures and introducing a few idiomatic expressions;

3. *Sentences,* expanding on the vocabulary and phrases from previous lessons, using the grammar you've learned to form complete sentences; and

4. *Conversations,* highlighting how everything in the Unit works together in a realistic conversational dialogue.

The lessons each comprise the following sections:

WORD LIST/PHRASE LIST/SENTENCE GROUP/CONVERSATION
Every lesson begins with a list of words, phrases, or sentences, or a conversation. The grammar and exercises will be based on these components, so it's important to spend as much time reading and rereading these as possible before getting into the heart of the lesson.

NOTES

A brief section may appear after the list or dialogue to highlight any points of interest in the language or culture.

NUTS & BOLTS

This is the nitty-gritty of each lesson, where you'll learn the grammar of the language, the nuts and bolts that hold the pieces together. Pay close attention to these sections; this is where you'll get the most out of the language and learn what you need to know to become truly proficient in Russian.

PRACTICE

It's important to practice what you've learned on a regular basis. You'll find practice sections throughout each lesson; take your time to complete these exercises before moving on to the next section. How well you do on each practice will determine whether or not you need to review a particular grammar point before you move on.

TIP!

In order to enhance your experience, you'll find several tips for learning Russian throughout the course. This could be a tip on a specific grammar point, additional vocabulary related to the lesson topic, or a tip on language learning in general. For more practical advice, you can also refer to the *Language learning tips* section that follows this introduction.

CULTURE NOTES AND LANGUAGE LINKS

Becoming familiar with Russian culture is nearly as essential to learning Russian as its grammar. These sections allow you to get to know Russian culture better through facts about Russia and other bits of cultural information. You'll also find the links to various websites you can visit to learn more about a particular topic or custom, or to find a language learning tool that may come in handy.

DISCOVERY ACTIVITY

Discovery activities are another chance for you to put your new language to use. They will often require you to go out into the world and interact with other Russian speakers, or simply to use the resources around your own home to practice your Russian.

UNIT ESSENTIALS

Finally, each Unit ends with a review of the most essential vocabulary and phrases. Make sure you're familiar with these phrases, as well as their structure, before moving on to the next Unit.

The coursebook also contains *Grammar summary* and *Additional internet resources* sections to be used for further reference.

LEARNER'S DICTIONARY

If you've purchased this book as a part of the complete audio package, you also received a Learner's dictionary with more than 15,000 of the most frequently used Russian words, phrases, and idiomatic expressions. Use it as a reference any time you're at a loss for words in the exercises and discovery activities, or as a supplemental study aid. This dictionary is ideal for beginner or intermediate level learners of Russian.

AUDIO

This course works best when used along with the four audio CDs included in the complete course package. These CDs feature all the word lists, phrase lists, sentence lists, and dialogues from each unit, as well as key examples from the *Nuts & bolts* sections. This audio can be used along with the book, or on the go for hands-free practice.

And it's as easy as that! To get even more out of *Living Language Complete Russian: The Basics,* you may want to read the *Language learning tips* section that follows this introduction. If you're confident that you know all you need to know to get started and prefer to head straight to Unit 1, you can always come back to this section for tips on getting more out of your learning experience.

Good luck!

If you're not sure about the best way to learn a new language, take a moment to read this section. It includes lots of helpful tips and practical advice on studying languages in general, improving vocabulary, mastering grammar, using audio, doing exercises, and expanding your learning experience. All of this will make learning more effective and more fun.

GENERAL TIPS

Let's start with some general points to keep in mind about learning a new language.

1. FIND YOUR PACE

The most important thing to keep in mind is that you should always proceed at your own pace. Don't feel pressured into thinking that you only have one chance to digest information before moving on to new material. Read and listen to parts of lessons or entire lessons as many times as it takes to make you feel comfortable with the material. Regular repetition is the key to learning any new language, so don't be afraid to cover material again, and again, and again!

2. TAKE NOTES

Use a notebook or start a language journal so you can have something to take with you. Each lesson contains material that you'll learn much more quickly and effectively if you write it down, or rephrase it in your own words once you've understood it. That includes vocabulary, grammar points and examples, expressions from conversations, and anything else that you find noteworthy. Take your notes with you to review whenever you have time to kill—on the bus or train, waiting at the airport, while dinner is cooking, whatever suits you best. Remember: practice and lots of review are perfect tools when it comes to learning languages.

3. MAKE A REGULAR COMMITMENT

Make time for your new language. The concept of hours of exposure is a key to learning a language. When you expose yourself to a new language frequently, you'll pick it up more easily. On the other hand, the longer the intervals between your exposure to a language, the more you'll forget. It's best to set aside regular time for learning. Imagine that you're enrolled in a class that takes place at certain times during the week, and set that time aside. Or use your lunch break. It's better to spend less time several days a week than a large chunk of time once or twice a week. In other words, spending thirty or forty minutes on Monday, Tuesday, Wednesday, Friday, and Sunday will be better than spending two and a half or three hours just on Saturday.

4. DON'T HAVE UNREALISTIC EXPECTATIONS

Don't expect to start speaking a new language as if it were your native language. It's certainly possible for adults to learn new languages with amazing fluency, but that's not a realistic immediate goal for most people. Instead, make a commitment to become functional in a new language, and start to set small goals: getting by in most daily activities, talking about yourself and asking about others, following TV and movies, reading a newspaper, expressing your ideas in basic language, and learning creative strategies for getting the most out of the language you know. Functional doesn't mean perfectly fluent, but it's a great accomplishment!

5. DON'T GET HUNG UP ON PRONUNCIATION

Losing the accent is one of the most challenging parts of learning a language. If you think about celebrities, scientists, or political figures whose native language isn't English, they probably have a pretty recognizable accent. But that hasn't kept them from becoming celebrities, scientists, or political figures. Very young children are able to learn the sounds of any language in the world, and they can reproduce them perfectly. That early ability is part of the process of learning a native language. In an adult, or even in an older child, this ability is reduced, so if you agonize over sounding like a native speaker in your new language, you're just setting yourself up for disappointment. That's not to say that you can't learn pronunciation well. Even adults can get pretty far through mimicking the sounds that they hear. So, listen carefully to the audio several times. Listening is a very important part of the learning process: you can reproduce the sound only after you learn to distinguish it. Then mimic what you hear. Don't be afraid of sounding strange at first. Just keep at it, and soon enough you'll develop good pronunciation.

6. DON'T BE SHY
Learning a new language inevitably involves speaking out loud, and making mistakes before you get better. Don't be afraid of sounding strange, or awkward, or silly. You won't; you'll impress people with your attempts. The more you speak, and the more you interact, the faster you'll learn to correct the mistakes you do make.

TIPS ON LEARNING VOCABULARY
You obviously need to learn new words in order to speak a new language. Even though this step may seem straightforward compared with learning how to actually put these words together in sentences, it's really not as simple as it appears. Memorizing words is difficult, even to remember them just for a short term is a challenge. But long term memorization takes a lot of practice and repetition. You won't learn vocabulary simply by reading through the vocabulary lists once or twice. You need to practice.

There are a few different ways to store a word in your memory, and some methods may work better for you than others. The best thing to do is to try a few different techniques until you feel that one is right for you. Here are a few suggestions and pointers:

I. AUDIO REPETITION
Fix your eye on the written form of a word, and listen to the audio several times. Remind yourself of the English translation as you do this.

2. SPOKEN REPETITION

Say a word several times aloud, keeping your eye on the written word as you hear yourself speak it. It's not a race—don't rush to blurt out the word over and over again so fast that you're distorting its pronunciation. Just repeat it, slowly and naturally, being careful to pronounce it as well as you can. And run your eye over the shape of the word each time you say it. You'll be stimulating two of your senses at once—hearing and sight—so you'll double the impact on your memory.

3. WRITTEN REPETITION

Write a word over and over again across a page, speaking it slowly and carefully each time you write it. Don't be afraid to fill up entire sheets of paper with your new vocabulary words.

4. FLASH CARDS

They may seem elementary, but they're effective. Cut out small pieces of paper (no need to spend a lot of money on index cards) and write the English word on one side and the new word on the other. Just this act alone will put a few words in your mind. Then read through your deck of cards. It's easier to go first from the target (new) language into English. Turn the target language side faceup, read each card, and guess at its meaning. Once you've guessed, turn the card over to see if you're right. If you are, set the card aside in your learned pile. If you're wrong, repeat the word and its meaning and then put it at the bottom of your "to learn" pile. Continue through until you've moved all of the cards into your learned pile.

Once you've completed the whole deck from your target language into English, turn the deck over and try to go from English into your target language. You'll see that this is harder, but also a better test of whether or not you've really mastered a word.

5. MNEMONICS

A mnemonic is a device or a trick to trigger your memory, like "King Phillip Came Over From Great Spain," which you may have learned in high school biology to remember that species are classified into kingdom, phylum, class, order, family, genus, and species. They work well for vocabulary, too. When you hear and read a new word, look to see if it sounds like anything familiar—a place, a name, a nonsense phrase. Then form an image of that place or person or even nonsense scenario in your head. Imagine it as you say and read the new word. Remember that the more sense triggers you have—hearing, reading, writing, speaking, picturing a crazy image—the better you'll remember.

6. Groups

Vocabulary should be learned in small and logically connected groups whenever possible. Most of the vocabulary lists in this course are already organized this way. Don't try to tackle a whole list at once. Choose your method—repeating a word out loud, writing it across a page, etc.—and practice it with a small group of words.

7. Practice

Don't just learn a word out of context and leave it hanging there. Go back and practice it in the context provided in this course. If the word appears in a conversation, read it in the full sentence and call to mind an image of that sentence. If possible, substitute other vocabulary words into the same sentence structure ("John goes to the *library*" instead of "John goes to the *store*"). As you advance through the course, try writing your own simple examples of words in context.

8. Come back to it

This is the key to learning vocabulary—not just holding it temporarily in your short term memory, but making it stick in your long term memory. Go back over old lists, old decks of flash cards you made, or old example sentences. Listen to vocabulary audio from previous lessons. Pull up crazy mnemonic devices you created at some point earlier in your studies. And always be on the lookout for old words appearing again throughout the course.

TIPS ON USING AUDIO

The audio in this course doesn't only let you hear how native speakers pronounce the words you're learning, but it also serves as a second kind of input to your learning experience. The printed words serve as visual input, and the audio serves as *auditory* input. There are a few different strategies that you can use to get the most out of the audio. First, use the audio while you're looking at a word or a sentence. Listen to it a few times along with the visual support. Then, look away and just listen to the audio. You can also use the audio from previously studied lessons as a way to review. Put the audio on your computer or an MP3 player and take it along with you in your car, on the train, while you walk, while you jog, or anywhere you have free time to listen to it. Remember that the more exposure and contact you have with your target language, the better you'll learn.

TIPS ON USING CONVERSATIONS

The conversations, or dialogues, in this book are a great way to see language in action, as it's really used by people in realistic situations. To get the most out of a dialogue, think of it as a cycle rather than a linear passage. First read through the dialogue once in the target language to get the gist. Don't agonize over the details just yet. Then, go back and read through it a second time, but focus on individual sentences. Look for new words or new constructions. Challenge yourself to figure out what they mean by the context of the dialogue. After all, that's something you'll be doing a lot of in the real world, so it's a good skill to develop! Once you've worked out the details, read the dialogue again from start to finish. Now that you're very familiar with the dialogue, turn on the audio and listen to it as you read. Don't try to repeat yet; just listen and read along. This will build your listening comprehension. Then, go back and listen again, but this time pause to repeat the phrases or sentences that you're hearing and reading. This will build your spoken proficiency and pronunciation. Now listen again without the aid of the printed dialogue. By now you'll know many of the lines inside out, and any new vocabulary or constructions will be very familiar.

TIPS ON DOING EXERCISES

The exercises are meant to give you a chance to practice the vocabulary and structures that you learn in each lesson, and of course to test yourself on retention. Take the time to write out the entire sentences to get the most out of the practice. Don't limit yourself to just reading and writing. Read the sentences and answers aloud, so you'll also be practicing pronunciation and spoken proficiency. As you gain more confidence, try to adapt the practice sentences by substituting different vocabulary or grammatical constructions, too. Be creative, and push the practices as far as you can to get the most out of them.

TIPS ON LEARNING GRAMMAR

Each grammar point is designed to be as small and digestible as possible, while at the same time complete enough to teach you what you need to know. The explanations are intended to be simple and straightforward, and one of the best things you can do is to take notes on each grammar section, putting the explanations into your own words, and then copying the example sentences or tables slowly and carefully. This will do two things. It will give you a nice clear notebook that you can take with you, so you can review and practice, and it will also force you to take enough time with each section, so that it's really driven home. Of course, a lot of grammar is memorization—verb endings, irregular forms, pronouns, and so on. So a lot of the vocabulary learning tips will come in handy for learning grammar as well.

1. AUDIO REPETITION

Listen to the audio several times while you're looking at the words or sentences. For example, for a verb conjugation, listen to all of the forms several times, reading along to activate your visual memory as well.

2. SPOKEN REPETITION

Listen to the audio and repeat several times for practice. For example, to learn the conjugation of an irregular verb, repeat all of the forms of the verb until you're able to produce them without looking at the screen. It's a little bit like memorizing lines for a play—practice until you can make it sound natural. Practice the example sentences that way as well, focusing, of course, on the grammar section at hand.

3. WRITTEN REPETITION
Write the new forms again and again, saying them slowly and carefully as well. Do this until you're able to produce all of the forms without any help.

4. FLASH CARDS
Copy the grammar point, whether it's a list of pronouns, a conjugation, or a list of irregular forms, on a flashcard. Stick the cards in your pocket so you can practice them when you have time to kill. Glance over the cards, saying the forms to yourself several times, and when you're ready to test yourself, flip the card over and see if you can produce all of the information.

5. GRAMMAR IN THE WILD
Do you want to see an amazing number of example sentences that use some particular grammatical form? Well, just type that form into a search engine. Pick a few of the examples you find at random, and copy them down into your notebook or language journal. Pick them apart, look up words you don't know, and try to figure out the other grammatical constructions. You may not get everything 100% correct, but you'll definitely learn and practice in the process.

6. COME BACK TO IT
Just like vocabulary, grammar is best learned through repetition and review. Go back over your notes, go back to previous lessons and read over the grammar sections, listen to the audio, or check out the relevant section in the grammar summary. Even after you've completed lessons, it's never a bad idea to go back and keep the old grammar fresh.

HOW TO EXPAND YOUR LEARNING EXPERIENCE

Your experience with your new language should not be limited to this course alone. Like anything, learning a language will be more enjoyable if you're able to make it a part of your life in some way. And you'd be surprised to know how easily you can do it these days!

1. USE THE INTERNET

The internet is an absolutely amazing resource for people learning new languages. You're never more than a few clicks away from online newspapers, magazines, reference material, cultural sites, travel and tourism sites, images, sounds, and so much more. Develop your own list of favorite sites that match your needs and interests—business, cooking, fashion, film, kayaking, rock climbing, or . . . well, you get the picture. Use search engines creatively to find examples of vocabulary or grammar "in the wild." Find a favorite blog or periodical and take the time to work your way through an article or entry. Think of what you use the internet for in English, and look for similar sites in your target language.

2. CHECK OUT COMMUNITY RESOURCES

Depending on where you live, there may be plenty of practice opportunities in your own community. There may be a cultural organization or social club where people meet. There may be a local college or university with a department that hosts cultural events such as films or discussion groups. There may be a restaurant where you can go for a good meal and a chance to practice a bit of your target language. Of course, you can find a lot of this information online, and there are sites that allow groups of people to get organized and meet to pursue their interests.

3. FOREIGN FILMS

Films are a wonderful way to practice hearing and understanding a new language. With English subtitles, pause, and rewind, they're practically really long dialogues with pictures, not to mention the cultural insight and experience they provide! And nowadays it's simple to rent foreign DVDs online or even access films online. So, if you're starting to learn a new language today, go online and rent yourself some movies that you can watch over the next few weeks or months.

4. Music
Even if you have a horrible singing voice, music is a great way to learn new vocabulary. After hearing a song just a few times, the lyrics somehow manage to plant themselves in the mind. And with the internet, it's often very easy to find the entire lyric sheet for a song online, print it out, and have it ready for whenever you're alone and feel like singing.

5. Television
If you have access to television programming in the language you're studying, including, of course, anything you can find on the internet, take advantage of that! You'll most likely hear very natural and colloquial language, including idiomatic expressions and rapid speech, all of which will be a healthy challenge for your comprehension skills. But the visual cues, including body language and gestures, will help. Plus, you'll get to see how the language interacts with the culture, which is also a very important part of learning a language.

6. Food
A great way to learn a language is through the cuisine. What could be better than going out and trying new dishes at a restaurant with the intention of practicing your newly acquired language? Go to a restaurant, and if the names of the dishes are printed in the target language, try to decipher them. Then try to order in the target language, provided, of course, that your server speaks the language! At the very least, you'll learn a few new vocabulary items, not to mention sample some wonderful new food.

1. THE CYRILLIC ALPHABET

The first thing that often intimidates anyone learning Russian is the alphabet.

Russian uses the Cyrillic alphabet, which is derived from the Greek, whereas English is written with the Latin alphabet. There are a few letters that are shared by both languages, and some letters may be familiar to you from basic mathematics and the names of college fraternities and sororities. As you use this book, you will quickly become familiar with the different letters and sounds, and soon you'll be able to recognize them instantly, reducing the intimidation factor.

Russian letter	Script	Name
Аа	*А а*	*ah*
Бб	*Б б*	*beh*
Вв	*В в*	*veh*
Гг	*Т г*	*geh*
Дд	*Д д*	*deh*
Ее	*Є е*	*yeh*
Ёё	*Ё ё*	*yoh*
Жж	*Ж ж*	*zheh*
Зз	*З з*	*zeh*
Ии	*И и*	*ee*
Йй	*Й й*	*ee kratkoye*

Russian letter	Script	Name
Кк	*К к*	*kah*
Лл	*Л л*	*ell*
Мм	*М м*	*em*
Нн	*Н н*	*en*
Оо	*О о*	*oh*
Пп	*П п*	*peh*
Рр	*Р р*	*err*
Сс	*С с*	*ess*
Тт	*Т т*	*teh*
Уу	*У у*	*ooh*
Фф	*Ф ф*	*eff*
Хх	*Х х*	*khah*
Цц	*Ц ц*	*tseh*
Чч	*Ч ч*	*cheh*
Шш	*Ш ш*	*shah*
Щщ	*Щ щ*	*shchah*
Ыы	*Ы ы*	*ih*
Ъь	*ъ ъ*	*hard sign*
Ьъ	*ь ь*	*soft sign*
Ээ	*Э э*	*eh*

Russian letter	Script	Name
Юю	*Ю* *ю*	*yoo*
Яя	*Я* *я*	*yah*

2. COGNATES

Now that you've learned the alphabet, let's begin to see how the sounds of Russian work by looking at some cognates. These are words that are similar in both Russian and English and descended from the same root.

абсолютизм	*absolutism*
авангард	*avant-garde*
авиация	*aviation*
автобиография	*autobiography*
атмосфера	*atmosphere*
бактериология	*bacteriology*
баллада	*ballad*
барометр	*barometer*
батарея	*battery*
библиография	*bibliography*
вакансия	*vacancy*
вандализм	*vandalism*
витамины	*vitamins*
гарантия	*guarantee*
генератор	*generator*
геология	*geology*
гладиатор	*gladiator*
дарвинизм	*Darwinism*
декларация	*declaration*
демократия	*democracy*
диагноз	*diagnosis*

диалект	*dialect*
диета	*diet*
дисциплина	*discipline*
жонглёр	*juggler*
зигзаг	*zigzag*
игнорировать	*ignore*
идея	*idea*
имитация	*imitation*
индивидуализм	*individualism*
инспектор	*inspector*
инструктор	*instructor*
инструмент	*instrument*
калейдоскоп	*kaleidoscope*
карикатура	*caricature*
композитор	*composer*
кооперация	*cooperation*
корреспондент	*correspondent*
критика	*criticism*
лабиринт	*labyrinth*
лаборатория	*laboratory*
либерализм	*liberalism*
литература	*literature*
марксизм	*Marxism*
медицина	*medicine*
методика	*method*
микроскоп	*microscope*
негатив	*negative*
обсерватория	*observatory*
опера	*opera*
операция	*operation*
оппозиция	*opposition*
оптимист	*optimist*

павильон	*pavilion*
панорама	*panorama*
паразит	*parasite*
перспектива	*perspective*
пикник	*picnic*
пирамида	*pyramid*
популярный	*popular*
привилегия	*privilege*
прогресс	*progress*
радиатор	*radiator*
ракета	*rocket*
резервуар	*reservoir*
репутация	*reputation*
рефлектор	*reflector*
статистика	*statistics*
тактика	*tactics*
телескоп	*telescope*
теория	*theory*
терминология	*terminology*
увертюра	*overture*
университет	*university*
эволюция	*evolution*

It may also help to look at some geographical names in Russian to get a better idea of how the language works.

Австралия	*Australia*
Австрия	*Austria*
Азия	*Asia*
Алжир	*Algeria*
Америка	*America*
Англия	*England*
Архангельск	*Arkhangelsk*

Аргентина	*Argentina*
Байкал	*Baikal (Lake)*
Баку	*Baku*
Бельгия	*Belgium*
Болгария	*Bulgaria*
Бразилия	*Brazil*
Вашингтон	*Washington*
Варшава	*Warsaw*
Великобритания	*Great Britain*
Владивосток	*Vladivostok*
Волга	*Volga*
Германия	*Germany*
Греция	*Greece*
Грузия	*Georgia*
Дания	*Denmark*
Дунай	*Danube*
Днепр	*Dnieper*
Европа	*Europe*
Египет	*Egypt*
Индия	*India*
Испания	*Spain*
Ирландия	*Ireland*
Иртыш	*Irtysh (River)*
Израиль	*Israel*
Италия	*Italy*
Кавказ	*Caucasus*
Калифорния	*California*
Канада	*Canada*
Киев	*Kiev*
Китай	*China*
Корея	*Korea*
Крым	*Crimea*

Люксембург	*Luxembourg*
Марокко	*Morocco*
Македония	*Macedonia*
Мексика	*Mexico*
Москва	*Moscow*
Нева	*Neva*
Нидерланды	*Netherlands*
Новая Зеландия	*New Zealand*
Норвегия	*Norway*
Одесса	*Odessa*
Ока	*Oka*
Псков	*Pskov*
Португалия	*Portugal*
Россия	*Russia*
Рязань	*Ryazan*
Самара	*Samara*
Севастополь	*Sevastopol*
Таиланд	*Thailand*
Турция	*Turkey*
Шотландия	*Scotland*
Швейцария	*Switzerland*
Швеция	*Sweden*
Япония	*Japan*

3. PRONUNCIATION

Russian pronunciation will be easy once you learn the rules of pronunciation and reading, which hold true with very few exceptions. It is just as easy to say *ah* as it is to say *oh*, or to say *vast* as it is to say *fast*. But if you pronounce *f* where it should be *v*, or *oh* where it should be *ah*, or *eh* where it should be *ee*, you will speak with a foreign accent. Knowing these rules will help you to have a sound picture of the word you are learning and will help you to recognize it when it is spoken by the native; you want to understand as well as to speak!

Russian is not phonetic. You don't read it the way it is spelled. Many native Russians think they do; most of them are sure they do—they are wrong! Learn word units. Always try to pronounce pronouns, prepositions, and adjectives together with the words they modify.

Russian punctuation varies little from that of English in the use of the semicolon, colon, exclamation point, question mark, and period. However, the use of the comma is determined by concrete grammatical rules and generally does not, as in English, indicate a pause in speech.

Remember that the Russian language is not phonetic. Most letters represent several sounds. It is important to keep this in mind at the beginning of your study and to acquire the proper speech habits at the very start.

The Russian language has twenty consonant letters representing thirty-five consonant sounds, because fifteen of these twenty letters can represent either soft or hard (palatalized or nonpalatalized) sounds. Three are hard only; two are soft only. There are ten vowels and one semi-vowel.

Softness, or palatalization, of consonants is indicated by the vowels: **е, ё, и, ю, я,** and **ь** (soft sign). When a consonant is followed by one of these vowels, the consonant is palatalized—i.e., it is soft. In palatalization, the articulation of a consonant in its alphabet (nonpalatalized) form is altered in a specific way: the place and manner of articulation remain the same, but the middle part of the speaker's tongue moves up to the palate to produce palatalization. Palatalization in the Russian language has particular significance and should therefore be carefully studied, as the meaning of a word can be changed through palatalization.

Vowels

Now that you've looked at the difference between Russian and English on a broad scale, let's get down to the specifics by looking at individual sounds, starting with Russian vowels.

Letter	Pronunciation	Examples
Аа	when stressed, like *a* in *father*	**армия** *(army)*, **лампа** *(lamp)*, **мало** *(little)*
	when unstressed, like *a* in *father*, but shorter	**командир** *(commander)*, **кадет** *(cadet)*
	otherwise, like the *a* in *sofa*	**карандаш** *(pencil)*, **магазин** *(store)*, **авангард** *(avant-garde)*
Оо	when stressed, like the *o* in *gone*	**он** *(he)*, **добрый** *(kind)*
	when unstressed, either in first place before the stressed syllable or used initially, like the *o* in *sob*	**Борис** *(Boris)*, **она** *(she)*, **оно** *(it)*, **отвечать** *(to answer)*
	otherwise, like the *a* in *sofa*	**хорошо** *(well)*, **плохо** *(badly)*, **молоко** *(milk)*

Letter	Pronunciation	Examples
Уу	like the *oo* in *food*	**стул** *(chair)*, **суп** *(soup)*, **утро** *(morning)*, **туда** *(there [in that direction])*, **урок** *(lesson)*, **узнавать** *(to find out)*, **учитель** *(teacher)*
ы	similar to the *i* in *sit*	**ты** *(you)*, **мы** *(we)*, **вы** *(pl., you)*, **мыло** *(soap)*, **малы** *(short, small)*, **столы** *(tables)*, **была** *(she was)*
Ээ	like the *e* in *echo*	**это** *(this)*, **эти** *(these)*, **поэт** *(poet)*, **этап** *(period, stage)*

The function of the vowels **е, ё, и, ю, я,** which are preceded by a glide (the sound similar to the final sound in the English word *may),* is the palatalization of the previous consonant, to which they lose the above-mentioned glide. However, when they follow a vowel or soft or hard signs, or when they appear initially, they are pronounced as in the alphabet—i.e., with the initial glide.

Letter	Pronunciation	Examples
Ее	when stressed, like the *ye* in *yet;* it always palatalizes the preceding consonant, except the letters **ж, ц,** and **ш**	**нет** *(no)*, **Вера** *(Vera, faith)*, **сесть** *(to sit down)*
	when unstressed, like the *i* in *sit*	**всегда** *(always)*, **сестра** *(sister)*, **жена** *(wife)*
	initially, or after another vowel, with the glide stressed, like *ye* in *yet*, or unstressed, like *ye*	**ей** *(to her)*, **её** *(her)*, **поездка** *(trip)*
Ёё	like the *yo* in *yoke;* always palatalizes the preceding consonant and is always stressed	**мёд** *(honey)*, **тётя** *(aunt)*, **ёлка** *(fir tree)*, **моё** *(my [n.])*, **ещё** *(yet, still)*
Ии	like *ee* in *beet;* always palatalizes the preceding consonant	**сила** *(strength)*, **Лиза** *(Liza)*, **никогда** *(never)*, **иногда** *(sometimes)*
	after the letters **ж, ц,** and **ш**, like the Russian sound **ы**	**шина** *(tire)*, **жить** *(live)*
Йй	like the *y* in *boy*	**мой** *(my)*, **пойти** *(to go)*, **спокойно** *(quietly)*, **Нью-Йорк** *(New York)*

Letter	Pronunciation	Examples
Юю	in the middle of a word, like *oo* in *food;* it always palatalizes the preceding consonant	**Люба** *(Lyuba),* **люблю** *(I love),* **любить** *(to love)*
	when used initially, it retains its glide and is pronounced like *you*	**юбка** *(skirt),* **юбилей** *(jubilee)*
Яя	when stressed in the middle of the word, like *ya* in *yacht;* it always palatalizes the preceding consonant	**мясо** *(meat),* **маяк** *(lighthouse)*
	when unstressed, it is pronounced either like the short *i* of *sit* or like the neutral *a* of *sofa* if it is the last letter of a word; it always palatalizes the preceding consonant	**тётя** *(aunt),* **десять** *(ten)*
	when stressed, like the *ya* in *yacht;* when used initially, it retains its glide	**яблоко** *(apple),* **январь** *(January)*
	when unstressed, like the *yi* in *yippy*	**язык** *(language, tongue)*

Letter	Pronunciation	Examples
ь	the soft sign; it palatalizes the preceding consonant, allowing the following vowel to retain its glide, and indicates that the preceding consonant is soft when written at the end of a word	**пьеса** (*play*), **пьяный** (*drunk*), **свинья** (*pig*)
ъ	the hard sign; it indicates that the preceding consonant remains hard and that the following vowel retains its glide	**объём** (*volume*), **объяснять** (*explain*)

CONSONANTS

Russian consonants, like those in every language, may be voiced or voiceless. The distinction between voiced and voiceless consonants is based on one aspect of otherwise identical articulation: in voiced consonants, the vocal cords are involved in articulation, while in voiceless consonants, they are not.

б в г д ж з	(voiced)	*b v g d zh z*
п ф к т ш с	(voiceless)	*p f k t sh s*

When two consonants are pronounced together, both must be either voiced or voiceless. In Russian, the second one always remains as it is and the first one changes accordingly.

всё, все, вчера	в = *v*, pronounced *f*
сделать, сдать	с = *s*, pronounced *z*

The preposition в *(in)* is very often pronounced *f.* **В школе** *(in school)* is pronounced *f shkoh-leh.*

Russian consonants can also be soft or hard, i.e., palatalized or nonpalatalized, when followed by the letters **е, ё, и, ю, я,** or **ь.** Exceptions are the consonants **ж, ш,** and **ц,** which are always hard.

These rules seem complicated, but it is much easier to learn them in the beginning and to start speaking correctly than it is to try to correct erroneous pronunciation later on. Listen carefully and try to hear the aforementioned differences.

Letter	Pronunciation	Examples
Бб	like *b* in *bread*	**брат** *(brother),* **бумага** *(paper),* **багаж** *(baggage)*
	palatalized	**белый** *(white),* **бинокль** *(binoculars)*
	at the end of a word or before a voiceless consonant, like the *p* in *hip*	**юбка** *(skirt),* **зуб** *(tooth),* **хлеб** *(bread)*
	voiceless palatalized	**дробь** *(buckshot),* **зыбь** *(ripple)*

Letter	Pronunciation	Examples
Вв	like the *v* in *very*	**ваш** *(your)*, **вот** *(here)*, **вода** *(water)*
	palatalized	**вера** *(faith)*, **конверт** *(envelope)*, **весь** *(all)*
	at the end of a word or before a voiceless consonant, like the *f* in *half*	**Киев** *(Kiev)*, **в школе** *(in school)*, **вчера** *(yesterday)*, **кров** *(shelter)*
	voiceless palatalized	**кровь** *(blood)*
Гг	like the *g* in *good*	**газета** *(newspaper)*, **где** *(where)*, **гармония** *(harmony)*
	palatalized	**гитара** *(guitar)*, **геометрия** *(geometry)*
	before **к**, like the Russian **x** (see below)	**легко** *(lightly, easily)*, **мягко** *(softly)*
	between **е** and **о**, like the *v* in *victor*	**его** *(his)*, **ничего** *(nothing)*, **сегодня** *(today)*
	at the end of a word, voiceless, like the *k* in *rock*	**рог** *(horn)*, **четверг** *(Thursday)*
Дд	like the *d* in *door*	**дом** *(house)*, **родной** *(relatives)*

Letter	Pronunciation	Examples
	palatalized	дерево *(tree)*, один *(one)*
	at the end of a word or before a voiceless consonant, like the *t* in *take*	обед *(dinner)*, подкова *(horseshoe)*, подпись *(signature)*
	voiceless palatalized	грудь *(chest, breast)*
Жж	like *s* in *measure*	жар *(heat)*, жена *(wife)*, жить *(to live)*, пожар *(fire)*
	at the end of a word or before a voiceless consonant, like the *sh* in *shake*	ложка *(spoon)*, муж *(husband)*
Зз	like the *z* in *zebra*	здание *(building)*, знать *(to know)*
	palatalized	зелёный *(green)*, зима *(winter)*
	at the end of a word or before a voiceless consonant, like the *s* in *sit*	ползти *(crawl)*, воз *(cart)*
Кк	like the *k* in *kept*	книга *(book)*, класс *(class)*, карандаш *(pencil)*
	palatalized	кепка *(cap)*, керосин *(kerosene)*, Киев *(Kiev)*, кино *(movie)*

Letter	Pronunciation	Examples
	before a voiced consonant, voiced, like the *g* in *good*	**вокзал** *(railroad station)*, **экзамен** *(examination)*, **к брату** *(to the brother)*
Лл	like the *l* in *look*	**ложка** *(spoon)*, **лампа** *(lamp)*, **мел** *(chalk)*
	palatalized, a bit like the *ll* in *million*	**любовь** *(love)*, **лёгкий** *(light)*, **мель** *(shoal)*, **боль** *(pain)*
Мм	like the *m* in *man*	**мама** *(mama)*, **магнит** *(magnet)*, **дом** *(house)*, **паром** *(ferry)*
	palatalized	**мясо** *(meat)*, **мина** *(mine)*
Нн	like the *n* in *noon*	**нос** *(nose)*, **нож** *(knife)*, **балкон** *(balcony)*
	palatalized	**небо** *(sky)*, **неделя** *(week)*, **няня** *(nurse)*, **конь** *(horse)*
Пп	palatalized	**первый** *(first)*, **письмо** *(letter)*, **цепь** *(chain)*

Letter	Pronunciation	Examples
Рр	like the *r* in *root*	**русский** (*Russian*), **парад** (*parade*), **подарок** (*gift*), **рука** (*hand*)
	palatalized	**рис** (*rice*), **порядок** (*order*), **дверь** (*door*)
Сс	like the *s* in *see*	**сон** (*dream*), **суп** (*soup*), **свет** (*light*), **мясо** (*meat*), **масло** (*butter*)
	palatalized	**север** (*north*), **село** (*village*), **весь** (*all*)
	before a voiced consonant, voiced, like the *z* in *zebra*	**сделать** (*to do*), **сгореть** (*to burn down*)
Тт	like the *t* in *table*	**табак** (*tobacco*), **тот** (*that*), **стол** (*table*), **тогда** (*then*)
	palatalized	**тень** (*shade*), **стена** (*wall*)
	before a voiced consonant, like the *d* in *dark*	**отдать** (*to give away*), **отгадать** (*to guess*)
Фф	like the *f* in *friend*	**фабрика** (*factory*), **Франция** (*France*), **фарфор** (*porcelain*)

Letter	Pronunciation	Examples
	palatalized	**афиша** (*poster*)
	before a voiced consonant, like the *v* in *victor*	**афганец** (*Afghan*)
Хх	like the *ch* in *loch*	**тихо** (*quietly*), **хорошо** (*well*), **техника** (*technique*), **блоха** (*flea*)
	palatalized	**хина** (*quinine*), **химия** (*chemistry*)
Цц	like the *ts* in *gets*	**цветок** (*flower*), **цепь** (*chain*), **цирк** (*circus*), **пациент** (*patient* [*n.*]), **перец** (*pepper*)
Чч	before a vowel, like the *ch* in *church*	**чай** (*tea*), **час** (*hour*), **часто** (*often*), **чемодан** (*suitcase*)
	exceptionally, like the *sh* in *shall*	**что** (*what*), **конечно** (*of course*)
Шш	like the *sh* in *shall*	**шаг за шагом** (*step after step*), **шахматы** (*chess*), **шина** (*tire*), **шёлк** (*silk*), **шерсть** (*wool*), **ты говоришь** (*you speak (sing.)*)

Letter	Pronunciation	Examples
Щщ	like the *shch* in fre*sh* *ch*eese	**щека** *(cheek),* **щётка** *(brush),* **помощь** *(help),* **посещение** *(visit)*

4. SPELLING RULES

All Russian endings fall under two general categories: hard and soft. Hard endings follow hard consonants and soft endings follow soft consonants to maintain vowel correspondence.

Vowels in hard endings	Vowels in soft endings
а	я
о	ё
у	ю
ы	и
э	е

However, an additional complication interferes with this fairly straightforward system and overrides it. This complication is usually referred to as the spelling rule. The spelling rule concerns only eight consonants: four hushers (because they produce a hushing sound)—**ж, ш, щ, ч;** three gutturals (because they are pronounced in the back of your mouth)—**г, к, х;** and the letter **ц.**

All gutturals and all hushers must be followed by the letters: **а, у,** and **и** (and never by **я, ю, ы**)!

All hushers and **ц** must be followed by either a stressed **о** or an unstressed **е**!

Memorize this spelling rule and always keep it in mind along with the above chart! They will take the mystery out of the

Russian endings and will reduce in half what you otherwise would have to memorize mechanically.

Keep in mind the following points:

- **жо** and **жё**, and **цэ** and **це**, are pronounced alike.

- **цы** and **ци**, **шо** and **шё**, and the letters **ж**, **ц**, and **ш** are always hard.

- **чо** and **чё**, **що** and **щё**, and the letters **ч** and **щ** are always soft.

Read these rules over and over again. Listen to the recordings several times. You have learned them not when you have read and understood the rules, but when you can remember and repeat the sounds and words correctly without looking at the book. Master these, and you will speak Russian well.

Five fundamental rules

1. Remember which syllable is stressed.

2. Remember that unstressed **o** is pronounced *ah* in prestressed positions and as *uh* in unstressed positions.

3. Remember that when two consonants are next to each other, the first changes according to the second.

4. Remember that unstressed **e** is pronounced *ih*.

5. Remember that the letters **е, ё, и, ю, я,** and **ь** palatalize the preceding consonant, unless it has no palatalized counterpart.

Unit 1

Talking about yourself and making introductions

Здравствуйте! In Unit 1, you will begin by learning how to introduce yourself and others and how to say such useful things as where you are from, as well as how to ask other people for basic information about themselves. Naturally, you will learn greetings and other essential courtesy expressions, along with other important conversational phrases.

——————————— Lesson 1 (Words) ———————————

WORD LIST 1

здравствуйте *(pl./sg. fml.)*	*hello*
здравствуй *(sg. infml.)*	*hello*
господин	*Mr.*
госпожа	*Ms., Mrs.*
Очень приятно!	*Nice to meet you! (lit., Very pleasant!)*
бизнесмен	*businessman/businesswoman*
бизнесменка, бизнесвумен	*businesswoman (less common)*
журналист	*journalist (male)*
журналистка	*journalist (female)*
американец	*American (male)*
американка	*American (female)*
Добро пожаловать!	*Welcome! (to a visitor)*
До свидания.	*Good-bye.*
Спасибо.	*Thank you.*

NUTS & BOLTS 1
Singular pronouns

The Russian greeting **здравствуйте** *(hello)* is a command that literally means *be healthy*. Notice that there are two ways of saying *hello*. One is formal; you'd use it with strangers and in formal situations; it has the plural/formal imperative ending, **-те**. The other, **здравствуй,** is informal; it is used in the singular with family members, close friends, and children. This distinction between formal and informal is also made in Russian between the different pronouns for the word *you*. Let's take a look at all of the subject pronouns in Russian. We will start with those that refer to one person.

я	*I*
ты *(infml.)*	*you*
он	*he*
она	*she*
оно	*it*
вы *(fml.)*	*you*

As you can see, there are two forms of the singular *you* in the table above. **Ты** is informal; **вы** is formal.

Notice that the third person singular pronoun is either masculine (**он**) or feminine (**она**). It can also be neuter (**оно**) when it replaces a neuter inanimate noun, such as **вино**. The Russian pronouns **он, она,** and the plural form, **они** *(they),* can refer to human beings as well as to inanimate objects; **оно** refers only to inanimate objects. So **он** can stand either for **бизнесмен** or for **ресторан,** because both are masculine, just as the English *they* can refer to both people and things. Only third person Russian pronouns have gender; all others are "gender blind." Russian pronouns are rarely omitted from the sentence even though they may seem redundant, as the verb ending clearly indicates the referent.

PRACTICE 1
Which Russian pronoun would you use in each of the following situations?

1. Talking to your best friend Иван

2. Asking directions from an older stranger you see on the street

3. Talking about your brother

4. Talking about yourself

5. Talking about your boss, господин Петров

6. Telling your waiter in a restaurant what you would like to order

NUTS & BOLTS 2
INTRODUCTION TO GENDER
Notice that the words **бизнесмен, господин,** and **американец***
all end in a consonant, while the words **журналистка, госпожа,**
and **американка** end in the vowel **a.** This is so because the words
in the first group are masculine, referring to males, while the
words in the second group are feminine, referring to females.
Most masculine nouns end in a consonant (they have a "zero"
ending); most feminine nouns have the ending **a.** There are also
neuter nouns, but we'll focus on those later. For now, we'll use
only masculine and feminine nouns in our vocabulary.

*All nationalities, as well as the pronoun *I* **(я),** are not capitalized in Russian unless at the
beginning of a sentence.

PRACTICE 2

What gender is each of the following nouns?

1. господин

2. американка

3. госпожа

4. журналистка

5. журналист

6. американец

WORD LIST 2

студент	*student (male)*
студентка	*student (female)*
пожалуйста	*please*
извините *(pl./sg. fml.)*	*excuse me*
извини *(sg. infml.)*	*excuse me*
откуда	*where from*
русский	*Russian (male)*
русская	*Russian (female)*
университет	*university*
здесь	*here*
давайте *(fml.)*	*let's*
давай *(infml.)*	*let's*
Счастливо!	*So long! (lit., Happily!)*

NUTS & BOLTS 3
Plural pronouns

Now let's look at the personal pronouns that refer to more than one person.

мы	*we*
вы *(pl.)*	*you*
они	*they*

Russian plural forms don't have gender. **Мы, вы,** and **они** refer equally to males and females. Notice that the pronoun **вы** can be either singular or plural. When it is singular, it refers to one person in the formal sense. When it is plural, there is no distinction between formal and informal.

PRACTICE 3
Now replace the people in the following list with the appropriate Russian pronouns.

1. Николай и Наталья
2. Ольга
3. Борис и Джон
4. Yourself and your friends
5. Джон
6. You *(fml./pl.)*

PRACTICE 4
Which Russian pronoun would you use when addressing the following people? There are two second person pronouns to choose from: **ты,** informal for one person, and **вы,** formal for one person, and either formal or informal for more than one person.

1. a child
2. two students
3. a waiter/waitress
4. your sister
5. your brothers
6. a police officer

Tip!
There are many different ways to memorize new vocabulary, so it's a good idea to try a few to see what works for you. Simply reading a word in a list isn't going to make you remember it. Write down your new vocabulary in a notebook, and then try to repeat it out loud and write each word several times to make it sink in. Use the recordings to give yourself even more repetition. You could also make flash cards, with Russian on one side and English on the other. Start by trying to guess the translations of the words from Russian into English, and once you've mastered that, go from

English to Russian, which will be harder. The most effective way to memorize your new vocabulary, however, is by writing out the words as you repeat them. This makes you focus longer on a given word and reinforces your visual memory with sound. You could also label things in your home or office. Experiment and explore, but whatever you do, try to make vocabulary learning as active as possible!

ANSWERS

PRACTICE 1: 1. ты; **2.** вы; **3.** он; **4.** я; **5.** он; **6.** я

PRACTICE 2: 1. masculine; **2.** feminine; **3.** feminine; **4.** feminine; **5.** masculine; **6.** masculine

PRACTICE 3: 1. они; **2.** она; **3.** они; **4.** мы; **5.** он; **6.** вы

PRACTICE 4: 1. ты; **2.** вы; **3.** вы; **4.** ты; **5.** вы; **6.** вы

—————— Lesson 2 (Phrases) ——————

PHRASE LIST 1

Я американец.	*I'm an American. (male)*
Я американка.	*I'm an American. (female)*
Извините. *(pl./sg. fml.)*	*Excuse me.*
Извини. *(sg. infml.)*	*Excuse me.*
Пойдёмте! *(pl./sg. addressee fml.)*	*Let's go!*
Пойдём! *(sg. addressee infml.)*	*Let's go!*
с удовольствием	*gladly (lit., with pleasure)*
Большое спасибо!	*Thank you very much! (lit., Big thank you!)*
Пожалуйста!	*Please!, You're welcome!*
Правда?	*Really? (lit., Truth?)*
недавно	*recently*
Мне очень понравилось.	*I liked it very much. (lit., It was very pleasing to me.)*

NUTS & BOLTS 1
OMISSION OF *TO BE*
Notice that the sentence *I'm an American* has only two words in Russian. This is because Russian doesn't have articles *(a, an,* or *the)* and doesn't use the verb *to be* in the present tense. So the sentence **Я американец** is grammatically correct although it literally translates as *I American.*

PRACTICE 1
How would you rephrase the following sentences in Russian?

1. I'm an American *(male)*.
2. I'm a student *(female)*.
3. He's a student.
4. She's a journalist.
5. She's an American.
6. I'm a businessperson *(male)*.
7. She's Russian.

NUTS & BOLTS 2
FORMAL AND INFORMAL GREETINGS AND COMMANDS
You may have noticed some differences in the commands and greetings you saw in the phrase list. **Извини(те), давай(те)**, and **пойдём(те)** are all command forms, similar to the greeting **здравствуй(те)**. Again, notice how the ending **-те** is used in formal situations or in the plural but dropped in the informal singular. This is especially important in the following expressions that you've seen so far.

Informal: To a good friend	Formal: To a person you don't know well
здравствуй	**здравствуйте**
пойдём	**пойдёмте**
давай	**давайте**
извини	**извините**

PRACTICE 2

Choose **здравствуйте** or **здравствуй** as appropriate to the following situations.

1. Greeting your tour guide.
2. Greeting your friends.
3. Greeting your sister.
4. Greeting a child.
5. Greeting several children.

PRACTICE 3

Choose **пойдёмте** or **пойдём** as appropriate to the following situations.

1. Saying "Let's go" to your colleagues.
2. Saying "Let's go" to your husband.
3. Saying "Let's go" to your daughter.
4. Saying "Let's go" to your good friend.
5. Saying "Let's go" to your parents.

PHRASE LIST 2

Как вас зовут? *(pl./sg. fml.)*	*What is your name?*
Как тебя зовут? *(sg. infml.)*	*What is your name?*
Меня зовут . . .	*My name is . . .*
Приятно познакомиться!	*Nice to meet you! (lit., Pleasant to meet you!)*
по профессии	*by profession*
из Москвы	*from Moscow*
конечно	*of course*
на "ты"	*on familiar terms (saying "ты" to each other)*
на "вы"	*on formal terms (saying "вы" to each other)*
да	*yes*

| нет | *no* |
| **Где вы были?** *(pl./sg. fml.)* | *Where were you?* |

NOTES

When people are on familiar terms with each other, Russians say that they are на **"ты"**—literally, *on* **"ты"** *terms.* Conversely, with somebody you don't know very well, you need to be *on* **"вы"** *terms:* на **"вы."**

NUTS & BOLTS 3
ASKING QUESTIONS
Now, let's look at some question words in Russian.

кто	*who*
что	*what*
как	*how*
где	*where*
откуда	*where from*
куда	*where to*

The English question *What is your name?* corresponds to the Russian expression **Как вас зовут?** which literally means *How do they call you?* To ask the same question informally, you need to replace **вас** with **тебя: Как тебя зовут?** The answer to both questions is:

Меня зовут Борис.

My name is Boris. (lit., They call me Boris.)

The Russian question word **что** *(what)* never refers to human beings; therefore, the English question *What are you?* corresponds to the Russian expression **Кто вы?** *(Who are you?).* To make this question less ambiguous, Russian speakers often add **по профессии.**

Кто вы по профессии?
What do you do? (lit., Who are you by profession?)

The question word **где** refers only to stationary reference points: *where you live, where you are, where you stand, where you were,* etc. Any time there's any movement from a place or to a place, Russian speakers use either **откуда** *(where from)* or **куда** *(where to)*. If it helps, you can compare this to the antiquated English forms *whence (where from)* and *whither (where to)*.

PRACTICE 4
Ask the following people what their names are. Use either a formal or an informal question. Also provide their answers.

1. Your fellow traveler on the plane, Natalia.

2. Her child, Misha.

3. Her husband, Nikolai.

4. Your tour guide, Olga.

5. The driver, Vladimir.

PRACTICE 5
Take a look at the following answers. What are the questions being answered?

1. Я журналистка.

2. Я из Москвы.

3. Меня зовут Джон.

4. Я бизнесмен.

5. Да, я русская.

Culture note

Russian first names are rarely shortened in formal situations or when accompanied by a last name. Thus **Наталья Петрова** will be **Наталья** rather than **Наташа; Владимир** will be **Владимир** rather than **Володя; Борис** will be **Борис** instead of **Боря**, etc. When meeting Russians, you should call them by their full first names (**Наталья, Владимир, Борис**) and switch to nicknames only after they have suggested you do so.

For your reference, here are some common Russian names and nicknames. Full first names are given first.

Female	
Full name	Nickname
Александра	**Саша, Шура**
Анна	**Аня**
Елена	**Лена**
Ирина	**Ира**
Мария	**Маша**
Наталья	**Наташа**
Ольга	**Оля**
Светлана	**Света**
Татьяна	**Таня**
Юлия	**Юля**

Male	
Full name	Nickname
Александр	Саша, Шура
Алексей	Алеша, Лёша
Борис	Боря
Владимир	Володя
Иван	Ваня
Константин	Костя
Михаил	Миша
Николай	Коля
Пётр	Петя
Юрий	Юра

ANSWERS

PRACTICE 1: 1. Я американец. **2.** Я студентка. **3.** Он студент. **4.** Она журналистка. **5.** Она американка. **6.** Я бизнесмен. **7.** Она русская.

PRACTICE 2: 1. Здравствуйте. **2.** Здравствуйте. **3.** Здравствуй. **4.** Здравствуй. **5.** Здравствуйте.

PRACTICE 3: 1. Пойдёмте. **2.** Пойдём. **3.** Пойдём. **4.** Пойдём. **5.** Пойдёмте.

PRACTICE 4: 1. Как вас зовут? Меня зовут Наталья. **2.** Как тебя зовут? Меня зовут Миша. **3.** Как вас зовут? Меня зовут Николай. **4.** Как вас зовут? Меня зовут Ольга. **5.** Как вас зовут? Меня зовут Владимир.

PRACTICE 5: 1. Кто вы по профессии? **2.** Откуда вы? **3.** Как вас зовут? **4.** Кто вы по профессии? **5.** Вы русская?

SENTENCE LIST 1

Откуда вы?	*Where are you (pl./sg. fml.) from?*
Я из Москвы.	*I am from Moscow.*
Я из Америки.	*I am from America.*
Где вы были в Америке?	*Where were you (pl./sg. fml.) in America?*
Я был(а) в Вашингтоне.	*I was in Washington.*
Я был(а) один месяц в Нью-Йорке.	*I was in New York for one month.*
Я был(а) две недели в Москве.	*I was in Moscow for two weeks.*
Очень интересно!	*Very interesting!*
Вот как?	*Really? (Is that so?)*

NUTS & BOLTS 1
INTRODUCTION TO CASES

Я из Америки.	**Где вы были в Америке?**
I am from America.	*Where were you (pl./sg. fml.) in America?*

Notice the change in the word ending in the Russian word for *America* in the previous two sentences. These changes to the endings of nouns or adjectives are called "cases."

Russian has many distinctions of this kind to mark a particular meaning. Here, the distinctions are location (**в Америке**—*in America*) and origin (**из Америки**—*from America*). Let's look at another similar phrase.

Я был(а) в Вашингтоне.
I was in Washington.

В Вашингтоне *(in Washington)* has the location ending **-е** added to the noun **Вашингтон** *(Washington)* because in this sentence, it denotes *being in* a place rather than *coming from* or *going to* one.

You will eventually learn all of the Russian cases; for now, however, it will do just to memorize these forms as they are. We'll come back to them in later lessons.

PRACTICE 1
Answer the question **Где вы были?** using the cues provided.

1. Америка
2. Нью-Йорк
3. Москва
4. Вашингтон

Answer the question **Откуда вы?** using the cues provided.

5. Москва
6. Америка

NUTS & BOLTS 2
MORE ON GENDER
All Russian nouns have gender—masculine, feminine, or neuter. As we mentioned in the previous lesson, nouns that denote human beings (animate nouns) can only be either masculine or feminine.

Masc.	Fem.
студент	студентка
"zero" ending	-а ending

Nouns that denote things (inanimate nouns) can be masculine, feminine, or neuter, and their gender is meaningless.

Masc.	Fem.	Neuter
университет *(university)*	правда *(truth)*	пиво *(beer)*
месяц *(month)*	неделя *(week)*	вино *(wine)*

Most masculine nouns end in a consonant (have a "zero" ending), most feminine nouns end in **a,** and most neuter nouns end in **-o** or **-e.**

Now let's look at the numerals 1 and 2 in Russian.

один (одна, одно)	*one*
два (две)	*two*

The numerals *one* and *two* in Russian change to match the gender of the word that follows.

Singular	Plural
один университет *(one university, m.)*	**два университета*** *(two universities, m.)*
одна неделя *(one week, f.)*	**две недели** *(two weeks, f.)*
одно пиво *(one beer, n.)*	**два пива** *(two beers, n.)*

* We'll discuss plural endings and endings of nouns with numerals in future units.

Notice that the number *two* has only two forms in Russian: **два** (masculine and neuter) and **две** (feminine).

PRACTICE 2
Choose the correct Russian numeral *one* **(один, одна, одно)** for the following nouns.

1. журналистка
2. бизнесмен
3. месяц
4. университет
5. пиво
6. студентка
7. вино

PRACTICE 3

Choose the correct Russian numeral *two* (**два, две**) for the following items.

1. two female students
2. two beers
3. two male Americans
4. two weeks

5. two wines
6. two girls
7. two universities

SENTENCE LIST 2

Я тоже студент.	*I'm a student too.*
Извините, пожалуйста.	*Excuse me, please.*
Я вас познакомлю. (*pl./sg. fml.*)	*I'll introduce you.*
Я тебя познакомлю. (*sg. infml.*)	*I'll introduce you.*
Как вас зовут? (*pl./sg. fml.*)	*What is your name?*
Давайте на "ты."	*Let's be on informal terms. (Let's be on "ты" terms.)*
Мне очень понравилось!	*I liked (it) very much!*
Я надеюсь, вам тоже понравится. (*pl./sg. fml.*)	*I hope you like (it) too.*

NUTS & BOLTS 3

THE ADVERB тоже

The Russian adverb **тоже** means *too* when comparing one person to another.

Я студент(ка).

I'm a student.

Я тоже студент(ка).

I'm a student too.

Тоже is not used for listing things you like, do, or know, etc.; for these expressions, you'd use another Russian adverb, **ещё.**

PRACTICE 4
Respond to the following statements saying that you are one of those things too.

1. Я американка.

2. Я из Америки.

3. Я был в Москве.

4. Я бизнесмен.

5. Мне очень понравилось!

NUTS & BOLTS 4
NUMBERS 1–10
You already learned the numbers 1 and 2; let's review them and add the rest of the numbers up to 10.

один (одна, одно)	*one*
два (две)	*two*
три	*three*
четыре	*four*
пять	*five*
шесть	*six*
семь	*seven*
восемь	*eight*
девять	*nine*
десять	*ten*

Russian numerals after 2 are "gender blind"—they have only one form for all three genders.

PRACTICE 5

Place the following Russian numerals in ascending order.

семь, три, пять, один, девять, четыре

Discovery activity

Do you exercise? If you do, count your first ten repetitions in Russian: one to ten steps, one to ten sit-ups, one to ten squats, one to ten push-ups, etc. This will help you remember the Russian numerals as well as keep you in shape!

ANSWERS

PRACTICE 1: 1. Я был в Америке. **2.** Я был в Нью-Йорке. **3.** Я был в Москве. **4.** Я был в Вашингтоне. **5.** Я из Москвы. **6.** Я из Америки.

PRACTICE 2: 1. одна; **2.** один; **3.** один; **4.** один; **5.** одно; **6.** одна; **7.** одно

PRACTICE 3: 1. две; **2.** два; **3.** два; **4.** две; **5.** два; **6.** две; **7.** два

PRACTICE 4: 1. Я тоже американка. **2.** Я тоже из Америки. **3.** Я тоже был в Москве. **4.** Я тоже бизнесмен. **5.** Мне тоже очень понравилось!

PRACTICE 5: 1. один; **2.** три; **3.** четыре; **4.** пять; **5.** семь; **6.** девять

CONVERSATION 1

John Bradley, an American businessman, is meeting a Russian journalist, Natalia Petrova, at the airport in Moscow.

Джон:	Здравствуйте. Я Джон Брэдли. А вы?
Наталья:	Здравствуйте, господин Брэдли. Очень приятно. Я Наталья Петрова.
Джон:	Очень приятно, госпожа Петрова. Кто вы по профессии?
Наталья:	Я журналистка. А кто вы по профессии?
Джон:	Я бизнесмен. Вы русская?
Наталья:	Да, я русская. Я из Москвы. А откуда вы?
Джон:	Я из Америки.
Наталья:	Вот как? Очень интересно! Я недавно была в Америке.
Джон:	Где вы были в Америке?
Наталья:	Я была один месяц в Нью-Йорке и две недели в Вашингтоне. Мне очень понравилось. Добро пожаловать в Россию! Я надеюсь, вам тоже понравится.
Джон:	Большое спасибо! До свидания.
Наталья:	Счастливо!

John:	*Hello. I'm John Bradley. And you?*
Natalia:	*Hello, Mr. Bradley. Nice to meet you. I'm Natalia Petrova.*
John:	*Nice to meet you, Ms. Petrova. What do you do?*
Natalia:	*I'm a journalist. And what do you do?*
John:	*I'm a businessman. Are you Russian?*
Natalia:	*Yes, I am (Russian). I'm from Moscow. Where are you from?*
John:	*I'm from America.*
Natalia:	*Oh, really? Very interesting. I was recently in America.*
John:	*Where were you in America?*

> *Natalia:* *I was in New York for a month and in Washington for two weeks. I liked it very much. Welcome to Russia! I hope you like it too.*
> *John:* *Thank you very much! Good-bye!*
> *Natalia:* *So long! (lit., Happily!)*

NOTES

Natalia and John are on formal terms at their first introduction. They say to each other **здравствуйте** and **вы**.

The endings of **Москва** *(Moscow)* and **Америка** *(America)* change when you say **из Москвы** *(from Moscow)* and **из Америки** *(from America)*.

Notice the masculine ("zero") and feminine **(-a)** endings in **господин, госпожа, бизнесмен,** and **журналистка**.

NUTS & BOLTS 1
PAST TENSE OF быть

You may have noticed in the dialogue that the sentence **Я недавно была в Америке** is translated with the past tense of the verb **быть** *(to be)*. Although this verb is always left out in the present tense, it is necessary to include in the past tense. It changes according to the natural gender of the speaking person or, more generally, to the gender of the subject of *was/were*. Natalia is a woman, so she adds the feminine ending **-a** when she says **я была** *(I was)*, as above. Let's look at the paradigm of the verb *to be* in the past tense.

был	*was (masculine)*
была	*was (feminine)*
было	*was (neuter)*
были	*were (pl.)*

Я был(а) в Америке.
I was in America.

Я был(а) в Москве.
I was in Moscow.

PRACTICE 1
Insert the correct past form of the verb **быть (был, была, было, были)** in the following sentences.

1. Наталья Петрова ____ в Америке.

2. Джон Брэдли ____ в Москве.

3. Джон и Наталья ____ в Нью-Йорке.

4. Мы тоже ____ в Нью-Йорке.

5. Я ____ в Петербурге. *(female)*

6. Я ____ в Москве. *(male)*

CONVERSATION 2
Sean, an American student, is visiting a Russian university and meeting a Russian student there, Olga.

Шон: **Извините, пожалуйста, вы студентка?**

Ольга: **Да, я студентка. Это мой университет.**

Шон: **Я тоже студент.**

Ольга: **Откуда вы?**

Шон: **Я из Нью-Йорка. Я американец.**

Ольга: **Правда? А как вас зовут?**

Шон: **Меня зовут Шон. А как вас зовут?**

Ольга: **Очень приятно, Шон. Меня зовут Ольга, или просто Оля. Давайте на "ты."**

Шон: **Приятно познакомиться, Оля. Конечно, давай на "ты." Это твои друзья там?**

Ольга: **Да, они тоже студенты. Пойдём, я тебя познакомлю.**

Шон: **С удовольствием! Пойдём.**

Sean:	*Excuse me please, are you a student?*
Olga:	*Yes, I'm a student. This is my university.*
Sean:	*I'm also a student.*
Olga:	*Where are you from?*
Sean:	*I'm from New York. I'm an American.*
Olga:	*Really? And what's your name?*
Sean:	*My name is Sean. And what is your name?*
Olga:	*Nice to meet you, Sean. My name is Olga or simply Olya. Let's be informal.*
Sean:	*Nice to meet you, Olya. Of course, let's be informal. Are those your friends over there?*
Olga:	*Yes, they are students too. Let's go, I'll introduce you.*
Sean:	*Sure (with pleasure). Let's go.*

Notes

Notice how Olga and Sean switch to the informal mode after the first introduction. They are both students and peers, so they quickly do away with formalities. Yet they were on formal terms at the very first moment of introduction. When they switch to на "ты," Olga also changes her full name to a shorter variant, Оля.

When Sean asks Olga what her name is, he starts his question with a *(and, but),* which shows that this is not the first question but rather a continuation of their conversation: *My name is Sean. And/But what is your name?*

NUTS & BOLTS 2
THE BASIC PLURAL OF NOUNS

Note the ending -ы in the word студенты. When Olga says of her friends, Они тоже студенты, she uses the standard masculine plural ending, -ы, in order to make the singular noun студент plural: студенты.

Они тоже студенты.

They are students too.

The ending **-ы** (or its soft counterpart, **и**) is used to pluralize most nouns. However, **друзья** is the irregular plural form of the singular masculine noun **друг**. Remember these forms for now as they are. We will take a look at more plural forms in the next Unit.

Это твои друзья там?
Are those your friends over there?

PRACTICE 2
What are the plural forms of the following nouns?

1. студент
2. университет
3. друг

4. бизнесмен
5. журналист

Culture note

In addition to a first name (**имя**) and a last name (**фамилия**), all complete Russian personal names also have another formal part, called a patronymic (**отчество**). The patronymic always consists of the person's father's first name with a particular suffix: **-ович (-евич)** for males, and **-овна (-евна)** for females. For example, if **Николай's** father's first name was, say, **Иван**, his patronymic would be **Иванович.** We know from the first dialogue that **Наталья's** last name is **Петрова**; so, if her father's first name was **Борис,** her patronymic would be **Борисовна,** and her complete **фамилия, имя, отчество** *(last name, first name, patronymic)* would be **Петрова Наталья Борисовна.** Notice also that in formal situations and all legal documents, Russian names are given in this order: 1. **фамилия** *(last or family name)* 2. **имя** *(first name)* 3. **отчество** *(patronymic).*

The **имя** and **отчество** can be initialized, so instead of **Пушкин Александр Сергеевич,** you will often see **А. С. Пушкин.** These initials are never pronounced as individual letters but are either left out altogether from pronunciation or deciphered as the full name and patronymic.

ANSWERS

PRACTICE 1: 1. была; 2. был; 3. были; 4. были; 5. была; 6. был

PRACTICE 2: 1. студенты; 2. университеты; 3. друзья; 4. бизнесмены; 5. журналисты

UNIT 1 ESSENTIALS

Здравствуйте. *(fml.)*	*Hello.*
Здравствуй. *(infml.)*	*Hello.*
Как вас зовут? *(fml.)*	*What's your name?*
Меня зовут . . .	*My name is . . .*
Очень приятно.	*Nice to meet you. (Very pleasant.)*
Приятно познакомиться.	*Nice to meet you. (Pleasant to meet you.)*
Я американец.	*I'm an American. (male)*
Я американка.	*I'm an American. (female)*
Откуда вы?	*Where're you from?*
Я из Москвы.	*I'm from Moscow.*
Я из Нью-Йорка.	*I'm from New York.*
Где вы были?	*Where were you?*
Я был(а) в Москве.	*I was in Moscow.*
Я был(а) в Вашингтоне.	*I was in Washington.*
Пойдёмте. *(fml.)*	*Let's go.*
Пойдём. *(infml.)*	*Let's go.*
Давайте на "ты."	*Let's be on informal terms. ("ты" terms)*
С удовольствием!	*Sure! (With pleasure!)*
Большое спасибо!	*Thank you very much!*
Пожалуйста.	*Please., You're welcome.*
один (одна, одно)	*one*
два (две)	*two*
три	*three*
четыре	*four*
пять	*five*

шесть	*six*
семь	*seven*
восемь	*eight*
девять	*nine*
десять	*ten*

Unit 2
Food

In Unit 2, you will learn Russian verb conjugation and two cases—the prepositional and the accusative—and will begin to learn the instrumental case as well. You will also learn how to talk about food, how to say where, what, and when you'd like to eat and drink, what you ate and drank, as well as how to make plans for breakfast, lunch, and dinner in the future. By the end of this lesson, you'll also be able to use the expression *I have . . .* in Russian to express possession.

—————— Lesson 5 (Words) ——————

WORD LIST 1

завтрак	*breakfast*
завтракать	*to have breakfast*
обед	*lunch*
обедать	*to have lunch*
ужин	*dinner, supper*
ужинать	*to have dinner, supper*
омлет	*omelet*
бутерброд	*sandwich (open-faced sandwich)*
вода	*water*
кофе	*coffee*
молоко	*milk*
мюсли	*cereal (the name comes from the popular Swiss cereal Muesli)*
буфет	*cafeteria*
ресторан	*restaurant*
центр	*downtown, center*

| гостиница | hotel |
| фойе | lobby (of a hotel or theater; from the word "foyer") |

NUTS & BOLTS 1
VERBS: CONJUGATION I

There are three daily meals in Russia: **завтрак** *(breakfast)*, **обед** *(lunch)*, and **ужин** *(dinner/supper)*. The Russian verbs **завтракать** *(to have breakfast)*, **обедать** *(to have lunch)*, and **ужинать** *(to have dinner/supper)* are derived from the above nouns. Notice that their infinitive forms are marked by the Russian ending **-ть,** which corresponds to the English particle *to,* as in *to have.* In order to say *I have breakfast* rather than *to have breakfast,* you need to change the verb's ending: this alteration according to the rules of grammar is called conjugation. A verb's conjugation depends on the person and number of the subject performing an action *(I have breakfast, she has breakfast)* and on the time when the action takes place *(I have breakfast, I had breakfast).* There are two regular conjugation types in Russian along with a few exceptions, and some irregular verb conjugations. In this lesson, we'll learn the first type of verb conjugation, which we'll call Conjugation I.

Let's take a look at the standard present tense conjugation endings. Memorize these forms; most Russian verbs will have the same or very similar endings when conjugated.

Conjugation I			
я	-ю/-у	мы	-ем
ты	-ешь	вы	-ете
он/она	-ет	они	-ют/-ут

The **-ю** (first person singular) and **-ют** (third person plural) Conjugation I endings are actually a combination of the stem ending

й and the conjugation endings **-у** and **-ут;** we'll look at how and why this happens in Unit 3. Most of the Conjugation I verbs you'll see in the next few lessons will have **-ю** and **-ют** endings.

Now let's look at how these endings work with the Conjugation I verb **завтракать** *(to have breakfast).* Notice that the **-ть** is dropped. The above endings are then attached to conjugate the verb—in this case **завтракать**—in the present tense.

завтракать *(to have breakfast)*

я	завтракаю	мы	завтракаем
ты	завтракаешь	вы	завтракаете
он/она/оно	завтракает	они	завтракают

PRACTICE 1
Match the following conjugation forms with the correct personal pronoun: **я, ты, он/она, мы, вы, они.**

1. завтракаю

2. обедаешь

3. ужинаем

4. обедает

5. завтракаете

6. ужинают

PRACTICE 2
Using the pronouns below as clues, conjugate the three different mealtimes **завтракать, обедать, ужинать** in the present tense.

1. мы

2. вы

3. я

4. Наталья

5. ты

6. Наталья и Джон

WORD LIST 2

супермаркет	*supermarket*
рыба	*fish*
мясо	*meat*
зелёный салат	*lettuce (lit., green salad)*
лук	*onion (sg. only)*
картошка	*potatoes (colloquial)*
макароны	*pasta (lit., macaroni; pl. only)*
сыр	*cheese*
чай	*tea*
сок	*juice*
сегодня	*today*
кафе	*café*
столовая	*cafeteria*
дома	*at home*
вместе	*together*
хотеть	*to want*
купить	*to buy*
еда	*food*

NUTS & BOLTS 2

THE PREPOSITIONAL CASE (SINGULAR)

To denote a location where something is happening (*at a restaurant, in a cafeteria, in Moscow, in New York,* etc.), the preposition **в** (*in* or *at*) is used and the ending of a Russian singular noun typically changes to **-е**. This change of the form reflects the prepositional case of the singular noun in question. Location (*at* or *in* a place) is one possible meaning of the prepositional case. Remember not to confuse location with direction in Russian. Direction (*to* a place) requires another case, which we'll discuss later. The prepositional ending **-е** is added to masculine consonant endings and replaces the feminine **-а/я** endings and the neuter **-о** ending.

Prepositional singular	Ending	Example
m./n./f.	**-e**	**в Нью-Йорке, в Москве, в ресторане, в кафе**

Compare the following.

Nominative		Prepositional	
Москва *(f.)*	*Moscow*	**в Москве**	*in Moscow*
Нью-Йорк *(m.)*	*New York*	**в Нью-Йорке**	*in New York*
ресторан *(m.)*	*restaurant*	**в ресторане**	*at/in the restaurant*
кафе *(n.)*	*café*	**в кафе**	*at/in the café*

One exception: **дома** means *at home.* You don't need to use the prepositional case when you say *at home* in Russian.

Я дома.
I'm home./I'm at home.

Another locative preposition, the preposition **на** *(on* or *at),* usually refers to open locations, such as floors, streets, avenues, stadiums, fields, squares, etc. It also refers to work or social gatherings, such as parties and picnics. **На** with a noun in the prepositional case means *on* rather than *in,* but there are exceptions, so it's best to learn which individual words in Russian take **на** or **в** as their preposition.

Prepositional case with **на** and **в**	
на первом этаже	*on the first floor*
на Невском проспекте	*on Nevsky Prospect*
на работе	*at work*
в университете	*at the university*

PRACTICE 3

Say that the following people were in the following places. Use
был *(m.)*, **была** *(f.)*, or **были** *(pl.)*.

1. я–буфет
2. Джон–Москва
3. Ирина–ресторан
4. мы–центр

5. вы–гостиница
6. Оля–Америка
7. она–дома

Culture note

Lunch **(обед)** in Russia is traditionally the largest meal of the day. It usually consists of a small salad, a bowl of soup, an entrée, a drink, and possibly even a dessert! Russian **обед** is taken later than American lunch. It rarely starts earlier than at 1:00 p.m. and can be as late as at 2:30 and 3:00 p.m. Dinner **(ужин)** is usually around 7:00 p.m.

Learn to differentiate among Russian eateries. **Буфет** is a small café where you go up to the counter, order your food and/or drink, and then take it to your table. You can find this type of restaurant in theaters, universities, hotels, and offices. **Столовая** is a cafeteria, much like dining halls in American colleges. The Russian word **ресторан** refers to a more formal and expensive eating place, distinct from **кафе,** which usually means a more casual restaurant.

ANSWERS

PRACTICE 1: 1. я завтракаю; **2.** ты обедаешь; **3.** мы ужинаем; **4.** он/она обедает; **5.** вы завтракаете; **6.** они ужинают

PRACTICE 2: 1. мы завтракаем, мы обедаем, мы ужинаем; **2.** вы завтракаете, вы обедаете, вы ужинаете; **3.** я завтракаю, я обедаю, я ужинаю; **4.** Наталья завтракает, Наталья обедает, Наталья ужинает; **5.** ты завтракаешь, ты обедаешь, ты ужинаешь; **6.** Наталья и Джон завтракают, Наталья и Джон обедают, Наталья и Джон ужинают

PRACTICE 3: 1. Я был(а) в буфете. **2.** Джон был в Москве. **3.** Ирина была в ресторане. **4.** Мы были в центре. **5.** Вы были в гостинице. **6.** Оля была в Америке. **7.** Она была дома.

———————————— Lesson 6 (Phrases) ————————————

PHRASE LIST 1

Как у вас дела? *(fml./pl.)*	*How are you doing?*
на первом этаже	*on the first floor*
только что	*just (recently)*
на завтрак	*for breakfast*
Что там (есть)?	*What's there?*
фрукт(ы)	*fruit(s)*
бутерброд с сыром	*open-faced sandwich with cheese*
кофе с молоком	*coffee with milk*
есть	*to eat*
пить	*to drink*
в центре города	*in the center of the city (downtown)*
Приятного аппетита!	*Bon appétit!*
увидимся	*see you*
Спасибо за помощь!	*Thank you for (your) help!*
Не за что.	*Not at all (don't mention it).*

NUTS & BOLTS 1
Conjugation of the verbs пить *(to drink)*, есть *(to eat)*, хотеть *(to want)*

The verb **пить** *(to drink)* in the present tense follows the Conjugation I paradigm. Note that the letter -ё replaces -e when it is stressed.

пить *(to drink)*

я	пью	мы	пьём
ты	пьёшь	вы	пьёте
он/она/оно	пьёт	они	пьют

Not all Russian verbs stick to the same pattern. There are several irregular verbs, and you will simply need to memorize their conjugation. The verb **есть** *(to eat)* is one of these irregular verbs. Let's look at its conjugation table in the present tense.

есть *(to eat)*

я	ем	мы	едим
ты	ешь	вы	едите
он/она/оно	ест	они	едят

Another irregular verb is **хотеть** *(to want)*. Let's look at its present tense conjugation.

хотеть *(to want)*

я	хочу	мы	хотим
ты	хочешь	вы	хотите
он/она/оно	хочет	они	хотят

It is uncommon to say *I would like* in Russian. Most people prefer a more direct expression **я хочу** *(I want)*. This expression is perfectly polite and acceptable.

Что вы хотите? –Я хочу . . .

What would you like? –I would like . . .

PRACTICE 1

Match the correct forms of the verb **есть** *(to eat)* with the following pronouns.

1. ты

2. я

3. мы

4. они

5. вы

PRACTICE 2

Match the correct forms of the verb **пить** *(to drink)* with the following subjects.

1. Лиза и Коля

2. Наташа

3. я

4. Джон и я

5. студенты

PRACTICE 3

Insert the correct forms of the verb **хотеть** *(to want)* in the following sentences.

1. Я _____ завтракать.

2. Мы _____ вместе обедать в столовой.

3. Что вы _____ купить в супермаркете?

4. Они _____ ужинать в ресторане.

5. Где ты _____ обедать?

PHRASE LIST 2

что-нибудь	*something, anything*
что-нибудь на завтрак	*something, anything for breakfast*
Что-нибудь ещё?	*Anything else?*
У меня много работы.	*I have a lot of work (to do).*
сегодня	*today*
завтра	*tomorrow*
завтра вечером	*tomorrow night*
в столовой	*in the cafeteria*
с друзьями	*with friends*
может быть	*maybe, probably, perhaps*
я куплю сыр	*I will buy cheese*
в холодильнике	*in the refrigerator*
обычно	*usually, normally*

NUTS & BOLTS 2

THERE IS/THERE ARE: есть

Now, let's learn how to say *there is/there are* and *I have* in Russian. You remember the expression **Что там есть?** *(What is there?)*. The verb **есть** is the only possible form of the verb *to be* in the present tense and is often omitted in the present.

In order to say that something is somewhere in Russian, you need to start with the location (**там, в супермаркете, в холодильнике,** etc.), then **есть**, and then the thing that is or the things that are at this location. This Russian construction corresponds to the English construction *there is/there are*.

В холодильнике есть молоко.
There is milk in the refrigerator. (lit., In the refrigerator is milk.)

Notice that the subject **молоко** appears at the end of the sentence, because the word order in Russian is not as strict as in English. The subject of the sentence is normally in the nominative case and answers the questions **кто? что?** Instead of **в холодильнике** you can also say **у меня** *(lit., by me)* and still have the same kind of sentence. (**Меня** is the genitive case of the pronoun **я**. We will study it later.)

У меня есть молоко.
I have milk. (lit., By me [there] is milk.)

У меня много работы.
I have a lot of work (to do). (lit., By me [there is] a lot of work.)

Notice the omission of **есть** in the second example; it is not necessary when the emphasis is on the quality or quantity of item in possession rather than on the fact of its possession. (Also note the noun **работы**, which is in the genitive sg. case. Memorize it for now as it is.)

PRACTICE 4
Что там есть? *(What is there?)* Answer this question matching the following items with their locations. Remember to keep the locations in the prepositional case and the available items in the nominative!

1. буфет—бутерброд с сыром

2. холодильник—рыба и мясо

3. супермаркет—лук, картошка и помидоры

4. столовая—омлет и фрукты

5. центр—рестораны и кафе

PRACTICE 5
Что у вас есть на завтрак, на обед, на ужин? *(What do you have for breakfast, lunch, dinner?)* Use the construction **у меня есть** and the following prompts in your answers.

1. на завтрак—омлет и бутерброд с сыром

2. на завтрак—сок и кофе с молоком

3. на обед—суп и мясо

4. на обед—салат и сок

5. на ужин—рыба и зелёный салат

6. на ужин—макароны, салат и вино

Discovery activity

What do you usually have for breakfast, lunch, and dinner? Where do you have your meals? Try to say as much as you can in Russian using as many words and phrases from above as possible. Every time you have a meal, try to describe what you're doing and what you're eating in Russian.

ANSWERS
PRACTICE 1: 1. ешь; **2.** ем; **3.** едим; **4.** едят; **5.** едите

PRACTICE 2: 1. пьют; **2.** пьёт; **3.** пью; **4.** пьём; **5.** пьют

PRACTICE 3: 1. хочу; **2.** хотим; **3.** хотите; **4.** хотят; **5.** хочешь

PRACTICE 4: 1. В буфете есть бутерброд с сыром. **2.** В холодильнике есть рыба и мясо. **3.** В супермаркете есть лук, картошка и помидоры. **4.** В столовой есть омлет и фрукты. **5.** В центре есть рестораны и кафе.

PRACTICE 5: 1. У меня есть омлет и бутерброд с сыром на завтрак. **2.** У меня есть сок и кофе с молоком на завтрак. **3.** У меня есть суп и мясо на обед. **4.** У меня есть салат и сок на обед. **5.** У меня есть рыба и зелёный салат на ужин. **6.** У меня есть макароны, салат и вино на ужин.

--- **Lesson 7 (Sentences)** ---

SENTENCE LIST 1

Скажите, пожалуйста, где мы завтракаем?	*Tell me, please, where are we having breakfast?*
Пойдёмте, я покажу.	*Let's go, I'll show (you).*
Что там есть на завтрак?	*What do they have for breakfast? (lit., What is there for breakfast?)*
Я ел(а) омлет и бутерброд с сыром.	*I ate an omelet and a sandwich (lit., butter-bread) with cheese.*
Я пил(а) воду и кофе с молоком.	*I drank water and coffee with milk.*
Я люблю русскую кухню!	*I like (lit., love) Russian cuisine!*
Днём мы будем обедать в русском ресторане.	*In the daytime, we'll have lunch in a Russian restaurant.*
Какой это ресторан?	*What kind of restaurant is it?*
Увидимся в фойе гостиницы.	*See you in the lobby of the hotel.*

NUTS & BOLTS 1
THE PAST TENSE OF ЕСТЬ *(TO EAT)* AND ПИТЬ *(TO DRINK)*

Although the present tense conjugation of the verbs **есть** *(to eat)* and **пить** *(to drink)* is irregular, the past tense is rather straightforward. Remember that Russian verbs change in the past tense according to the gender and number of the subject. There is no distinction regarding person as in the present tense.

Past tense of **есть** *(to eat)*

ел	*masculine*
ела	*feminine*
ело	*neuter*
ели	*plural*

Past tense of **пить** *(to drink)*

пил	*masculine*
пила	*feminine*
пило	*neuter*
пили	*plural*

Я ел(а) омлет и бутерброд с сыром.
I ate an omelet and a sandwich with cheese.

Я пил(а) воду и кофе с молоком.
I drank water and coffee with milk.

As you can see, these forms don't differ from the past tense forms of the verb *to be*, which we discussed in Unit 1. Most Russian verbs form their past tense by dropping the ending -**ть** of the infinitive and adding -**л/-ла/-ло/-ли** with the respect to the gender/number of the noun. Notice that the stress shifts to the ending -**а** in the feminine past of **пить (пила)** but then goes back to its place for the other forms. This type of stress shift is common in the past tense.

PRACTICE 1
Say the following in Russian.

1. What did you (**ты**) have for breakfast?

2. What did they eat for lunch?

3. What did she eat for dinner?

4. Where did you (**вы**) eat breakfast?

5. He had lunch at the hotel.

6. We had dinner in a restaurant.

NUTS & BOLTS 2
THE ACCUSATIVE CASE
Notice that the verbs **есть** *(to eat)* and **пить** *(to drink)* take direct objects. Direct objects are <u>what</u> you are eating and <u>what</u> you are drinking. Direct objects are expressed in Russian by the accusative case. The accusative of singular masculine inanimate (ending in a consonant or **-ь**) and neuter nouns (ending in **-о** or **-е**) as well as of their plural forms is like the nominative case. Feminine nouns denoting direct objects drop their **-а/-я** endings and add **-у/-ю** endings respectively.

Accusative case	Ending	Example
m inanim./n./sg./pl.	same as the nominative	**омлет, молоко, фрукты, соки**
f.	**-у/-ю**	**воду, Олю**

Я ел(а) омлет и пил(а) молоко и воду.
I ate an omelet and drank milk and water.

Я ел(а) фрукты и пил(а) соки.
I ate fruits and drank juices.

Remember that the Russian verbs **завтракать** *(to have breakfast)*, **обедать** *(to have lunch)*, and **ужинать** *(to have dinner)*, just like their English counterparts, don't take direct objects. If you need to specify <u>what</u> you had for breakfast, lunch or dinner, you should say

Я ел(а) омлет на завтрак.
I ate an omelet for breakfast.

PRACTICE 2
Что вы ели и пили на завтрак? Answer this question using the following prompts. Remember to put the things you ate and drank into the accusative case!

1. omelet and juice
2. fruits and coffee with milk
3. cheese sandwich and water
4. cereal and milk
5. omelet and water

SENTENCE LIST 2

Я обычно завтракаю дома.	*I usually have breakfast at home.*
Что ты хочешь купить?	*What do you want (would you like) to buy?*
Я хочу купить рыбу, помидоры, зелёный салат, лук и мясо.	*I want (would like) to buy fish, tomatoes, lettuce, onion(s), and meat.*
Всё это есть в супермаркете.	*All of this is (available) in the supermarket.*
Я знаю одно хорошее и недорогое кафе в центре.	*I know one good and inexpensive café downtown (in the center).*
Извини, сегодня у меня много работы.	*Forgive me, I have a lot of work (to do) today.*
Давай пойдем туда завтра вечером.	*Let's go there tomorrow night.*
Пойдём в клуб.	*Let's go to a club.*
Договорились.	*Okay. (lit., agreed)*

NUTS & BOLTS 3
CONJUGATION II VERBS

Now let's learn the conjugation of another type of verb, Conjugation II verbs. Conjugation II verbs take the following endings.

Conjugation II endings			
я	-ю/-у	мы	-им
ты	-ишь	вы	-ите
он/она/оно	-ит	они	-ят/-ат

Let's look at how this works with the verb **любить** *(to like, to love)*.

любить *(to like, to love)*			
я	люблю	мы	любим
ты	любишь	вы	любите
он/она/оно	любит	они	любят

Notice that the 1st person singular form has an additional consonant л before the ending. This type of stem change is called mutation. This is an -л mutation. Now remember the following rule: if there's a mutation in a Conjugation II verb, it occurs only in the 1st person singular form, not in any of the others.

The verb **любить** takes direct objects (in the accusative case) or can be followed by the infinitive form of another verb.

Я люблю фрукты.	I like fruit(s).
Я люблю омлет.	I like omelet(s)./(lit., I like an omelet.)
Я люблю русскую* кухню. (f. sg.)	I like Russian cuisine.

*The adjective **русская** (f. sg.) is also in the accusative case. Memorize it for now as it is; we will discuss the declension of adjectives later.

The verb **любить** works with infinitives just as in English.

Я люблю завтракать дома.
I like to have breakfast at home.

PRACTICE 3

Что вы любите? *(What do you like?)* Using the prompts below, say that these people like the following things.

1. Irina—sandwich with cheese and coffee

2. they—water

3. I—have breakfast at home

4. you *(fml.)*—omelet and fruits

5. you *(infml.)*—have dinner in a restaurant

6. we—Russian cuisine

PRACTICE 4

Что вы хотите купить в супермаркете? *(What would you like to buy in a supermarket?)* Make a shopping list of the following items using the construction **я хочу купить**. Remember to put the nouns in the accusative case!

1. зелёный салат   4. помидоры и лук

2. чай и кофе   5. сыр и вино

3. рыба и мясо

Tip!

Although Russian pronunciation stress patterns can be confusing, they aren't entirely random or arbitrary. In the past tense, there are three basic stress patterns: 1) stable stress, 2) feminine stress shift, and 3) end stress shift. For example, **ел, ела, ело, ели** have stress on the same vowel **-e**; this is the stable stress pattern. In **пил, пила, пило, пили** the stress shifts to the feminine ending **-а**, but then goes back to the root vowel **–и-** in the neuter and plural forms; this is the feminine stress shift. Stress can also always fall on the last vowel in the ending as, for instance, in the past tense of the verb **провёл, провела, провело, провели** (spent [time]). There are also three basic stress patterns in the present tense. We'll discuss them later. Learn to differentiate the types of stress patterns in Russian, this will help you remember how to pronounce Russian verbs properly.

ANSWERS

PRACTICE 1: 1. Что ты ел на завтрак? **2.** Что они ели на обед? **3.** Что она ела на ужин? **4.** Где вы завтракали? **5.** Он обедал в гостинице. **6.** Мы ужинали в ресторане.

PRACTICE 2: 1. Я ел(а) омлет и пил(а) сок. **2.** Я ел(а) фрукты и пил(а) кофе с молоком. **3.** Я ел(а) бутерброд с сыром и пил(а) воду. **4.** Я ел(а) мюсли и пил(а) молоко. **5.** Я ел(а) омлет и пил(а) воду.

PRACTICE 3: 1. Ирина любит бутерброд с сыром и кофе. **2.** Они любят воду. **3.** Я люблю завтракать дома. **4.** Вы любите омлет и фрукты. **5.** Ты любишь ужинать в ресторане. **6.** Мы любим русскую кухню.

PRACTICE 4: 1. Я хочу купить зелёный салат. **2.** Я хочу купить чай и кофе. **3.** Я хочу купить рыбу и мясо. **4.** Я хочу купить помидоры и лук. **5.** Я хочу купить сыр и вино.

─────────── Lesson 8 (Conversations) ───────────

CONVERSATION 1

An American tourist, John Adams, is meeting his Russian tour guide, Irina Vasilieva, in the lobby of his hotel in St. Petersburg in the morning. They are discussing their meal arrangements for the day.

Джон:	Здравствуйте, Ирина!
Ирина:	Здравствуйте, Джон.
Джон:	Как у вас дела?
Ирина:	Спасибо, хорошо. А как у вас?
Джон:	Всё отлично! Скажите, пожалуйста, где мы завтракаем?
Ирина:	Как, вы ещё не завтракали? Завтрак на первом этаже, в буфете. Пойдёмте, я вам покажу. Я только что оттуда.
Джон:	Большое спасибо. Что там есть на завтрак?
Ирина:	Я ела омлет и бутерброд с сыром и пила воду и кофе с молоком.
Джон:	Я не люблю много есть на завтрак. Там есть фрукты или мюсли?
Ирина:	Да, конечно есть. Вы знаете, что днём мы будем обедать в ресторане в центре города?
Джон:	Какой это ресторан?
Ирина:	Это русский ресторан на Невском проспекте. Там русская кухня.
Джон:	Отлично! Я люблю русскую кухню! Спасибо за помощь!
Ирина:	Не за что. Вот мы и в буфете. Приятного аппетита!

Джон: Спасибо, Ирина. Увидимся в фойе гостиницы.
Ирина: До встречи в фойе.

John: Hello, Irina!
Irina: Hello, John!
John: How are you doing?
Irina: Fine, thank you. And you?
John: Everything is great! Tell (me) please, where are we having breakfast?
Irina: Oh, you haven't had breakfast yet? Breakfast is on the first floor, in the café. Let's go, I'll show you. I'm just from there.
John: Thank you very much. What do they have for breakfast (what is there for breakfast)?
Irina: I had (ate) an omelet and a sandwich with cheese and drank water and coffee with milk.
John: I don't like to eat a lot for breakfast. Do they have (are there) fruits and cereal?
Irina: Yes, of course (there are). Do you know that we'll have lunch in a restaurant in the center of the city?
John: What restaurant is it?
Irina: It's a Russian restaurant on Nevsky Prospect (Avenue). It has Russian cuisine.
John: Great! I like Russian cuisine! Thanks for your help!
Irina: Not at all. Here's the café (here we are in the café). Bon appétit!
John: Thank you, Irina. See you in the lobby of the hotel.
Irina: See you (until our meeting) in the lobby.

NOTES

Notice the difference between the phrases **мы завтракаем** and **мы будем обедать.** The former is in the present tense and means *we have breakfast* (usually) or *we are having breakfast* (either right now or in the future). The latter, **мы будем обедать,** refers only to the future and means *we will have lunch.*

Notice the expressions **бутерброд с сыром** *(a sandwich with cheese)* and **кофе с молоком** *(coffee with milk)*. *With something* requires the instrumental case in Russian; we'll learn this case in a later Unit.

Remember to differentiate among the Russian cases you already know: the nominative, the accusative, and the prepositional.

NUTS & BOLTS 1
THE FUTURE TENSE OF быть *(TO BE)*

Let's take a look at the conjugation of the verb *to be* in the future tense.

Future tense of **быть** *(to be)*

я буду	мы будем
ты будешь	вы будете
он/она/оно будет	они будут

Formally, this conjugation fully coincides with the present tense Conjugation I. The verb **быть** usually functions as the auxiliary verb with the infinitive that follows it.

Я буду ужинать дома.
I will have dinner at home.

By itself, **я буду** can also mean *I will be.*

Я буду в гостинице.
I will be in the hotel.

PRACTICE 1

Say where the following people will have breakfast, lunch, or dinner using the prompts.

1. я (завтракать; дома)

2. мы (обедать; кафе)

3. они (ужинать; ресторан)

4. Николай (завтракать; буфет)

5. Вы (обедать; университет)

6. ты (ужинать; гостиница)

NUTS & BOLTS 2

THE DEMONSTRATIVE PRONOUN ЭТОТ

Notice the demonstrative pronoun **этот** *(this)* in the phrase **этот ресторан** *(this restaurant)*. Like adjectives, demonstrative pronouns agree in gender, number, and case with the nouns they modify. Learn the following forms of the demonstrative pronoun **этот** in the nominative and prepositional cases.

Nominative case	
этот ресторан *(m.)*	*this restaurant*
эта гостиница *(f.)*	*this hotel*
это кафе *(n.)*	*this café*
эти студенты *(pl.)*	*these students*

Prepositional case (singular only)	
в этом ресторане *(m.)*	*in this restaurant*
в этой гостинице *(f.)*	*in/at this hotel*
в этом кафе *(n.)*	*in this café*

PRACTICE 2
Say the following in Russian.

1. I am having breakfast at this hotel.

2. I will have breakfast at this hotel.

3. He has lunch downtown.

4. He will have lunch downtown.

5. We are having dinner in this Russian restaurant.

6. We will have dinner in this Russian restaurant.

CONVERSATION 2
An American exchange student, Lisa, is going food shopping with her Russian friend, Nikolai. They are discussing their dinner plans.

Николай: Лиза, что ты хочешь купить в супермаркете?

Лиза: Я хочу купить рыбу, помидоры, зелёный салат, лук, картошку, мясо и макароны.

Николай: Что-нибудь ещё?

Лиза: Да, ещё что-нибудь на завтрак. Может быть, я куплю сыр, яйца, сок, чай, кофе и молоко. Я обычно завтракаю дома.

Николай: Всё это есть в этом большом, новом супермаркете. А где ты обедаешь и ужинаешь?

Лиза: Обычно, я обедаю в университете, в столовой, а ужинаю или дома, или в ресторане с друзьями.

Николай: А где ты ужинаешь сегодня вечером? Я знаю одно хорошее и недорогое кафе в центре.

Лиза: Извини, Коля, сегодня у меня много работы и я буду ужинать дома. Но завтра пятница. Давай пойдём туда завтра вечером.

| Николай: | Договорились—завтра вечером мы вместе ужинаем в этом кафе. А потом пойдём в клуб. |
| Лиза: | С удовольствием! |

Nikolai:	Lisa, what would you like (do you want) to buy in the supermarket?
Lisa:	I'd like (I want) to buy fish, tomatoes, lettuce, onion(s), potato(es), meat, and pasta.
Nikolai:	Anything else?
Lisa:	Yes, also something for breakfast. Maybe I'll buy cheese, eggs, juice, tea, coffee, and milk. I usually have breakfast at home.
Nikolai:	All of this is available in this big, new supermarket. And where do you have lunch and dinner?
Lisa:	Usually, I have lunch at the university, in the cafeteria, and dinner either at home or in a restaurant with my friends.
Nikolai:	Where are you having dinner tonight? I know one good and inexpensive café downtown.
Lisa:	I'm sorry, Kolya, I have a lot of work (to do) today and I'll have dinner at home. But tomorrow is Friday. Let's go there tomorrow night.
Nikolai:	Agreed, tomorrow night we're having dinner in this café. And then we'll go to a club.
Lisa:	Great (with pleasure)!

Notes

Notice how Lisa calls **Николай** "**Коля.**" She does so because they are on informal terms—they are **на ты.**

Pay attention to some of the time expressions used: **утром, днём, вечером.** They mean *in the morning, in the afternoon,* and *in the evening* respectively. These expressions are the neuter noun **утро** *(morning),* the masculine nouns **день** *(afternoon/day)* and **вечер** *(evening)* in the instrumental case. In Russian, you don't need any preposition to say in the morning, in the afternoon, or in the evening. All you need are these nouns in the instrumental case. We'll look at this case later.

NUTS & BOLTS 3
CONJUNCTIONS

You have been introduced to some conjunctions in this dialogue: **и, а, но, или,** and **или . . . или.** The conjunction **или** means *or.* *Either . . . or* in Russian is **или . . . или.**

Или дома, или в ресторане.
Either at home or in a restaurant.

The Russian conjunction **и** means *and,* **но** means *but.* However, there's no direct equivalent for the Russian conjunction **а.** It is usually used to denote contrast rather than contradiction (for which the Russians use **но**).

Я обедаю в университете, а ужинаю дома.
I have lunch at the university and/but have dinner at home.

Here we have contrast rather than contradiction. But if you say **хороший, но недорогой ресторан** *(good but inexpensive restaurant),* you present it as a contradiction: from the fact that it's good, one would expect it to be expensive but it isn't. Of course, you can simply say **хороший и недорогой ресторан** *(good and inexpensive restaurant).*

и	and (enumeration)
а	and/but (contrast)
но	but (contradiction)

PRACTICE 3

Supply the sentences below with the appropriate time expressions in the instrumental case.

1. Я завтракаю дома.

2. Ты обедаешь в университете.

3. Они ужинают в ресторане.

4. Я куплю еду в супермаркете.

5. Вы обедаете в гостинице.

6. Мы вместе будем ужинать в этом кафе.

7. Мы вместе пойдём в клуб.

ANSWERS

PRACTICE 1: 1. Я буду завтракать дома. **2.** Мы будем обедать в кафе. **3.** Они будут ужинать в ресторане. **4.** Николай будет завтракать в буфете. **5.** Вы будете обедать в университете. **6.** Ты будешь ужинать в гостинице.

PRACTICE 2: 1. Я завтракаю в этой гостинице. **2.** Я буду завтракать в этой гостинице. **3.** Он обедает в центре города. **4.** Он будет обедать в центре города. **5.** Он ужинает в этом русском ресторане. **6.** Он будет ужинать в этом русском ресторане.

PRACTICE 3: 1. утром; **2.** днём; **3.** вечером; **4.** днём; **5.** днём; **6.** вечером; **7.** вечером

UNIT 2 ESSENTIALS

Как у вас дела? *(pl./sg. fml.)*	*How are you doing?*
Как у тебя дела? *(infml. sg.)*	*How are you doing?*
Утром я завтракаю дома.	*In the morning, I have breakfast at home.*
Где мы будем обедать днём?	*Where will we have lunch in the afternoon?*
Вечером я ужинаю в ресторане в центре города.	*In the evening, I have dinner in a restaurant in the center of the city.*
Что вы любите есть на завтрак, обед, ужин?	*What do you like to eat for breakfast, lunch, (and) dinner?*
Он на Невском проспекте.	*He/It is on Nevsky Prospect.*
Я люблю русскую кухню!	*I like (lit., love) Russian cuisine.*
Приятного аппетита!	*Bon appétit!*
Увидимся в фойе гостиницы.	*See you in the lobby of the hotel.*
Я хочу купить в супермаркете рыбу, мясо, зелёный салат и помидоры.	*I'd like (I want) to buy fish, meat, lettuce, and tomatoes in the supermarket.*
Что там есть на завтрак?	*What do they have (what is there) for breakfast?*
У меня много работы.	*I have a lot of work (to do).*
Давай(те) пойдём в клуб.	*Let's go to a club.*

Unit 3
Family and the home

In Unit 3, you'll learn how to talk about your family, age, occupations, residences, and accommodations. You'll learn the last three cases, the genitive, the instrumental, and the dative, as you continue to expand and master the ones you're already familiar with—the nominative, the accusative, and the prepositional. You'll also learn numerals, a little bit about reflexive verbs, as well as personal and possessive pronouns. Let's get going!

——————— Lesson 9 (Words) ———————

WORD LIST 1

Добрый вечер!	*Good evening!*
муж	*husband*
жена	*wife*
много дел	*lots of things to do (lit., lots of things)*
юрист	*lawyer*
консультант	*consultant*
финансовая компания	*financial company*
мальчик	*boy*
девочка	*girl*
сын	*son*
дочь *(f.)* (дочка—*dim.*)	*daughter*
старший	*older (elder)*
младший	*younger*
брат	*brother*
другой	*other (another)*

| детский сад | daycare |
| школа | school (elementary, middle, high) |

NUTS & BOLTS 1
SINGULAR POSSESSIVE PRONOUNS

Learn the following Russian equivalents of the 1st and 2nd person possessive pronouns my, your *(infml. sg.)*, our, and your *(fml. sg., pl)* in the nominative case. As modifiers, they have to agree with the nouns they define.

	Masculine	Feminine	Neuter	Plural
my	мой	моя	моё	мои
your (sg., infml.)	твой	твоя	твоё	твои
our	наш	наша	наше	наши
your (pl., fml.)	ваш	ваша	ваше	ваши

The 3rd person possessive pronouns **его** *(his, its)*, **её** *(her)*, and **их** *(their)*, agree in gender and number with the owner rather than with the object that is owned, just like their English counterparts *his, her,* and *their.*

мой сын
my son

наша дочь
our daughter

твой муж
your husband

PRACTICE 1

Modify the following nouns with the correct possessive pronoun.

1. my husband
2. his wife
3. our daughter

4. their boy
5. your *(infml.)* school
6. your *(fml.)* older brother

NUTS & BOLTS 2

NUMBERS 11–100 AND THE GENITIVE CASE (SINGULAR)

Before we discuss the genitive case, let's take a look at the Russian numerals from 11 to 100.

одиннадцать	11
двенадцать	12
тринадцать	13
четырнадцать	14
пятнадцать	15
шестнадцать	16
семнадцать	17
восемнадцать	18
девятнадцать	19
двадцать	20
тридцать	30
сорок	40
пятьдесят	50

шестьдесят	60
семьдесят	70
восемьдесят	80
девяносто	90
сто	100

The nouns that come after Russian numerals follow a strange and counterintuitive rule known as the Rule of Numbers. Take a look at the following chart to find out which number will use which case.

Number	Case
1, 21, 31, etc.	nominative sg. or accusative sg.
2–4, 22–24, 32–34, etc.	genitive sg.
5–20, 25–30, 35–40, etc.	genitive pl.

Before we can use this Rule of Numbers, you have to learn another case: the genitive case. Let's start with the genitive singular. The endings for the masculine and neuter nouns are **-а/-я,** while the feminine endings are **-ы/-и.**

Genitive	Ending	Example
m./n.	**-а/-я**	**сына, пива**
f.	**-ы/-и**	**жены, девочки**

The genitive case has many different functions in Russian, of which the rule of numbers is only one example. The quantitative word **много**—as in the expression you learned in Unit 1, **много работы** *(a lot of work)*—also requires the genitive case.

Let's now look at how these cases work with numbers. We'll begin with the numerals 1 through 4. Keep in mind that the numeral stays the same except in the accusative feminine singular.

	Masculine	Feminine	Neuter
Nominative	**сын**	**девочка, школа**	**пиво**
	один сын	**одна девочка, одна школа**	**одно пиво**
Genitive	**сына**	**девочки, школы**	**пива**
	два сына	**три девочки, три школы**	**четыре пива**

PRACTICE 2
Give Russian equivalents to the word combinations with numerals below. Remember to follow the Rule of Numbers! Also remember to agree the Russian numerals *one* and *two* in gender with the people or things you count.

1. one son

2. two daughters *(dim.)*

3. three mothers

4. four beers

5. three nights

6. twenty-one companies

7. four brothers

8. three girls

9. two boys

10. twenty-three schools

NUTS & BOLTS 3
Counting years

When you count years, use the noun **год** *(year)* in the nominative for years ending in 1 **(один год),** and its genitive singular form **года** for years ending in 2, 3, or 4 **(два года, три года, четыре года).** From 5 up, you need to use **лет,** a different form for years.

пять лет
five years

двенадцать лет
twelve years

девятнадцать лет
nineteen years

Remember that 21–24, 31–34, etc. will use **год** in its appropriate form according to the final number.

двадцать один год
twenty-one years

сорок четыре года
forty-four years

PRACTICE 3
Agree the noun **год** *(year)* with the numerals below.

1. 2   5. 43

2. 5   6. 74

3. 1   7. 66

4. 21

WORD LIST 2
общежитие	*dormitory*
родители *(pl.)*	*parents*

он родился	*he was born*
она родилась	*she was born*
они родились	*they were born*
сестра	*sister*
программист	*programmer*
библиотекарь *(m.)*	*librarian (male or female)*
год (года, лет)	*year*
двухэтажный дом	*two-story house*
за городом	*in the suburbs, in the country (lit., beyond the city)*
дача	*dacha (Russian cottage in the country)*
коттедж	*suburban house*
со всеми удобствами	*with all modern conveniences*
квартира	*apartment*
спальня	*bedroom*
гостиная	*living room*
столовая	*dining room (also cafeteria or dining hall)*
ванная	*bathroom*
туалет	*toilet, half-bath*

NOTES

The verb **родиться** *(to be born)* is a reflexive verb. We'll look at reflexive verbs in a later lesson in this unit; for now, please just remember this as an expression. Use **родился** for men, **родилась** for women, and **родились** for the plural. This expression will usually be followed by the prepositional case.

NUTS & BOLTS 4
PREPOSITIONAL PHRASES WITH ROOMS OF THE HOUSE

Now let's look at the names of rooms in the house and the prepositional phrases with them. Notice that some of them are nouns, but some are substantivized adjectives—modifiers of the implied noun **комната** *(room)*. You can tell the difference by their endings.

Remember that substantivized adjectives, such as **столовая** *(dining room)*, should be declined as adjectives although they're used in the sentence as nouns.

спальня, **в спальне**	*bedroom,* *in the bedroom*	noun
гостиная, **в гостиной**	*living room,* *in the living room*	substantivized adjective
столовая, **в столовой**	*dining room,* *in the dining room*	substantivized adjective
коридор, **в коридоре**	*corridor,* *in the corridor*	noun
кухня, **на кухне**	*kitchen,* *in the kitchen*	noun
ванная, **в ванной**	*bathroom*,* *in the bathroom*	substantivized adjective
туалет, **в туалете**	*toilet*,* *in the toilet*	noun
балкон, **на балконе**	*balcony,* *on the balcony*	noun
терраса, **на террасе**	*terrace/deck,* *on the terrace/deck*	noun

*Note that in Russian speaking countries, **туалет** refers to a room with only a toilet, while **ванная** is a room with a bathtub or shower, and often a toilet as well.

The neuter noun **общежитие** *(dorm)* belongs to a special subgroup of nouns that have two -**и**'s in the prepositional case. These nouns can be masculine **(кафетерий)**, feminine **(Россия)**, or neuter **(общежитие)**. However, all of them have the penultimate -**и**. So you should say **в кафетерии, в России, в общежитии.** This is good to remember because the names of many countries

and states in Russian end in **-ия.** Consequently, their preposi-
tional case is as follows: **Франция–во Франции** *(France, in
France)*, **Италия–в Италии** *(Italy, in Italy)*, **Япония–в Японии**
(Japan, in Japan), **Германия–в Германии** *(Germany, in Germany)*,
Калифорния–в Калифорнии *(California, in California)*, etc.

Я ел(а) в кафетерии.
I ate in the cafeteria.

Она была в России.
She was in Russia.

Он был в общежитии.
He was in the dorm.

PRACTICE 4

Где вы родились? *(Where were you born?)* Answer this question
using the following prompts. Remember to put the places of
birth (locations) in the prepositional case and make sure the verb
agrees with the subject!

1. Анна–Калифорния

2. Николай–Россия

3. мы–Америка

4. она–Вермонт

5. Вы–Москва

6. они–Италия

7. Иван–Петербург

Culture note

Most Russian families live in city apartments. As Christy notes in
Conversation 2, Russians count rooms in their apartments (rather
than bedrooms) and don't count bathrooms, kitchens, and corri-
dors. So a standard American one-bedroom apartment is a two-
room Russian apartment **(двухкомнатная квартира);** a
two-bedroom apartment is a three-room Russian one
(трёхкомнатная квартира), etc. It's fairly common to have the
bathroom separate from the toilet. The first is a **ванная,** the other

is a **туалет**. Besides the apartment in the city, most Russian families own a small country house with a small piece of land, one hour or so away from their city of residence. This country house is called a **дача** (dacha). It may or may not have all modern conveniences, such as hot and cold water, an in-house bathroom, or a heating system suitable for the Russian winter. However, many of the new dachas match all of the expected standards, and they are referred to as being **со всеми удобствами** (with all modern amenities). Some of the more affluent residents of Russian cities can afford buying a house in the suburbs comparable to an American single-family home, called a **коттедж** in Russian. This relatively new phenomenon of Russian life has lately become more popular among those who prefer, and can afford, a daily escape from the city.

ANSWERS

PRACTICE 1: 1. мой муж; **2.** его жена; **3.** наша дочь; **4.** их мальчик; **5.** твоя школа; **6.** ваш старший брат

PRACTICE 2: 1. один сын; **2.** две дочери; **3.** одна мать; **4.** четыре пива; **5.** три ночи; **6.** двадцать одна компания; **7.** четыре брата; **8.** три девочки; **9.** два мальчика; **10.** двадцать три школы

PRACTICE 3: 1. два года; **2.** пять лет; **3.** один год; **4.** двадцать один год; **5.** сорок три года; **6.** семьдесят четыре года; **7.** шестьдесят шесть лет

PRACTICE 4: 1. Анна родилась в Калифорнии. **2.** Николай родился в России. **3.** Мы родились в Америке. **4.** Она родилась в Вермонте. **5.** Вы родились в Москве. **6.** Они родились в Италии. **7.** Иван родился в Петербурге.

PHRASE LIST 1

она осталась дома	*she stayed at home*
она работает консультантом	*she works as a consultant*
если я не ошибаюсь	*if I'm not mistaken*
двое детей	*two children*
замужем	*married (about a woman)*
женат	*married (about a man)*
с нами живёт младший сын	*the younger son lives with us*
он ходит в школу	*he goes to school (secondary school)*
дочери учатся в университете	*daughters go to college (lit., study at university)*
в других штатах	*in other states*
они приезжают домой на каникулы	*they come home for breaks (school breaks)*
я вас обязательно познакомлю	*I'll definitely introduce you*
Всего хорошего!	*Take care! So long! (lit., All the best!)*

NOTES

The adverb **замужем** means *married* and refers only to women. Married men are referred to with the short adjective **женат**: **она замужем** *(she's married);* **он женат** *(he's married).*

NUTS & BOLTS 1
THE INSTRUMENTAL CASE
Now let's learn the noun endings in the instrumental case.

Instrumental case	Ending	Example
m./n.	-ом/-ём/-ем	консультантом словарём, мужем

Instrumental case	Ending	Example
f.	-ой/-ёй/-ей	журналисткой
pl.	-ами/-ями	консультантами врачами журналистками словарями

For masculine and neuter nouns, the hard ending **-ом** follows hard consonants and the consonants **ж, ш, щ, ч, ц,** if the ending is stressed. The soft stressed ending **-ём** follows soft consonants (**-ем** is the unstressed soft ending). The feminine endings are **-ой** or **-ёй/ей**. The plural instrumental endings are **-ами** (hard) or **-ями** (soft). The question words **кто?** and **что?** become **кем?** and **чем?** in the instrumental case.

NUTS & BOLTS 2
CONJUGATION I VERBS работать *(TO WORK)* AND жить *(TO LIVE)*
Let's look at the conjugation of two important verbs **работать** *(to work)* and **жить** *(to live)*.

работать *(to work)*

я работаю	мы работаем
ты работаешь	вы работаете
он/она/оно работает	они работают

Past: **работал, работала, работало, работали**

Работать is an imperfective, Conjugation I verb. Its conjugation is fully predictable and standard; it has no mutations or stress shifts. In fact, this verb is so regular that you can use it as a pattern for Conjugation I verbs whose stem end in **-ай**:

работа [й-у]=ю > работаю, etc. You can hear the last й of the stem in every present tense form, i.e., before all vowel endings (although you can't see it since it is a part of the following "iotated" vowel—either ю=[й+у] or е=[й+э]). However, the phonetic й disappears before all consonant endings, that is, in the past tense and in the infinitive: работал, работать. We'll refer to this subtype of Conjugation I verbs as -ай verbs throughout the rest of this course.

The verb работать can take different cases depending on the specific meaning of each phrase and is used with the instrumental case above. This case usually states the instrument with which or the manner in which something is done.

Она работает консультантом.
She works as a consultant.

There is an easier way to express the same idea.

Она консультант.
She's a consultant.

This pattern works with other occupations as well.

Он врач. Он работает врачом.
He's a doctor. He works as a doctor.

Она юрист. Она работает юристом.
She's a lawyer. She works as a lawyer.

Naturally, the verb **работать** can take the prepositional case that indicates the location, the place where one works.

Он работает в больнице.
He works at the hospital.

Она работает в финансовой компании.
She works at a finance company.

Now let's look at the conjugation of the verb **жить** *(to live)*.

жить *(to live)*

я живу	мы живём
ты живёшь	вы живёте
он/она/оно живёт	они живут

Past: жил, жила, жило, жили

This verb has a consonant stem **жив-**. All consonant stems stay intact before vowel endings, as in the present tense. However, they lose the last consonant before all consonant endings, as in the past tense or in the infinitive form. Consequently, the Russians say **живу,** but **жил** and **жить.**

As you can guess, this verb takes the prepositional case, which denotes the location where you live.

Я живу в Москве.
I live in Moscow.

Я живу в Нью-Йорке.
I live in New York.

Я живу в России.
I live in Russia.

Я живу в Калифорнии.
I live in California.

If this location is plural, you need to use the prepositional plural ending, either **-ах** (hard) or **-ях** (soft), e.g., **в городах** *(in cities).*

Они живут в других штатах.
They live in other states.

PRACTICE 1

Кем вы работаете? *(What do you do? lit., As who do you work?)* Say what the following people do for a living using the verb **работать.** Remember to use the instrumental case!

1. Михаил–бизнесмен

2. она–юрист

3. мой муж–консультант

4. моя жена–журналистка

5. их старший сын–врач

6. её родители–врачи

7. наша дочь–библиотекарь

PRACTICE 2

Где они живут? *(Where do they live?)* Say where these people live. Use the prompts below.

1. Bill–New York

2. his children–other states

3. Julia–Moscow

4. her parents–other cities

5. I–California

PHRASE LIST 2

моя семья *(sg.)*	*my family*
сейчас	*now*
я живу в студенческом общежитии	*I live in a student dorm*
она сидит дома	*she stays (lit., sits) home*
ей два года	*she's two years old*
у нас дом загородом	*we have a house in the suburbs*
Сколько?	*How much?/How many?*
например	*for example*
Как интересно!	*How interesting!*

NUTS & BOLTS 3
THE DATIVE CASE

Now let's look at the final Russian case, the dative. This case is used to express the indirect object. It's always associated with the act of giving and denotes the recipient of the giving action, its beneficiary. When you give something to someone, this *someone* is in the dative case, whereas the *something* is in the accusative as a direct object. Let's look how Russian nouns and pronouns change in the dative case.

	Singular	Plural
m. zero	-у/ю брату, библиотекарю	-ам/ям студентам, гостям
m. -а	-е папе	-ам/ям
f. -а	-е сестре	-ам/ям
f. soft	-и дочери, матери	-ам/ям

Personal pronouns have different forms in the dative case as well.

Nominative	Dative
я	мне
ты	тебе
он, оно	ему
она	ей

Nominative	Dative
мы	**нам**
вы	**вам**
они	**им**

When Russians give their age *(I am X years old)*, they use the dative case construction, which literally translates as *To me (is/are) X years.*

Мне двадцать пять лет.
I'm 25 years old. (lit., To me, twenty-five years.)

PRACTICE 3

Сколько вам лет? *(How old are you?)* Say how old these people are using the prompts below. Remember to follow the rule of numbers (see above), and use the correct form of the noun **год!**

1. my son—21
2. his daughter—5
3. her husband—42
4. their parents—65 and 64
5. I—30
6. our doctor—44
7. my older sister—25

Discovery activity

How big is your family? Think of every member of your family you can mention by his or her generic name: **муж, жена, сын, дочь, отец, мать,** or **родители. Сколько им лет?**

Try to determine the ages and occupations of the people you encounter during the day: **Сколько им лет? Кем они работают?** If you can't refer to people by their occupation or status in Russian, use pronouns, but remember to follow Russian grammar rules!

ANSWERS

PRACTICE 1: 1. Михаил работает бизнесменом. **2.** Она работает юристом. **3.** Мой муж работает консультантом. **4.** Моя жена работает журналисткой. **5.** Их старший сын работает врачом. **6.** Её родители работают врачами. **7.** Наша дочь работает библиотекарем.

PRACTICE 2: 1. Билл живёт в Нью-Йорке. **2.** Его дети живут в других штатах. **3.** Юля живёт в Москве. **4.** Её родители живут в других городах. **5.** Я живу в Калифорнии.

PRACTICE 3: 1. Моему сыну двадцать один год. **2.** Его дочери пять лет. **3.** Её мужу сорок два года. **4.** Их родителям шестьдесят пять лет и шестьдесят четыре года. **5.** Мне тридцать лет. **6.** Нашему врачу сорок четыре года. **7.** Моей старшей сестре двадцать пять лет.

——————— Lesson 11 (Sentences) ———————

SENTENCE LIST 1

Вы здесь один или с женой?	*Are you here alone or with (your) wife?*
У жены было много дел.	*(My) wife had a lot of work/things (to do).*
У вас есть дети?	*Do you have children?*
У нас двое детей.	*We have two kids.*
Они живут с вами?	*Do they live with you?*
Наш сын ходит в детский сад.	*Our son goes to daycare.*
Наша дочь ходит в школу.	*Our daughter goes to school (secondary education).*
Старшие дочери учатся в институте.	*The older daughters go to college.*
Вы, наверное, скучаете по ним.	*You probably miss them.*
Они часто приезжают домой на каникулы.	*They often come home for break.*

| Передавайте большой | *Say hello (lit., big greeting) to your wife.* |
| привет вашей жене. | |

Notes

In the sentence **у жены было много дел** *(my/the wife had a lot of things to do)*, the verb **было** *(was)* is in the past tense and agrees with **много** *(a lot of/many)*, which is considered neuter in Russian. The quantitative expression **много дел** (as well as its opposite, **мало дел**) is similar to the one in Unit 2 **много работы** *(a lot of work [to do])*, except that the following noun is in the genitive plural form. We'll learn the genitive plural in the next unit. For now, remember the simple rule: if the noun ends in a vowel in the nominative singular (regardless of the gender), the genitive plural drops it so that the final form is truncated as in **дел, школ, больниц,** etc.

NUTS & BOLTS 1
PERSONAL PRONOUNS IN THE GENITIVE AND EXPRESSING POSSESSION

In the last lesson you learned how to express the personal pronouns in the dative case. Now, let's look at the personal pronouns in the genitive case.

Nominative	Genitive
я	меня
ты	тебя
он, оно	его, него
она	её, неё
мы	нас
вы	вас
они	их, них

Notice that the third person pronouns in the genitive will begin with **н** after a preposition. In Russian, personal pronouns in the genitive case are used most often to express possession following the formula **у** + genitive pronoun + **есть**.

У вас есть дети?

Do you have children?

У нас двое детей.

We have two kids.

Notice in the answer **у нас двое детей** the verb **есть** is omitted. This occurs when there is clarification on the original question, in this case **двое**.

It's idiomatic to use the collective numerals **двое, трое,** and **четверо** in this context in Russian. The collective numerals from two to four are the most common in Russian. Remember that, as opposed to the standard numerals 2, 3, and 4, which take the genitive singular (see the rule of numbers above), the collective numerals take the genitive plural: **двое детей**. Memorize the nominative plural noun **дети** *(children, kids)* and its genitive plural form **детей**. The singular form of **дети** is **ребёнок** *(child, kid),* so you should say **один ребёнок** but **двое детей**.

PRACTICE 1

Сколько у вас детей? *(How many children do you have?)* Give the Russian equivalents to the following English sentences. Don't translate the possessive pronouns in brackets.

1. We have three kids **(дети).**

2. They have two kids.

3. (My) brother has three kids.

4. Do you *(fml.)* have one child?

5. (My) daughter has two kids.

SENTENCE LIST 2

Они живут в отдельном доме.	They live in a separate (single-family) home.
Они живут в квартире.	They live in an apartment.
Это не дача, а коттедж.	This isn't a dacha; it's a cottage.
Сколько у вас комнат в доме?	How many rooms do you have (are there) in your house?
У вас дом со всеми удобствами?	Does your house have all modern conveniences?
У нас в квартире есть горячая вода, ванная и туалет.	We have hot water, a bathroom, and a toilet in our apartment.
У нас на даче нет горячей воды.	We don't have hot water at (our) dacha.
Мы живём в двухкомнатной/ трёхкомнатной/ четырехкомнатной квартире в городе.	We live in a two-room/three-room/four-room apartment in the city.
Это значит, что у нас две спальни и одна гостиная.	This means that we have two bedrooms and one living room.
Приезжайте к нам в гости в Вермонт!	Come visit us in Vermont!

NUTS & BOLTS 2
NEGATION

Learn the following phrase **не дача, а коттедж. Не . . . , а . . .** is a common construction in Russian. Use it every time you contrast two things and choose one of them *(not X but Y)*. Notice that the Russian negative particle **не** comes immediately before the word it negates, be it a noun or a verb.

Я живу не в доме, а в квартире.
I live not in a house, but in an apartment.

When you want to express the absence of something or some-body in Russian, you need to use the genitive of negation. You do so by putting the missing object into the genitive case.

У нас нет горячей воды.
We don't have hot water.

У меня нет друга.
I don't have a friend.

У меня нет дачи.
I don't have a dacha.

The verb **есть** *(to be)* becomes **нет** in the negative.

PRACTICE 2
Restate the sentences below as one sentence using the phrase **не . . . , а. . . .**

1. Я не живу на даче. Я живу в квартире.

2. Он не из Канады. Он из Америки.

3. Моя дочь не учится в университете. Она учится в школе.

4. Его жена не работает юристом. Она работает консультантом.

5. Вашему брату не двадцать лет. Ему пятнадцать лет.

PRACTICE 3
Restate the following sentences in the negative. Remember to use the genitive of negation.

1. У нас есть дача.

2. В этом университете есть общежитие.

3. У нас есть горячая вода.

4. У вас есть спальня.

5. В этом доме есть столовая.

6. У них есть дочь.

> ### *Language link*
>
> Use an internet search engine to look for **квартиры в Москве** (*apartments in Moscow*) and check out some of the Russian websites that offer apartments in Moscow for rent. What types of apartments do they offer? **Сколько комнат?** (*How many rooms?*) **Какие комнаты?** (*What kind of rooms?*) Say as much as you can about them in Russian.

ANSWERS

PRACTICE 1: 1. У нас трое детей. **2.** У них двое детей. **3.** У брата трое детей. **4.** У вас один ребёнок? **5.** У дочери двое детей.

PRACTICE 2: 1. Я живу не на даче, а в квартире. **2.** Он не из Канады, а из Америки. **3.** Моя дочь учится не в университете, а в школе. **4.** Его жена работает не юристом, а консультантом. **5.** Вашему брату не двадцать, а пятнадцать лет.

PRACTICE 3: 1. У нас нет дачи. **2.** В этом университете нет общежития. **3.** У нас нет горячей воды. **4.** У вас нет спальни. **5.** В этом доме нет столовой. **6.** У них нет дочери.

—————— Lesson 12 (Conversations) ——————

CONVERSATION 1

At the reception after a conference, an American visitor, Bill Cooper, is talking to his Russian colleague and acquaintance, Yulia Igorevna Sidorova. They are discussing their families.

Билл Купер: Здравствуйте, Юлия Игоревна!

Ю. И. Сидорова: Добрый вечер, господин Купер! Вы здесь один или с женой?

Билл Купер:	Один. У жены было много дел и она осталась дома.
Ю. И. Сидорова:	А кем работает ваша жена?
Билл Купер:	Она юрист, но она работает консультантом в финансовой компании.
Ю. И. Сидорова:	А как ваши дети? Если я не ошибаюсь, у вас двое детей?
Билл Купер:	Нет, трое. У нас две девочки и один мальчик.
Ю. И. Сидорова:	А сколько им лет?
Билл Купер:	Старшей дочери, Джил, двадцать один год, Сюзане девятнадцать лет, а младшему сыну, Генри четырнадцать. А вы замужем?
Ю. И. Сидорова:	Да, замужем. Моего мужа зовут Николай Сергеевич. Он врач и работает в больнице.
Билл Купер:	А у вас есть дети?
Ю. И. Сидорова:	Да, у нас один сын. Ему четыре года. Он ходит в детский сад. Ваши дети живут с вами?
Билл Купер:	С нами живёт только младшийш Генри. Он еще ходит в школу. А старшие дочери учатся в университетах, в других штатах. Я вас познакомлю, когда вы будете в Америке.
Ю. И. Сидорова:	С удовольствием познакомлюсь с ними. Передавайте вашей жене большой привет. Всего хорошего!
Билл Купер:	Обязательно передам. До свидания, Юлия Игоревна. До встречи.

Bill Cooper:	Hello, Julia Igorevna!
J. I. Sidorova:	Good evening, Mr. Cooper! Are you here alone or with (your) wife?
Bill Cooper:	Alone. My wife had a lot of things to do and stayed home.
J. I. Sidorova:	And what does your wife do?
Bill Cooper:	She's a lawyer, but she works as a consultant in a finance company.

J. I. Sidorova:	*And how are your children? If I'm not mistaken, you have two kids?*
Bill Cooper:	*No, three. We have two girls and one boy.*
J. I. Sidorova:	*How old are they?*
Bill Cooper:	*The older daughter, Jill, is twenty-one, Susanne is nineteen, and the younger son, Henry, is fourteen. Are you married?*
J. I. Sidorova:	*Yes, I am married. My husband's name is Nikolai Sergeevich. He's a doctor and (he) works in a hospital.*
Bill Cooper:	*Do you have children?*
J. I. Sidorova:	*Yes, we have one son. He's four. He goes to daycare. Do your children live with you?*
Bill Cooper:	*Only our younger son, Henry, lives with us. He still goes to (high) school. But the older daughters go to colleges in other states. I'll introduce you when you come to America (lit., are in America).*
J. I. Sidorova:	*I'll be glad to meet them. Say hello to your wife. Take care!*
Bill Cooper:	*I definitely will. Good by, Julia Igorevna. See you!*

Notes

Note that Bill Cooper is calling Ms. Sidorova by her first name and patronymic. They are on formal terms. Calling her **госпожа Сидорова,** however, would have been too official and impersonal. Because English doesn't have a social equivalent to this type of address (formal yet not impersonal), Ms. Sidorova has no choice but to call Bill Cooper **господин Купер** (Mr. Cooper). Addressing him as Bill, while he's calling her **Юлия Игоревна,** would be uncomfortable for her.

The adverb **ещё** in the sentence **он ещё ходит в школу** translates as *still*.

It is common for Russians to invert the information in a sentence. Since Ms. Sidorova discussed the living arrangements in her previous statement (**Ваши дети живут в вами?**), Bill Cooper begins his reply where she left off: **С нами живёт только младший сын.**

NUTS & BOLTS 1
Reflexive verbs

Если я не ошибаюсь is an idiomatic expression equivalent to the English *if I'm not mistaken*. **Ошибаться** is a Conjugation I verb, and it's a reflexive verb. In Russian, reflexive verbs are conjugated using the same pattern as non-reflexive verbs with the particle **-ся/-сь** added to the end. The ending **-ся** follows consonants, and **-сь** is added after vowels.

ошибаться *(to be mistaken)*

я ошибаюсь	мы ошибаемся
ты ошибаешься	вы ошибаетесь
он/она/оно ошибается	они ошибаются

Past: **ошибался, ошибалась, ошибалось, ошибались.** The stress is stable.

The verb **родиться** *(to be born)* is also reflexive.

родиться *(to be born)*

я рожусь	мы родимся
ты родишься	вы родитесь
он/она/оно родится	они родятся

Past: **родился, родилась, родилось, родились.**

Notice the end stress shift in the past. You should say **родился** for males, **родилась** for females, and **родились** for plurals. Predictably, this verb takes the prepositional case, because the place where you were born is a location.

Он родился в России.
He was born in Russia.

Она родилась во Франции.
She was born in France.

Мы родились в Калифорнии.
We were born in California.

PRACTICE 1
Translate the following sentences into Russian.

1. You're mistaken *(fml.)*; she's twenty-one.

2. If I'm not mistaken, your children live with you *(fml.)*.

3. You're mistaken *(infml.)*; he works as a doctor.

4. He was born in Russia.

5. They were born in Cleveland.

NUTS & BOLTS 2
INSTRUMENTAL CASE OF PERSONAL PRONOUNS
Let's look at the instrumental case of personal pronouns. The instrumental case of pronouns is used especially to express *with someone or something*. Remember that you need the preposition **с** in the instrumental case only in the sense of accompaniment, as in **кофе с молоком** *(coffee with milk)* or **с женой** *(with [my] wife)*, and never in the purely instrumental sense, as in *I'm writing with a pen* (we'll discuss the instrumental of means later).

Nominative	Instrumental
я	со мной
ты	с тобой
он, оно	с ним

Nominative	Instrumental
она	**с ней**
мы	**с нами**
вы	**с вами**
они	**с ними**

PRACTICE 2

Rewrite the following sentences replacing the nouns in the instrumental case with the appropriate pronouns.

1. Мы живём с детьми в отдельном доме.

2. Я живу с братом в гостинице.

3. Я жил с родителями.

4. Они работают с юристом.

5. Вы здесь с женой?

NUTS & BOLTS 3

INSTRUMENTAL CASE OF ADJECTIVES

Let's also look at the adjectival endings in the instrumental case. They are **-ым/им** for masculine and neuter adjectives, **-ой/ей** for feminine adjectives, and **-ыми/ими** for plurals.

с моей младшей сестрой

with my younger sister

с моим младшим братом

with my younger brother

с моими русскими друзьями

with my Russian friends

Let's review the adjectival endings in the nominative, prepositional, and instrumental cases. Learn them through the familiar examples in the chart below.

	Masculine	Feminine	Neuter	Plural
Nom.	младший брат	младшая сестра	доброе утро	русские друзья
Prep.	в большом доме	в ванной комнате	в студенческом общежитии	в других штатах
Inst.	с русским другом	с младшей сестрой	с красным вином	с русскими друзьями

PRACTICE 3
Rewrite the following sentences and put the phrases in the parentheses in the instrumental case.

1. Я живу со (старший брат).

2. Вы работаете с (хороший юрист).

3. Я живу с (американский студент).

4. Она сидит дома с (младшая сестра).

5. Мы работаем с (русские врачи).

CONVERSATION 2
Christy Doyle, an American exchange student, is talking to her Russian host, Aleksei Gregorovich, in her apartment in Moscow. They are having tea and discussing their respective families.

Алексей: **Кристи, где ты живёшь в Америке?**
Кристи: **Я из Вермонта. Я там родилась, и моя семья живёт в Вермонте. Но сейчас я студентка в**

университете в Калифорнии. Я там живу в студенческом общежитии.

Алексей: А кто ваши родители? Кем они работают.

Кристи: Моего отца зовут Патрик. Он программист. Моя мама библиотекарь, но она сейчас не работает. Она сидит дома с моей младшей сестрой Дженнифер. Она ещё маленькая. Ей только два года.

Алексей: А они живут в доме или в квартире?

Кристи: У нас дом загородом.

Алексей: А сколько в нём комнат?

Кристи: У нас четыре спальни, гостиная, столовая, две ванных комнаты.

Алексей: Вы живете на даче?

Кристи: Нет, это не дача, а коттедж—большой двухэтажный дом со всеми удобствами.

Алексей: Значит, у вас шесть комнат?

Кристи: Да, но в Америке мы считаем только спальни. Например, у вас в Москве четырёхкомнатная квартира—это значит, что у вас три спальни и одна гостиная.

Алексей: Как интересно!

Кристи: Приезжайте к нам в гости в Вермонт!

Aleksei: Christy, where do you live in America?

Christy: I'm from Vermont. I was born there and my family lives in Vermont. But now, I'm a student at a university in California. I live in a student dorm there.

Aleksei: And who are your parents? What do they do?

Christy: My father's name is Patrick. He's a programmer. My mother is a librarian, but she's not working now. She's staying home with my younger sister, Jennifer. She's still small. She's only two (years old).

Aleksei: Do they live in a house or in an apartment?

Christy: We have a house in the country (suburbs).

Aleksei: Do you live at a dacha?

Christy:	No, this isn't a dacha; it is a house—a big, two-story house with all the conveniences.
Aleksei:	How many rooms are there (in it)?
Christy:	We have four bedrooms, a living room, a dining room, and two bathrooms.
Aleksei:	Then (this means) you have six rooms?
Christy:	Yes, but in America, we count only bedrooms. For example, you have a four-room apartment in Moscow—this means that you have three bedrooms and one living room.
Aleksei:	How interesting!
Christy:	Come to visit us in Vermont!

NUTS & BOLTS 4
Genitive of origin

Notice the genitive case in Christy's statement **Я из Вермонта.** This is the genitive of origin. You already learned the expressions **Я из Америки** and **Я из Нью-Йорка** in Unit 1. Now you know that all places of origin take the genitive case in Russian and are usually preceded by the preposition **из** *(from)*. The nouns that take the preposition **на** in the prepositional case have the preposition **с** in the genitive of origin.

For example, **на работе** *(at work)* becomes **с работы** *(from work)*. Remember to differentiate among different declensions. Masculine nouns (zero endings or **-ь**) take **-а** (or soft **-я**) in the genitive case **(из Вермонта)**; feminine nouns (**-а/я** endings and some exceptional masculine **-а** nouns) take **-ы** (or soft **-и**) in the genitive **(из Америки).** Also remember that the exceptional nouns in **-ия** (**Россия** and other countries ending in **-ия,** etc.) change their endings to **-ии** in the genitive singular (**из России, из Франции, из Германии,** etc.), just as they do in the prepositional case (**в России, во Франции,** etc.).

Я из Вермонта.

I'm from Vermont.

Я из Америки.
I'm from America.

Я из Нью-Йорка.
I'm from New York.

Он из России.
He's from Russia.

Она из Франции.
She's from France.

PRACTICE 4

Откуда вы? *(Where are you from?)* Restate the answers below using the genitive of origin.

1. Он родился в Москве.

2. Она родилась в Вермонте.

3. Они родились в России.

4. Я родилась в Америке.

5. Ты родился в Петербурге.

6. Вы родились в Германии.

Tip!

How do you use foreign geographical names in Russian? Well, if the foreign geographical name (American, English, French, etc.) fits into any Russian declension, meaning, if it ends in a consonant (1st declension) or the vowel -**a** (2nd declension), you decline it as a Russian noun of the same class: **Вермонт** *(Vermont)* becomes **в Вермонте/из Вермонта,** and **Аризона** *(Arizona)* becomes **в Аризоне/из Аризоны.** If the foreign name has any other ending, so that it doesn't fit the above patterns, it will stay indeclinable in Russian: **Огайо** *(Ohio)* becomes **в Огайо/из Огайо,** and **Миссисипи** *(Mississippi)* becomes **в Миссисипи/из Миссисипи,** etc. There is a way to avoid declining the foreign geographical name if you're not sure how to go about it: introduce the foreign name with a generic noun (**город, штат,** etc.). The generic noun assumes the case, relieving the following noun from the need to change.

Я живу в Мичигане.
I live in Michigan.

Я живу в штате Мичиган.
I live in the state of Michigan.

Я родился в Фениксе.
I live in Phoenix.

Я родился в городе Феникс.
I live in the city of Phoenix.

ANSWERS

PRACTICE 1: 1. Вы ошибаетесь, ей двадцать один (год). **2.** Если я не ошибаюсь, ваши дети живут с вами. **3.** Ты ошибаешься, он работает врачом. **4.** Он родился в России. **5.** Они родились в Кливленде.

PRACTICE 2: 1. Мы живём с ними в отдельном доме. **2.** Я живу с ним в гостинице. **3.** Я жил с ними. **4.** Они работают с ним. **5.** Вы здесь с ней?

PRACTICE 3: 1. Я живу со старшим братом. **2.** Вы работаете с хорошим юристом. **3.** Я живу с американским студентом. **4.** Она сидит дома с младшей сестрой. **5.** Мы работаем с русскими врачами.

PRACTICE 4: 1. Он из Москвы. **2.** Она из Вермонта. **3.** Они из России. **4.** Я из Америки. **5.** Ты из Петербурга. **6.** Вы из Германии.

У жены было много дел.	*(My) wife had a lot of things (to do).*
Моя жена работает консультантом.	*(My) wife works as a consultant.*
Она работает в финансовой компании.	*She works in a financial company.*
Я родился/родилась в Калифорнии.	*I was born in California. (m./f.)*
Я учусь в университете.	*I study in a university (go to college).*
Я живу в студенческом общежитии.	*I live in a student dorm.*
Я замужем/женат.	*I'm married. (f./m.)*
Сколько вам лет?	*How old are you?*
Мне двадцать один год.	*I'm 21 years old.*
Мне двадцать два года.	*I'm 22 years old.*
Мне двадцать пять лет.	*I'm 25 years old.*
У вас есть дети?	*Do you have children?*
У нас трое детей.	*We have three kids.*
Младший сын ещё ходит в школу.	*The younger son still goes to school.*
Он живёт с нами в двухэтажном доме загородом.	*He lives with us in a two-story house in the country.*
У нас четыре спальни, гостиная, столовая и две ванных комнаты.	*We have four bedrooms, a living room, a dining room, and two bathrooms.*
Приезжайте к нам в гости в Вермонт!	*Come visit us in Vermont!*

UNIT 4
Everyday life

In Unit 4, you'll learn to talk about your everyday life: going to work, going out, doing laundry and shopping, working out and playing sports, going on tours, meeting with friends, etc. You'll learn dates, days of the week, and months of the year in Russian, as well as how to use them in a sentence. We'll explain Russian perfective and imperfective verbs, and you'll learn how to express what you like doing in Russian.

———— Lesson 13 (Words) ————

WORD LIST 1

снимать—снять	*to rent (an apartment)*
станция метро	*metro station*
остановка	*stop (bus, trolley, streetcar)*
на метро	*by metro, by subway*
пешком	*on foot*
каждый день	*every day*
иногда	*sometimes*
театр	*theater*
музей	*museum*
удобно	*convenient, comfortable*
спортивный зал (спортзал)	*gym (lit., sports hall)*
спортивный клуб (спортклуб)	*gym (lit., sports club)*

NOTES

The Russian verb **снимать** has several meanings: 1) *to rent (to hire, not to rent out)* as in **снимать квартиру,** 2) *to take photographs,* and 3) *to take off* (an article of clothing). This is possible because the verb literally means *to take off,* so in the first case, you *take an apartment off* someone; in the second, you *take an image (photograph) off* someone; in the third, you *take off* your shoes, etc. This verb belongs to Conjugation I.

NUTS & BOLTS 1
IMPERFECTIVE AND PERFECTIVE VERBS
All Russian verbs can be either imperfective or perfective. This grammatical category is called "aspect," and it doesn't correspond directly to anything in English grammar. Of these two types of verbs, only imperfective verbs can be in the present tense. Imperfective verbs describe continuous or repeated actions. For example, when you want to emphasize the fact that you rented an apartment for several months (duration), or when you say that you rented the same apartment several times (repetition), you have to use the imperfective verb **снимать (я снимал квартиру).** Such adverbs as **часто** *(often),* **обычно** *(usually),* **всегда** *(always),* **иногда** *(sometimes),* and **никогда** *(never)* are good indicators of the imperfective aspect because they clearly point at the fact of repetition. Follow them and you'll never be wrong!

However, when you present the act of renting an apartment in such a way that this act either follows something (e.g., you told me to rent it and I did) or precedes something that your interlocutor is aware of (e.g., I rented this apartment and now we have a place to stay), you need to use the perfective aspect. One can say that perfective verbs in Russian denote a one-time action that is either a result of something prior to it or the basis for something following it. Perfective actions denote a link in a causal chain and indicate one-time, completed actions. Because perfective verbs don't occur in the present tense, they automatically become future tense when you conjugate them. The perfective aspect of *to rent* is **снять.**

Я снимал(а) квартиру.

I rented an apartment.

снять *(to rent)*

я сниму	мы снимем
ты снимешь	вы снимите
он/она/оно снимет	они снимут

Past: **снял, сняла, сняло, сняли**

Both the perfective and imperfective forms of this verb take the accusative case.

PRACTICE 1

Fill in the blanks using the correct perfective or imperfective form of the verb **снимать/снять** in the following sentences. Indicate the reason for your choice: present tense, repetition, duration, one-time action/sequence/result.

1. Когда я в Москве, я всегда _____ эту квартиру.

2. Сейчас я живу в цснтре, я _____ прекрасную двухкомнатную квартиру.

3. Моему другу понравилась *(my friend liked)* эта квартира, и он _____ её.

4. Ты обычно _____ квартиру около метро.

5. В прошлом году *(last year)* мы _____ эту квартиру всё лето *(during the whole summer)*.

6. Я _____ эту квартиру, когда у меня будет много денег *(when I have a lot of money)*.

WORD LIST 2

месяц	*month*
один/одна/одни *(m., f., pl.)*	*one, alone*
покупать *(conj. I; -ай)—*	*to buy*
купить *(conj. II; -и)*	

готовить	to cook
стиральная машина	washer (lit., washing machine)
стирать (conj. I; -ай)	to wash, to do laundry
—постирать	
сушилка	dryer
химчистка	dry cleaner
вещь (f.), вещи (pl.)	thing, things
зима	winter
весна	spring
лето	summer
осень	fall

NUTS & BOLTS 2
SEASONS AND MONTHS

Learn the four seasons in Russian. They are **зима** *(winter)*, **весна** *(spring)*, **лето** *(summer)*, **осень** *(fall)*. Notice that **зима** and **весна** are feminine nouns, **осень** is also the feminine noun ending in **-ь,** and **лето** is neuter. In order to say *in the winter, in the spring,* etc., you need to put these nouns into the instrumental case without prepositions.

зимой	in the winter
весной	in the spring
летом	in the summer
осенью	in the fall

Now let's learn the names of the months in Russian. In order to say *in January, in February,* etc., use the preposition **в** and the month in the prepositional case.

январь	January	**в январе**	in January
февраль	February	**в феврале**	in February
март	March	**в марте**	in March
апрель	April	**в апреле**	in April
май	May	**в мае**	in May
июнь	June	**в июне**	in June
июль	July	**в июле**	in July
август	August	**в августе**	in August
сентябрь	September	**в сентябре**	in September
октябрь	October	**в октябре**	in October
ноябрь	November	**в ноябре**	in November
декабрь	December	**в декабре**	in December

All Russian months are masculine and are never capitalized. Notice the following stress pattern in the prepositional case: all cold (fall and winter) months from September to February have end stress; all warm (spring and summer) months from March to August have stem stress.

PRACTICE 2

Когда они жили и работали в России? *(When did they live and work in Russia?)* Restate the sentences below replacing the seasons with the three appropriate months so that *in the winter* indicates *in December, in January, and in February; in the spring* indicates *in March, in April, and in May,* etc.

1. Грэг жил в России весной.

2. Мэри работала в Москве зимой.

3. Дженнифер жила в Петербурге осенью.

4. Билл работал в Ростове летом.

NUTS & BOLTS 3

THE VERBS покупать—купить *(TO BUY)*

To buy is **покупать—купить** in Russian. This is another aspectual pair where **покупать** is imperfective and **купить** is perfective. **Покупать** is a Conjugation I verb, just like the verbs **работать, снимать,** etc. **Купить,** on the other hand, is a Conjugation II verb. Notice in the chart below that it adds the letter -**л** in the first person singular and has a present tense stress shift. Look at the following future tense conjugation of the verb **купить** and note how it is identical to the verb **любить.**

купить *(to buy)*

я куплю	мы купим
ты купишь	вы купите
он/она/оно купит	они купят

Past: **купил, купила, купило, купили**

Remember that the same set of endings as in the imperfective present tense denotes the future tense with the perfective verbs. Compare the following sentences:

Я иногда покупаю продукты в этом магазине.

I sometimes buy groceries in this store. (present tense, imperfective, recurrent action)

Я завтра куплю продукты в этом магазине.

Tomorrow I will buy groceries in this store. (future, perfective, one-time action)

PRACTICE 3

Translate the following sentences into Russian. Pay attention to your choice of aspect and tense! Indicate the reason for your choice of aspect from the following list: present tense, repetition, duration, one-time action/result.

1. We buy groceries in this store.

2. Tomorrow, he will buy groceries in this store.

3. She sometimes bought (used to buy) groceries in this store.

4. They will do laundry tomorrow all day long (весь день).

5. I washed all of his clothes (все его вещи).

6. You *(infml.)* always do laundry at home.

Culture note

It's customary in Russia to consider the first day of the appropriate month to be the beginning of a new season, not the equinox or solstice. So winter officially starts on the 1st of December, spring, on the 1st of March, summer, on the 1st of June, and fall, on the 1st of September. In addition, September 1st is traditionally the first day of the new academic year for all schools and universities (unless, of course, it falls on the weekend), and the official **День знаний** *(Knowledge Day)*. Before 1918, Russia followed the Julian calendar, which is approximately two weeks behind the Gregorian calendar now commonly accepted everywhere in the world, including Russia. However, the Russian Orthodox Church still holds on to the old style Julian calendar. Consequently, Christmas in Russia falls on January 7. The entire week between New Year's Day and Christmas is a national holiday. Don't plan to do any business in Russia at this time, because most government and business institutions will be closed!

ANSWERS

PRACTICE 1: 1. снимаю *(repetition)*; **2.** снимаю *(present)*;
3. снял *(sequence/result)*; **4.** снимаешь *(repetition)*;
5. снимали *(duration)*; **6.** сниму *(sequence/result)*

PRACTICE 2: 1. Грэг жил в России в марте, в апреле и в
мае. **2.** Мэри работала в Москве в декабре, в январе, в
феврале. **3.** Дженнифер жила в Петербурге в сентябре, в
октябре и в ноябре. **4.** Билл работал в Ростове в июне, в
июле и в августе.

PRACTICE 3: 1. Мы покупаем продукты в этом магазине
(present tense). **2.** Завтра он купит продукты в этом
магазине *(one-time action)*. **3.** Она иногда покупала
продукты в этом магазине *(repetition)*. **4.** Они будут стирать
весь день *(duration)*. **5.** Я постирал все его вещи *(one-time
action/result)*. **6.** Ты всегда стираешь дома *(present tense)*.

——————— Lesson 14 (Phrases) ———————

PHRASE LIST 1

Как жизнь? *(infml.)*	*How's life?*
Рад тебя/вас видеть!	*Glad to see you!*
начинать *(conj. I; -ай)* —**начать** + *acc. or impr. inf.*	*to begin, to start*
кончать *(conj. I; -ай)* (**заканчивать**)—**кончить** + *acc. or impr. inf.*	*to end, to finish*
гулять по городу	*walk around the town*
отдыхать	*to rest*
читать *(conj. I; -ай)* **книгу**	*to read a book*
смотреть—посмотреть телевизор	*to watch TV*
делать—сделать + *acc.*	*to do*
после работы	*after work*
выходные (дни)	*weekend (lit., days off)*

дни недели	*days of the week*
по вечерам	*in the evenings*

NUTS & BOLTS 1
MORE IMPERFECTIVE-PERFECTIVE VERB PAIRS

The imperfective-perfective verbs **начинать—начать** *(to begin, to start)* and **заканчивать—закончить** *(to end, to finish)* can take either a compliment in the accusative case:

Он начал работу.

He started work.

or an imperfective infinitive:

Он начал работать.

He started to work.

Notice that the following infinitive must be imperfective. The conjugated verbs themselves, however, can be either perfective or imperfective depending on the context. Sometimes the alternative imperfective verb **кончать** is used instead of **заканчивать**. All three imperfective verbs **начинать, заканчивать, кончать** belong to Conjugation I. The perfective verb **начать** has the same endings as the present tense Conjugation I, but it is formed from the perfective infinitive with the stem **начн-**.

начать *(to begin)*

я начну	мы начнём
ты начнёшь	вы начнёте
он/она/оно начнёт	они начнут

The past tense **начал, начала, начало, начали** has feminine stress shift.

The perfective verb **закончить (кончить)** is Conjugation II.

закончить *(to end)*

я закончу	мы закончим
ты закончишь	вы закончите
он/она/оно закончит	они закончат

The past tense **закончил, закончила, закончило, закончили** has a stable stem stress.

PRACTICE 1
Translate the following sentences into Russian.

1. I'm starting a new job.

2. They started watching TV.

3. He finished working and started reading.

4. She will finish this job.

5. We start every day after work.

NUTS & BOLTS 2
THE DAYS OF THE WEEK
Now, let's learn **дни недели** *(the days of the week)* in Russian:

Дни недели	Days of the week	Когда?	When?
понедельник	*Monday*	в понедельник	*on Monday*
вторник	*Tuesday*	во вторник	*on Tuesday*
среда	*Wednesday*	в среду	*on Wednesday*

четверг	*Thursday*	**в четверг**	*on Thursday*
пятница	*Friday*	**в пятницу**	*on Friday*
суббота	*Saturday*	**в субботу**	*on Saturday*
воскресенье	*Sunday*	**в воскресенье**	*on Sunday*

Notice that the days of the week are not capitalized in Russian, just like the names of the months. Also, in order to say *on Monday, on Tuesday,* etc., you need to use the preposition **в/во** with the accusative case (not prepositional).

Выходные (дни) is the traditional Russian word for *weekend*. The term **уик-энд** is stylistically marked as trendy. **Выходные—это суббота** *(Saturday)* **и воскресенье** *(Sunday)*.

PRACTICE 2
Что вы делали в выходные? *(What did you do on the weekend?)* Complete the sentences using the activities from the above list, such as **читать книгу, смотреть телевизор, отдыхать, гулять по городу.** You can also use any of the expressions you learned in the previous lessons.

1. В пятницу вечером _____ .

2. В субботу утром _____ .

3. В субботу вечером _____ .

4. В воскресенье днём _____ .

PHRASE LIST 2
ходить в гости	*to visit someone, to drop in on someone*
ходить в магазин	*to go to the store*
ездить на экскурсии	*to go on a tour*
встречаться с друзьями	*to meet with friends*
заниматься *(conj. I; -ай)* спортом	*to do/play sports*

кататься (*conj. I;* -ай) на лыжах	to ski
кататься (*conj. I;* -ай) на велосипеде	to ride a bicycle
играть (*conj. I;* -ай) в теннис	to play tennis
сдавать—сдать вещи в химчистку	take things to the dry cleaner
некоторые вещи	some things
поэтому	therefore

NUTS & BOLTS 2
Verbs of motion

The Russian verb of motion **ходить** (e.g., **ходить в школу**) literally means *to walk*. All motion verbs in Russian are distinguished by two general criteria:

1. the method of motion—walking, riding a vehicle, sailing, flying, etc.;

2. the nature of movement—multidirectional (round-trip) or unidirectional (one way).

The verb **ходить** is a walking verb, whereas the verb **ездить** is a vehicular one. Remember that you'll almost always use vehicular motion verbs when a geographical name is mentioned, because this automatically implies traveling by vehicle rather than walking. Both **ходить** and **ездить** are multidirectional verbs. This means that they denote one of the following actions:

a. a recurrent action

Каждый день я хожу на работу.
Every day I go to work.

Каждое лето я езжу в Россию.
I go to Russia every summer.

b. a round-trip action in the past

Вчера я ходил(а) в кино.

I went to the movies yesterday (and I'm back now).

Летом я ездил(а) в Россию.

I went to Russia in the summer (and I'm back now).

c. a general physical action

Я люблю ходить пешком.

I like to walk.

Я люблю ездить на машине.

I like to drive.

Unidirectional verbs, on the other hand, denote an action that is happening at any given point in time: in the present, past, or future. The two unidirectional verbs you need to learn for now are **идти** *(to go on foot, to walk)* and **ехать** *(to go by vehicle, to ride, to drive)*. Let's look at how the verb **идти** is conjugated in the present tense.

идти *(to go on foot, to walk)*

я иду	**мы идём**
ты идёшь	**вы идёте**
он/она/оно идёт	**они идут**

As you can see, it is a Conjugation I verb. Its past tense, however, is irregular: **он шёл, она шла, оно шло, они шли.** Notice that the root vowel -**ё** flees in the past tense forms that have a vowel ending.

The verb **ехать** is also a Conjugation I verb.

ехать *(to go by vehicle, to ride, to drive)*

я еду	мы едем
ты едешь	вы едете
он/она/оно едет	они едут

The past tense is **он ехал, она ехала, оно ехало, они ехали.** No stress shifts either in the present or past.

You should only use the unidirectional motion verbs **идти** and **ехать** for background actions in the past or for current actions in the present.

Когда я шёл/шла на работу, я купил(а) газету.
As I was walking to work, I bought a newspaper.

The first action in the above example **когда я шла на работу** *(when I was walking to work)* serves as a background for the main action **я купила газету** *(I bought a newspaper)*. Use unidirectional verbs in the present tense when you catch an action as it unfolds in front of you as you would a snapshot.

Смотри, Ваня идёт!
Look, Vanya is coming/going!

In addition, remember that the walking verbs **ходить/идти** often refer to a local activity (within the city bounds), regardless of the exact mode of transportation. So it's normal to say **я вчера ходил в театр** *(I went to the theater yesterday),* even if you took the metro, because going to the theater is a local activity.

Naturally, all motion verbs take the accusative case of direction: you go to a place in contrast to being at one.

Я был(а) в театре.

I was at the theater. (prepositional, location)

Я ходил(а) в театр.

I went to the theater. (accusative, direction)

PRACTICE 3

Restate the following sentences replacing the past forms of the verb **быть** with the appropriate motion verbs. Remember to change the case of the destination noun from the prepositional to the accusative!

1. Вчера мы были в театре.

2. Летом они были в России.

3. Я сегодня была на работе.

4. Вы были в гостях в субботу?

5. Ты был на экскурсии в Новгороде?

6. Я был в магазине утром.

Tip!

The most efficient way to learn grammar is to learn it by example. Don't just memorize verbs, nouns, or expressions thematically (although this is also important), but try as well to see the grammatical patterns they represent. In this fashion, you will be learning grammar by analogy. For example, if you know the conjugation pattern of the verb **купить** (Conjugation II, л-mutation, present tense stress shift), you can store all other new verbs that belong to the same subtype under its grammatical heading, such as the verb **любить**. **Играть в теннис** *(acc.)* could be a formula for any sports game you play, **играть на гитаре** *(prep)*—for playing any musical instrument. This approach will help you organize and remember the seemingly endless variety of Russian words and expressions.

ANSWERS

PRACTICE 1: 1. Я начинаю новую работу. **2.** Они начали смотреть телевизор. **3.** Он закончил (кончил) работать и начал читать. **4.** Она закончит (кончит) эту работу. **5.** Мы начинаем каждый день после работы.

PRACTICE 2: (Possible answers) **1.** В пятницу вечером я смотрел(а) телевизор/был(а) в клубе. **2.** В субботу утром я читал(а) книгу/завтракал(а) в кафе. **3.** В субботу вечером я отдыхал(а)/ужинал(а) в ресторане. **4.** В воскресенье днём я гулял(а) по городу/покупал(а) продукты в магазине.

PRACTICE 3: 1. Вчера мы ходили в театр. **2.** Летом они ездили в Россию. **3.** Я сегодня ходила на работу. **4.** Вы ходили в гости в субботу? **5.** Ты ездил на экскурсию в Новгород? **6.** Я ходил в магазин утром.

—————— Lesson 15 (Sentences) ——————

SENTENCE LIST 1

Я снимаю квартиру в самом центре, около станции метро «Пушкинская».	*I'm renting an apartment in the center, near "Pushkinskaya" metro station.*
Я живу недалеко от работы.	*I live not far from work.*
Это далеко?	*Is it far?*
Нет, одна остановка на метро.	*No, one stop on the metro.*
Сколько сейчас времени?	*What time is it now?*
Сейчас девять часов утра.	*Now it's nine o'clock in the morning.*
Во сколько ты начинаешь работать?	*What time do you start work?*
Я начинаю работать в девять часов утра.	*I start work at nine o'clock in the morning.*
Я заканчиваю в пять часов тридцать минут.	*I finish at five-thirty.*

В центре много театров, музеев, магазинов, кафе, красивых улиц и площадей.	In the center, there are a lot of theaters, museums, stores, cafés, beautiful streets and squares.
Везде можно ходить пешком.	You can go everywhere on foot.
В эту субботу я иду на балет в Большой театр.	This Saturday I'm going to a ballet at the Bolshoi Theater.

NUTS & BOLTS 1
THE GENITIVE CASE (PLURAL)

We've already seen the genitive singular for nouns; now let's look at the genitive plural. There are three basic endings in the genitive plural **-ов, -ей,** or zero. The choice of the ending is simple; it generally depends on the nature of the last letter of the noun.

Nominative singular	Example	Genitive plural ending	Example
ending in a hard consonant	магазин час	**-ов**	магазинов часов
ending in **й, ь, ж, ш, щ, ч, ц**	трамвай месяц рубль	**-ев**	трамваев месяцев рублей
ending in **ь**	площадь	**-ей**	площадей (notice that the soft sign is replaced with a soft vowel)
ending in a vowel	минута улица яблоко окно письмо	**-**	минут улиц яблок окон писем

The adjectives in the genitive plural have the hard ending **-ых** or the soft ending **-их** (also following the spelling rule): **много красивых улиц, много больших музеев.**

The uncountable noun **вре́мя** *(time)* is an exception to this rule. Although it looks like a feminine noun, it's actually neuter, as all nouns ending in **-мя.** Consequently, many Russians mispronounce it in the genitive plural as **сколько "вре́мя"** *(what time is it),* instead of its proper form **сколько вре́мени (много вре́мени,** etc.).

PRACTICE 1
Say that the people or places below have a lot of the following. Remember to use the construction **у** + gen. **много** + gen. for people, and **в** + prep. + **много** + gen. for places.

1. Иван–работа

2. Москва–хорошие магазины

3. центр–интересные музеи

4. Петербург–красивые улицы

5. я–время

NUTS & BOLTS 2
TELLING TIME
There are several ways to tell time in Russian. The easiest one is to say the number of hours first and then the number of minutes. Remember to apply the rule of numbers: use the nominative/accusative singular after one; use the genitive singular after two, three, and four; use the genitive plural after five and higher.

Сколько сейчас вре́мени?
What time is it now?

Сейчас (один) час двадцать одна минута.
It's 1:21.

Сейчас два часа три минуты.

It's 2:03.

Сейчас пять часов десять минут.

It's 5:10.

Note that it is customary to leave out **один** before **час**.

Сейчас час двадцать одна.

It's 1:21.

To indicate a.m. and p.m., use either **утра, дня, вечера,** or **ночи**. For the hours between 4 and 11 a.m., you should say **утра** *(lit., of the morning)*. For the hours between 12 and 4 p.m., you should say **дня** *(lit., of the afternoon)*. For the hours between 5 and 11 p.m., you should say **вечера** *(lit., of the evening)*. And for the hours between 12 and 3 a.m., you should say **ночи** *(lit., of the night)*.

Я начинаю работу в девять часов утра.

I start work at nine a.m.

PRACTICE 2
Сколько сейчас времени? *(What time is it now?)*

1. 2:30

2. 6:15

3. 3:25

4. 1:42

5. 10:22 a.m.

SENTENCE LIST 2

Сколько времени ты жила в Америке?	*How long (lit., how much time) did you live in America?*
Я жил(а) в Америке девять месяцев.	*I lived in America for nine months.*
Я приехал(а) в Америку первого сентября.	*I arrived in America on the first of September.*

Я вернулся/вернулась в Россию десятого мая.	*I came back to Russia on the tenth of May.*
Она ездила в Россию в две тысячи шестом году.	*She went to Russia in 2006.*
Он родился в тысяча девятьсот восемьдесят втором году.	*He was born in 1982.*
Она жила одна.	*She lived alone.*
Она сама покупала продукты, готовила и стирала.	*She bought groceries, cooked, and did the laundry herself.*
У неё в доме была стиральная машина и сушилка.	*She had a washer and dryer in her house.*
Иногда она ходила в кафе и в ресторан.	*Sometimes she went to a café and to a restaurant.*

NUTS & BOLTS 3
THE ACCUSATIVE OF DURATION

When an action continues for a certain time, you should use the accusative case to indicate this time. This is called the accusative of duration.

Я жила в Америке один год/одну неделю/девять месяцев.
I lived in America for one year/one week/nine months.

If you need to ask about duration, you can use the expression **сколько времени**.

Сколько времени ты жил в Москве?
(For) how long did you live in Moscow?

Remember to use the rule of numbers for time periods with the numerals different than 1: **я жила в Америке два года/пять лет.**

NUTS & BOLTS 4
NUMBERS 100–1,000 AND ORDINAL NUMBERS

Before we learn how to say dates and years in Russian, let's look at the numerals from 100 to 1,000.

сто	100
двести	200
триста	300
четыреста	400
пятьсот	500
шестьсот	600
семьсот	700
восемьсот	800
девятьсот	900
тысяча	1,000

In order to say a year in Russian—for example, 1979—you need to say **тысяча девятьсот семьдесят девятый год,** literally, *(one) thousand nine hundred seventy-ninth year.* The numeral *one* in *one thousand* is usually left out in spoken Russian. The last digit of the year (if it's not a zero) becomes an ordinal numeral. If it's a zero, e.g., 1960, then the last digit before the zero forms one ordinal numeral: **тысяча девятьсот шестидесятый год** *([one] thousand nine hundred sixtieth year).* Ordinal numerals have adjectival endings and function just like adjectives. Let's look at the ordinal numbers in Russian.

первый	*first*
второй	*second*
третий	*third*
четвёртый	*fourth*
пятый	*fifth*
шестой	*sixth*
седьмой	*seventh*
восьмой	*eighth*
девятый	*ninth*
десятый	*tenth*
двадцатый	*twentieth*
тридцатый	*thirtieth*
сороковой	*fortieth*
пятидесятый	*fiftieth*
шестидесятый	*sixtieth*
семидесятый	*seventieth*
восьмидесятый	*eightieth*
девяностый	*ninetieth*
сотый	*hundredth*

In order to answer the question **когда?** *(when?)* with a given date, in a given month, and in a given year, you should follow the scheme below:

Когда?		
Число	**Месяц**	**Год**
		в + prepositional в тысяча девятьсот семьдесят девятом году
	в + prepositional в сентябре	genitive тысяча девятьсот семьдесят девятого года
genitive семнадцатого	genitive сентября	genitive тысяча девятьсот семьдесят девятого года

Я родился/Я родилась семнадцатого сентября тысяча девятьсот семьдесят девятого года.
I was born on September 17, 1979.

Notice that the date comes first. If there's a date, you should use no preposition and put the date in the genitive case of the ordinal numeral (as if it were the event of the seventeenth of September). The month and the year follow in the genitive case (because it was the date of a given month, of a given year). If you don't have the date, but just the month and the year or just the year, follow the examples in the chart above.

And finally, the year 2000 is **двухтысячный год/в двухтысячном году;** the year 2001—**две тысячи первый год/в две тысячи первом году,** etc.

PRACTICE 3

Когда вы родились? *(When were you born?)* Say when the following people were born, writing out the numerals in full words. Remember to choose the correct gender of the verb родиться *(to be born)* in the past tense.

1. Наталья—1 сентября 1975

2. её дочь—май 2002

3. мой муж—8 декабря 1965

4. моя мать—1950

5. мой друг—октябрь 1975

PRACTICE 4

Answer the following questions using the prompts below.

1. Когда Лена приехала в Америку? (сентябрь 2005 года)

2. Когда она вернулась в Россию? (10 мая)

3. Когда вы ездили в Петербург? (1999)

4. Когда вы начали работать в этой компании? (21 июня 2000)

5. Когда мы будем кататься на лыжах? (февраль)

Discovery activity

Practice dates and times in Russian: think of the things you need to do today, this week, and this month; say when you need to do them in Russian.

Then try to say when you and your family members and friends were born. Look at the people around you—can you guess when he or she was born? Even if you're wrong with the date, try to be correct with the grammar!

ANSWERS

PRACTICE 1: 1. У Ивана много работы. **2.** В Москве много хороших магазинов. **3.** В центре много интересных музеев. **4.** В Петербурге много красивых улиц. **5.** У меня много времени.

PRACTICE 2: 1. Сейчас два часа тридцать минут. **2.** Сейчас шесть часов пятнадцать минут. **3.** Сейчас три часа двадцать пять минут. **4.** Сейчас (один) час сорок две минуты. **5.** Сейчас десять часов двадцать две минуты утра.

PRACTICE 3: 1. Наталья родилась первого сентября тысяча девятьсот семьдесят пятого года. **2.** Её дочь родилась в мае две тысячи второго года. **3.** Мой муж родился восьмого декабря тысяча девятьсот шестьдесят пятого года. **4.** Моя мать родилась в тысяча пятидесятом году. **5.** Мой друг родился в октябре тысяча девятьсот семьдесят пятого года.

PRACTICE 4: 1. Лена приехала в Америку в сентябре две тысячи пятого года. **2.** Она вернулась в Россию десятого мая. **3.** Я ездил(а) в Петербург в тысяча девятьсот девяносто девятом году. **4.** Я начал(а) работать в этой компании двадцать первого июня двухтысячного года. **5.** Мы будем кататься на лыжах в феврале.

———————— Lesson 16 (Conversations) ————————

CONVERSATION 1

Greg Campbell, an American who has recently relocated to Moscow for a year, is telling his Russian friend, Inna Gribova, about his new life and daily routine there.

Инна: Привет, Грэг! Как жизнь в Москве? Как ты устроился?

Грэг: Привет, Инна! Рад тебя видеть! У меня всё отлично. Я прекрасно устроился. Я снимаю прекрасную двухкомнатную квартиру в центре, около станции метро «Пушкинская».

Инна: Здорово! Это недалеко от твоей работы?

Грэг: Всего одна остановка на метро. Иногда я даже хожу пешком.

Инна: Ты работаешь каждый день?

Грэг: Да, конечно, каждый день кроме субботы и воскресенья. Начинаю в девять часов утра и заканчиваю в пять часов тридцать минут, а иногда в шесть вечера.

Инна: Тебе нравится жить в центре?

Грэг: Очень! Здесь много интересных театров и музеев, хороших магазинов, ресторанов, кафе, красивых улиц и площадей, и везде можно ходить пешком. Это очень удобно. Я люблю ходить пешком.

Инна: А что ты делаешь после работы по вечерам и в выходные?

Грэг: В понедельник, среду и пятницу я хожу в спортивный зал, а потом или в магазин за покупками, или с друзьями в кино. А иногда я просто гуляю по городу или отдыхаю дома— читаю и смотрю телевизор. А в эту субботу я иду на балет в Большой театр.

Инна: Я уверена, что тебе очень понравится.

Inna: Hi, Greg! How's life in Moscow? Are you settled?

Greg: Hi, Inna! (I'm) glad to see you! Everything's great. I'm well settled. I'm renting a wonderful two-room apartment in the city center, near the metro station "Pushkinskaya."

Inna: Great! Is it close to (lit., not far from) your job?

Greg: Just one stop on the metro. Sometimes I even walk (lit., go on foot).

Inna: Do you work every day?

Greg: *Yes, of course, every day except Saturdays and*
Sundays. (I) start at nine in the morning and finish at
five-thirty, sometimes at six in the evening.

Inna: *Do you like living in the center?*

Greg: *Very much! There're many interesting theaters and*
museums, good stores, restaurants, cafés, beautiful
streets and squares here, and you can walk everywhere.
This is very convenient. I like walking.

Inna: *And what do you do after work in the evenings and on*
weekends?

Greg: *On Monday, Wednesday, and Friday, I go to the gym,*
and then either shopping (lit., to the store for goods) or
to the movies with friends. Sometimes I just walk
around the city or rest at home—read and watch TV.
And this Saturday, I'm going to a ballet at the Bolshoi
Theater.

Inna: *I'm sure you'll like it very much.*

NOTES

Устроиться is a reflexive perfective verb that doesn't have a direct equivalent in English. It can be translated as *get settled, set up one's accommodations.* When a person moves, it takes time before he or she is comfortable and settled. When this happens, you'd say that **он устроился** or **она устроилась, они устроились. Как вы устроились?** is a common courtesy question to a newcomer. This is why Inna is asking her friend Greg, who recently arrived in Moscow, **как ты устроился?** And Greg responds, **я прекрасно устроился** *(I'm set up nicely).*

Notice the difference between the adverb **прекрасно (я прекрасно устроился)** and the adjective **прекрасный (я снимаю прекрасную квартиру).** Adjectives and adverbs are strictly differentiated in Russian. Russian adverbs usually end in **-о/е;** they only change in the comparitive degree. Adverbs modify actions, they tell you how you do something: **хорошо** *(well),* **плохо** *(bad/badly),* **быстро** *(fast),* **отлично** *(great),* **прекрасно** *(nicely/wonderfully)*, etc. On the other hand, Russian adjectives modify nouns and change in accordance with the gender, number, and case of the nouns they modify: **прекрасная квартира, я снял прекрасную квартиру, я живу в прекрасной квартире,** etc.

NUTS & BOLTS 1
EXPRESSING LIKES AND DISLIKES

You already know the verb **любить** (see Unit 2). It is most commonly used with infinitives when you like doing something: **я люблю гулять; я люблю ходить пешком** *(I like to go for a walk; I like to go on foot)*. You should also use it with food and drinks, as in **я люблю кофе** *(I like coffee)* and with aesthetic preferences, as in **я люблю балет** *(I like ballet)*. However, when used to refer to people, this verb actually means *to love:* **он любит её** *(he loves her)*.

There's another way of expressing likes and dislikes in Russian. For this, you can also use the Conjugation II reflexive verb **нравиться** *(to like)*. It takes nouns in the nominative case (objects/subjects of liking) or verb infinitives (whatever is being liked) and pronouns or nouns in the dative case (the person who is doing the liking).

Мне нравится жить в центре.
I like living in the city center. (lit., Living in the center pleases me.)

Мне нравится моя новая жизнь в Москве.
I like my new life in Moscow. (lit., My new life in Moscow pleases me.)

The verb **нравиться** is less common than the verb **любить.** You should primarily use it in the present tense when you are in the middle of a new experience and you like it. For example, if you recently moved to Moscow and you're enjoying it, then you should say: **Мне нравится жить в Москве.** Conversely, if you've always liked walking (it's not a new experience for you), then you should say: **Я люблю ходить пешком.**

When you put the verb **нравиться** in the perfective form **понравиться,** then it refers to your impression of any completed experience–tasting some food, seeing a show, meeting a friend.

Мне понравился балет.
I liked the ballet (the one I just saw).

Мне понравилась твоя сестра.
I liked your sister (after I met her).

Мне понравилось вино.
I liked the wine (the one I just tried).

Мне понравились музеи в Москве.
I liked the museums in Moscow (the ones I went to).

Notice how the gender of the thing you liked affects the gender of the past perfective verb **понравиться.** If the thing you liked is expressed by an infinitive, the verb **понравиться** should be neuter.

Мне понравилось гулять по городу.
I liked walking/strolling around the city (after I tried it).

If you conjugate the perfective verb **понравиться,** it denotes the future tense and means *will like something*.

Тебе понравится балет.
You'll like the ballet.

The Russian adverb **удобно** means both convenient and comfortable. It's often used with the semantic subject in the dative case **мне удобно** *(lit., [it is] convenient for me)*. In the past tense, you simply insert the past tense of the verb *to be* in the neuter form (because the subject *it* is implied): **мне/ей/ему было удобно;** or in the future, third person singular: **мне/ей/ему будет удобно.**

PRACTICE 1

Say what the following people like doing. Use the conjugated verb **любить** with the prompts below.

1. Мы _____ смотреть телевизор вечером.

2. Я _____ гулять по городу.

3. Володя _____ театр.

4. Моя дочь _____ читать книги.

5. Вы _____ ходить пешком.

PRACTICE 2

Translate the following sentences into Russian according to the clue in parentheses.

1. I like ballet. (любить)

2. I liked the ballet. (нравиться)

3. My wife likes Russian cuisine. (любить)

4. I love my wife. (любить)

5. I like (I'm enjoying) my new job. (нравиться)

6. Do you like walking? (любить)

7. Yesterday I went to the museum and I liked it. (нравиться)

8. I like Russian. (любить)

9. You'll be comfortable in this apartment. (infml.)

CONVERSATION 2

A Russian graduate student, Igor Zubov, spent a year in the U.S. as an exchange student. He's talking to his friend Tanya Petrova about his daily life in America.

Таня: Сколько времени ты жил в Америке в прошлом году?

Игорь:	Я приехал в Америку первого сентября и вернулся в Россию в мае—всего девять месяцев.
Таня:	Ты жил один или в общежитии?
Игорь:	Я снимал комнату в отдельном доме.
Таня:	Значит, ты сам ходил в магазин, покупал продукты и готовил?
Игорь:	Да, но иногда я ходил в столовую, кафе или ресторан.
Таня:	А у тебя в доме была стиральная машина?
Игорь:	Да, конечно! И стиральная машина, и даже сушилка. Поэтому я обычно стирал дома, а некоторые вещи сдавал в химчистку.
Таня:	А что ты делал вечером, и в субботу и в воскресенье?
Игорь:	Я много занимался, но ещё я ходил в гости, встречался с друзьями и ездил на экскурсии в другие города.
Таня:	А ты занимался спортом в Америке?
Игорь:	Да, все американцы много занимаются спортом. И я тоже зимой катался на лыжах, а весной и осенью играл в теннис и катался на велосипеде.
Таня:	Я рада, что тебе понравилось в Америке!

Tanya:	*For how long did you live in America last year?*
Igor:	*I came to America on the first of September and came back to Russia in May—nine months total.*
Tanya:	*Did you live alone or in a dorm?*
Igor:	*I rented a room in a separate house.*
Tanya:	*This means you went to the store by yourself, bought groceries, and cooked?*
Igor:	*Yes, but sometimes, I went to the dining hall, a café, or a restaurant.*
Tanya:	*Did you have a washer in your house?*

Igor: Yes, of course! Both a washer and (even) a dryer. This is why I usually did laundry (washed) at home, but I took some (of my) things to the dry cleaner.

Tanya: What did you do in the evenings and on Saturday and Sunday (on weekends)?

Igor: I studied a lot, but I also went to parties, met with friends, and went on tours to other cities.

Tanya: Did you do sports (exercise) in America?

Igor: Yes, all Americans exercise a lot. I also skied in the winter, and played tennis and rode a bicycle in the spring and fall.

Tanya: I'm glad you liked (it) in America!

NOTES

The pronoun **сам** means *by oneself, by myself, by yourself,* etc. It agrees with the gender of the person it refers to. In the question **Ты сама ходила в магазин?** *(Did you go to the store yourself?)*, **сама** is feminine, because this inquiry is addressed to Lena. Had it been addressed to a man, it would've been **Ты** *(sg. infml.)* **сам ходил в магазин?** or **Вы** *(pl. or sg. fml.)* **сами ходили в магазин?**

Similarly, **один, одна,** and **одни,** when used to mean *alone,* reflect the gender and number of the person(s) they refer to. You should say **он жил один** *(he lived alone)* about a male person, **она жила одна** *(she lived alone)* about a female person, and **они жили одни** *(they lived alone)* about two or more people.

When the conjunction **и** is repeated twice **и . . . и,** it usually means *both.* **Там была и стиральная машина и даже сушилка.** *(There were both a washer and [even] a dryer.)* Lena is making a point that there was a dryer, because dryers are relatively uncommon in Russia: people usually wash clothes in a washer and then hang them out to dry.

The verb **кататься** denotes the general *riding for fun.* Consequently, it's used to describe such activities as **кататься на** велосипеде *(riding a bicycle)*, **кататься на лыжах** *(skiing, lit., riding on skis)*, and **кататься на коньках** *(skating, lit., riding on skates)*.

NUTS & BOLTS 2
THE VERBS заниматься *(TO STUDY)* AND играть *(TO PLAY)*
The verb **заниматься** refers to the actual process of studying. It's a Conjugation I verb. Being a reflexive verb, it doesn't take a direct object. **Заниматься** is usually modified by location (**где?**/*where?*) or by an adverb (**как?**/*how?*): **заниматься в кафе, дома**, etc., or **много, мало, хорошо заниматься.** You can also use it by itself.

–**Что ты делал вчера вечером? –Я занимался.**
–What did you do last night? –I studied.

It's important to differentiate the above verb from the verb **учиться** *(to be a student in a school, to go to school)*.

The verb **заниматься** is also used in another expression, **заниматься спортом,** which refers to any kind of sport and means *to do sports* or *to play sports*. Notice that the noun **спорт** is in the instrumental case. The verb **играть** *(to play)* is used strictly with games and is followed by the preposition **в** and the name of the sport in the accusative: **играть в теннис** *(to play tennis)*, **играть в футбол** *(to play soccer)*, **играть в баскетбол** *(to play basketball)*, etc.

You can also use the verb **играть** with musical instruments. In this case, **играть** will be followed by the preposition **на** and the musical instrument in the prepositional case: **играть на пианино** *(to play the piano)*, **играть на гитаре** *(to play the guitar)*, etc.

PRACTICE 3

Fill in the blanks using the correct studying verb: **заниматься** or **учиться.**

1. Вчера вечером мы _____ в кафе.

2. Она студентка, она _____ в университете.

3. Вы отличные студенты, вы много _____ .

4. Обычно я _____ один дома.

5. Сегодня у меня много дел, я буду _____ весь вечер.

PRACTICE 4

Чем они занимаются? *(What do they busy themselves with?)* Say what the following people do as their hobby. Use the prompts below, and conjugate the appropriate verbs in the present tense.

1. моя сестра—велосипед

2. мои родители—лыжи

3. мы—теннис

4. американцы—спорт

5. мой брат—гитара

6. мои дети—пианино

PRACTICE 5

Describe Lena's life in America. Mention at least five activities she did while there. Use any expressions from the above dialogue and/or from the entire unit.

Discovery activity

Think of your schedule. What do you do on different days of the week? What do you do in the winter, spring, summer, and fall? What sports do you play? Try to say as much as you can about your lifestyle. What about your family members and friends? What do they do for fun? Use as many expressions as you can from this unit.

ANSWERS

PRACTICE 1: 1. Мы любим смотреть телевизор вечером.
2. Я люблю гулять по городу. **3.** Володя любит театр.
4. Моя дочь любит читать книги. **5.** Вы любите ходить пешком.

PRACTICE 2: 1. Я люблю балет. **2.** Мне понравился балет.
3. Моя жена любит русскую кухню. **4.** Я люблю (мою) жену. **5.** Мне нравится моя новая работа. **6.** Ты любишь ходить пешком? **7.** Вчера я ходил в музей, и он мне понравился. **8.** Я люблю русский. **9.** Тебе будет удобно в этой квартире.

PRACTICE 3: 1. занимались; **2.** учится; **3.** занимаетесь; **4.** занимаюсь; **5.** заниматься

PRACTICE 4: 1. Моя сестра катается на велосипеде. **2.** Мои родители катаются на лыжах. **3.** Мы играем в теннис.
4. Американцы занимаются спортом. **5.** Мой брат играет на гитаре. **6.** Мои дети играют на пианино.

PRACTICE 5: (Possible answers) **1.** В Америке Лена каталась на лыжах зимой. **2.** Лена снимала комнату в отдельном доме. **3.** Лена сама покупала продукты и готовила. **4.** Лена стирала дома, а некоторые вещи сдавала в химчистку.
5. Лена занималась спортом.

UNIT 4 ESSENTIALS

Я работаю каждый день.	*I work every day.*
Я начинаю работать в девять часов утра.	*I start work at nine in the morning.*
Я заканчиваю работать в пять часов тридцать минут.	*I finish work at five-thirty.*
Мне нравится жить в центре.	*I like living in the (city) center.*
Я люблю много ходить пешком.	*I like walking a lot.*
Я вчера ходил на балет. Он мне очень понравился.	*I went to (see) a ballet yesterday. I liked it very much.*

В понедельник, среду и пятницу я хожу в спортивный зал.	On Monday, Wednesday, and Friday, I go to the gym.
Я занимаюсь спортом.	I play sports., I exercise.
Зимой я катаюсь на лыжах, летом—на велосипеде.	I ski in the winter, (and) ride (my) bicycle in the summer.
Вечером после работы я отдыхаю, читаю и смотрю телевизор.	I rest, read, and watch TV in the evening after work.
Я родился/родилась первого мая тысяча девятьсот семьдесят пятого года.	I was born on the first of May in nineteen seventy-five.
У меня дома есть стиральная машина.	I have a washer at home.
Я сам(а) покупаю продукты и готовлю.	I buy groceries and cook by myself.
Иногда я хожу в гости.	Sometimes, I go on a visit.

Unit 5
Health and the human body

In Unit 5, we'll talk about physical health. You'll learn how to talk with doctors, how to explain common symptoms such as fever, headache, sore throat, and cough, as well as the names of the basic body parts. In addition to the basic vocabulary, you will also learn perfective and imperfective imperatives, negative imperatives, negation, negative pronouns, indefinite pronouns with the particles **-то** and **-нибудь,** more time expressions, impersonal sentences, comparatives, more plural forms of nouns, and more verbs of motion.

———— Lesson 17 (Words) ————

WORD LIST 1

всё нормально	*everything is okay (lit., normal)*
температура	*temperature*
болеть	*to be sick*
заболеть	*to fall sick*
голова	*head*
горло	*throat*
нос	*nose*
рот	*mouth*
живот	*abdomen, stomach, belly*
зуб	*tooth*
рука	*hand, arm*
нога	*foot, leg*
спина	*back*
лицо	*face*
ухо	*ear*

глаз	*eye*
теплее	*warmer*
лучше	*better*
больше	*more*
побольше	*a little more (colloquial)*
меньше	*less*
поменьше	*a little less (colloquial)*
аптека	*drug store, pharmacy*
если	*if*
молодец	*"Good job!"*

NOTES

Лучше and **теплее** are comparatives. Most Russian comparatives end in **-ee**. However, some have just one **-e** following one of the following "hushers": **ж, ш, щ,** or **ч,** as in the comparative **лучше.**

Молодец is a term of approval of a person. It can roughly be translated as *you do/did a great/good job.* Although it's a masculine noun, it equally refers to males and females. The plural form is **молодцы** (notice the fleeting **-e,** just like in the plural noun **американцы).**

NUTS & BOLTS 1
THE ADVERB нормально

The adverb **нормально** often refers to the *normal* state of affairs. **Всё нормально** means *everything is okay* in the most general sense.

The adjective **нормальный** is a modifier in such set phrases as **нормальная температура** *(normal temperature),* **нормальное давление** *(normal [blood] pressure),* **нормальный пульс** *(normal pulse),* **нормальные результаты анализа** *(normal test results),* etc.

Notice the change in the ending of the adjective, as it agrees in number and gender with the nouns it modifies. All of the examples above, of course, are in the nominative case. If the noun appears in any other case, the modifying adjective will change accordingly.

NUTS & BOLTS 2
Body parts and the plural of neuter nouns
First, let's learn the following basic body parts in the nominative singular and plural.

Singular	Plural	Translation
нос	носы	*nose, noses*
рот	рты	*mouth, mouths*
живот	животы	*stomach, stomachs*
зуб	зубы	*tooth, teeth*
рука	руки	*hand/arm, hands/arms*
нога	ноги	*foot/leg, feet/legs*
спина	спины	*back, backs*
лицо	лица	*face, faces*
ухо	уши	*ear, ears*
глаз	глаза	*eye, eyes*

Notice the irregular plurals for **ухо—уши** (**х/ш** mutation) and **глаз—глаза** (-**а** plural); some other -**а/я** plurals are **дом—дома, учитель—учителя.**

Most neuter nouns end in -**а** in the plural form (often with a stress shift): **лицо—лица, письмо—письма, окно—окна.**

The noun **рот–рты** has a fleeting **о** in the root. All other plurals in the above chart are regular: they end in **-ы** (for hard endings) or **-и** (for soft endings and the spelling rule).

PRACTICE 1

What are the nominative plural forms of the nouns below? Remember to follow the spelling rule.

1. ухо
2. дом
3. голова
4. лицо
5. нога
6. молодец
7. рука
8. зуб

NUTS & BOLTS 3

The verb болеть *(TO BE SICK)*

The imperfective verb **болеть** means *to be sick*. It belongs to Conjugation I.

болеть *(to be sick)*

я болею	**мы болеем**
ты болеешь	**вы болеете**
он/она/оно болеет	**они болеют**

The past tense is **болел, болела, болело, болели.** The verb has no mutations or stress shifts.

Its perfective counterpart **заболеть** means *to fall sick* and denotes the beginning of the action rather than its duration. **Он заболел** means that he has fallen ill in the past, and he's still sick (**он ещё болеет).**

The verb **болеть** *(to be sick)* can be followed by the name of the illness in the instrumental case: **я болею гриппом** *(I'm sick/came down with the flu)*, **он болел воспалением лёгких** *(he was sick/he had pneumonia)*, etc. When you ask, what a person is sick with, you need to put the interrogative **что** *(what)* into the instrumental case as well: **Чем вы болеете/заболели/болели?** *(lit., What are you sick/have you been sick/were you sick with?)*

PRACTICE 2
Translate the following sentences into Russian.

1. I'm often sick in the winter.

2. She has normal temperature.

3. He fell sick yesterday.

4. It's warmer today.

5. We were sick for the whole winter.

WORD LIST 2

Что у вас болит?	*What's hurting you?*
больно	*painful*
больница	*hospital*
насморк	*nasal congestion*
кашель *(m.)*	*cough*
кашлять *(imperf., conj. I, -ай)*	*to cough*
воспаление лёгких	*pneumonia*
грипп	*flu*
простуда	*common cold*
простудиться *(perf., conj. II, -и)*	*to catch a cold*
выздороветь *(perf., conj. I, -ей)*	*to get healthy*
лекарство от	*medication for (lit., from)*
многие	*many (people)*

The genitive form of **кашель** *(cough)* is **кашля.**

The noun **лекарство** *(medication)* takes the preposition **от**+*genitive,* when it denotes *medication for something.* So you would say **лекарство от гриппа** *(flu medication),* which literally means *medication from the flu.* This makes sense on its own terms because this medication helps get *away from* the illness.

NUTS & BOLTS 4
THE VERB болеть *(TO HURT)*

Что у вас болит? *(lit., What do you have hurting?)* is the most common question you would hear in the doctor's office. Notice that **болит** *(hurts)* is different from **болеет** *(is sick),* which is the 3rd person singular of **болеть** you learned before. Even though both infinitives seem to be the same—**болеть** *(to be sick)* and **болеть** *(to hurt)*—the first **болеть** *(to be sick)* is a Conjugation I verb with the stem ending in **-еи**, while the second **болеть** (to hurt) belongs to Conjugation II with the stem ending in **-е**. This **-е** disappears before vowel endings (in the present tense) but stays before consonant endings (in the past and in the infinitive). The verb **болеть** *(to hurt)* has only two forms in the present tense—the third person singular and plural **(болит, болят).**

Голова болит.

I have a headache. (lit.,[My] head hurts.)

Зубы болят.

I have a toothache. (lit., [My] teeth hurt.)

The past tense forms are just like those for *to be sick:* **болел, болела, болело, болели.**

Russian has one uniform expression for all aches and pains. This is how it works: you mention the bodily organ at fault, and say that it hurts, then locate this ailment by the suffering person (**у** + *genitive),* and put everything in the reverse order.

У меня болит голова.

My head hurts.

У неё болят зубы.

Her teeth hurt.

У него болела спина.

His back hurt.

У вас болели ноги.

Your legs hurt.

Больно is an adverb meaning *painful,* as in the impersonal expression **мне больно** *(it hurts; lit., it's painful to me).* Compare this expression with the one you learned in Unit 4: **мне удобно** *(it's convenient to me).*

PRACTICE 3

Что у вас болит? *(What hurts?/Where does it hurt?)* Answer this question using the prompts below. Remember to put personal pronouns into the genitive case after the preposition **y.**

1. я—голова

2. он—зубы

3. вы—спина

4. она—нога

5. ты—живот

NUTS & BOLTS 5
EXPRESSING AILMENTS

The nouns **насморк, кашель, воспаление лёгких, грипп** and **простуда** are the names of common ailments. In order to say that you have any of them, you need to use the expression **у меня** *(I have).*

У меня кашель.

I have a cough.

У меня грипп.

I have the flu.

У меня простуда.

I have a cold.

The adjectives **сильный** *(strong, severe)* and **небольшой** *(light, minor)* can be used to modify the nouns: **сильный насморк, небольшой кашель.** There are also verbs corresponding to the nouns **кашель** and **простуда: кашлять (кашляю, кашляешь, кашляют**—*to cough)* and **простудиться (он простудился, она простудилась**—*to catch a cold).* **Сильно** and **немного** are the commonly used adverbs in these situations.

Я сильно кашляю.

I'm coughing heavily.

У меня немного болит голова.

I have a minor headache.

PRACTICE 4
Translate the following sentences into Russian.

1. I feel ill. I have the flu.

2. He caught a cold. He has a running nose and he coughs.

3. I was sick, but I recovered now.

4. They bought the flu medication in the pharmacy.

5. What do you have for (from) a cough?

6. This is a cold medication.

Culture note

In the nineteenth century, pharmacies in Russia also offered first aid. In a way, this tradition has been carried over into the modern day pharmacy, where, in addition to medication, customers often receive medical advice. It's common to approach the pharmacist with a detailed description of symptoms and expect that he or she will suggest the suitable remedy. So customers often say: **что у вас есть от гриппа, у меня болит живот,** etc. In more serious cases, the pharmacist will recommend that the customer see a doctor. As a mnemonic device, compare the English word *apothecary* to the Russian **аптека.**

ANSWERS

PRACTICE 1: 1. уши; **2.** дома; **3.** головы; **4.** лица; **5.** ноги; **6.** молодцы; **7.** руки; **8.** зубы

PRACTICE 2: 1. Я часто болею зимой. **2.** У неё нормальная температура. **3.** Он вчера заболел. **4.** Сегодня теплее. **5.** Мы болели всю зиму.

PRACTICE 3: 1. У меня болит голова. **2.** У него болят зубы. **3.** У вас болит спина. **4.** У неё болит нога. **5.** У тебя болит живот.

PRACTICE 4: 1. Я заболел(а). У меня грипп. **2.** Он простудился. У него насморк, и он кашляет. **3.** Я болел(а), но я сейчас выздоровел(а). **4.** Они купили лекарство от гриппа в аптеке. **5.** Что у вас есть от кашля? **6.** Это лекарство от простуды.

——— Lesson 18 (Phrases) ———

PHRASE LIST 1

мне кажется	*it seems to me*
я себя плохо чувствую	*I feel bad (sick)*
(из)мерить температуру	*take (lit., measure) the temperature*
на всякий случай	*just in case*
мочь	*be able to, can or may*
пить чай с мёдом	*to drink tea with honey (as a traditional remedy)*

он прав	*he's right*
она права	*she's right*
они правы	*they're right*
Мне лучше пойти домой.	*I'd better go home.*
одеваться *(imperf., conj. I, -ай)*	*to dress/to get dressed*
(с)делать зарядку	*to exercise in the mornings*
брать пример с (кого?) + *gen.*	*to follow one's example*

NOTES

The Russian expression **делать зарядку** doesn't have a good English equivalent. Nevertheless, it's more than common in Russian. It means to exercise for 5–20 minutes in the morning in order to get "charged" for the day. **Зарядка** literally means *charge* (as in "battery charge"). This is a Russian cultural phenomenon that should be taken for what it is: it's generally believed in Russia that, in order to have good physical and mental health, one needs to start the day with a set of morning exercises. The Soviet government even used to broadcast a short exercise program on the national radio every day, early in the morning, in order to keep the entire country motivated and fit.

NUTS & BOLTS 1

THE IMPERFECTIVE VERBS казаться *(to seem)* AND чувствовать *(to feel)*

The imperfective verb **казаться** means *to seem*. The phrase **мне кажется** means *it seems to me*. Notice that it's subjectless: the English subject *it* is left out in Russian, and the semantic subject, the person who experiences this action, is in the dative case. Literally, the phrase reads *to me (it) seems* (**мне кажется**).

The earlier sentence **мне больно** was also subjectless: **больно** (an adverb that denotes a certain state of being) is *given to me,* and I experience it—**мне больно** *(it's painful to me)*.

Мне лучше пойти домой.
It's better for me to go home.

This sentence is also subjectless and works exactly the same way, but with a comparative **лучше**.

The imperfective verb **чувствовать** means *to feel*. However, if you want to express a general state of being (**хорошо, плохо**, etc.), rather than a specific sensation, you should add the reflexive particle **себя** *(self)*.

Я хорошо себя чувствую.
I feel good.

Я плохо себя чувствую.
I feel bad.

Remember that the first **в** in the verb **чувствовать** is silent. **Чувствовать** is a Conjugation I verb with the stem ending in **-ова**. The verbs of this kind are called **ова**-verbs. All of them have one peculiarity: the suffix **-ова-** becomes **-у(й)-** in the present tense (the **й** will be absorbed by the following soft vowel: **чувству(й)у > чувствую**). Let's look at its present tense conjugation.

чувствовать *(to feel)*

я чувствую	мы чувствуем
ты чувствуешь	вы чувствуете
он/она/оно чувствует	они чувствуют

The stem reverts to its original form in the past tense: **он чувствовал, она чувствовала, оно чувствовало, они чувствовали**. Once again, remember to add **себя** when you're speaking about the way you or other people are feeling.

Как вы себя чувствуете?
How are you feeling?

Я хорошо себя чувствую.
I feel good.

Я плохо себя чувствую.
I feel bad.

Я лучше себя чувствую.
I feel better.

Я хуже себя чувствую.
I feel worse.

PRACTICE 1

Match the phrases below so that they form meaningful and grammatically correct sentences.

1. Когда я болел,	a. поэтому мне лучше пойти домой.
2. Каждое утро	b. и я буду брать с тебя пример!
3. Я плохо себя чувствую,	c. я пил чай с мёдом.
4. Мне кажется,	d. он делает зарядку.
5. Ты молодец	e. что я заболел.

NUTS & BOLTS 2

THE MODAL VERB мочь

Modal verbs in Russian act in a similar way to those in English and almost always appear followed by another verb. Now let's learn the conjugation of the modal verb **мочь** *(be able to/can/may)*.

мочь *(be able to/can/may)*

я могу	мы можем
ты можешь	вы можете
он/она/оно может	они могут

Past: мог, могла, могло, могли

Notice the **г/ж** mutation before the **-е** endings (the middle forms), but not before the **-у** endings (the first and last forms). Also remember the present tense stress shift here. The modal verb **мочь** can be used by itself, as in **если можешь** *(if you can),* or with infinitives, as in **я могу заболеть** *(I may get sick).*

PRACTICE 2
Translate the following sentences into Russian.

1. She's right; I'd better go home.

2. Just in case, I took the temperature. It was normal.

3. I like drinking tea with honey.

4. It seems to me that he's gotten sick.

5. She's getting dressed.

PHRASE LIST 2

у меня сильный насморк и кашель	*I have bad (lit., strong) nasal congestion and a cough*
у меня немного болит живот	*my stomach hurts a little*
у меня высокая температура	*I have a fever (lit., high temperature)*
болеть гриппом	*to be sick with the flu*
выписывать—выписать рецепт	*to write (out) a prescription*

принимать—принять лекарство	*to take medication*
два раза в день	*twice a day*
после еды	*after meals*
до еды	*before meals*
во время еды	*with (during) meals*
кашель пройдёт	*(the) cough will pass*
Поправляйтесь!	*Get well!*
быть у врача	*to be at the doctor's (locational)*
ходить к врачу	*to go to the doctor's (directional)*

NUTS & BOLTS 3
IRREGULAR GENITIVE PLURALS

Look at the phrase **два раза в день** *(two times a day)*. The noun **раз** *(time, occasion)* is irregular: its nominative singular **раз** coincides with its genitive plural **раз** *(times, occasions)*. This is what this noun looks like when you apply the rule of numbers to it.

Nom. sg.	один раз	one time (once)
Gen. sg.	два/три/четыре раза	two/three/four times
Gen. pl.	пять раз	five times

The question **Сколько раз в день . . . ?** *(How many times a day . . . ?)* uses the quantitative word **сколько** and the genitive plural of **раз**. Two more common nouns follow the same irregular genitive plurals: **человек** *(person)* and **солдат** *(soldier)*.

один человек, два человека, десять человек
one person, two people, ten people

один солдат, три солдата, пятнадцать солдат
one soldier, three soldiers, fifteen soldiers

Learn the time expressions with the prepositions **до, после, во время**. All three are followed by the genitive case: **до еды** *(before meals)*, **до пятницы** *(before Friday)*, **до обеда** *(before lunch)*; **после еды** *(after meals)*, **после работы** *(after work)*, **после ужина** *(after dinner)*; **во время еды** *(during/with meals)*, **во время работы** *(during work)*, **во время каникул** *(during the break/vacation)*, etc.

PRACTICE 3
Give Russian equivalents to the following English sentences.

1. I'm sick with the flu.

2. He has a bad cough and a high temperature.

3. I take this medication twice a day after meals.

4. I have a stomachache.

5. Take *(fml.)* this medication and your cough will pass. Get well!

Language link

In the cases of emergency, the Russians call three different phone numbers: 01 for fire emergency, 02 for police emergency, and 03 for medical emergency. 03 **(ноль три)** is synonymous with the ambulance in Russian. It's also written on all state owned ambulances. Although Russia provides free health care for all of its citizens, the care is not always reliable. Alternatively, there're many privately owned medical and dental facilities for all types of medical care. The level of service they provide is adequate to the Western standards, and so are the fees. One of the oldest privately owned health care companies is "American Medical Centers" in Moscow. Visit their website by going to *http://amc.rbc.ru.* Compare the English and Russian versions.

ANSWERS

PRACTICE 1: 1-c. Когда я болел, я пил чай с мёдом.
2-d. Каждое утро он делает зарядку. **3-a.** Я плохо себя
чувствую, поэтому мне лучше пойти домой. **4-e.** Мне
кажется, что я заболел. **5-b.** Ты молодец, и я буду брать с
тебя пример!

PRACTICE 2: 1. Она права, мне лучше пойти домой. **2.** На
всякий случай я измерил температуру. Она была
нормальная. **3.** Я люблю пить чай с мёдом. **4.** Мне
кажется, что он заболел. **5.** Она одевается.

PRACTICE 3: 1. Я болею гриппом. **2.** У него сильный
кашель и высокая температура. **3.** Я принимаю это
лекарство два раза в день после еды. **4.** У меня болит
живот. **5.** Принимайте это лекарство и ваш кашель
пройдёт. Поправляйтесь!

—————————— Lesson 19 (Sentences) ——————————

SENTENCE LIST 1

Я измерил(а) температуру.	*I took (my) temperature.*
Я ходил(а) к врачу.	*I went to the doctor (and I'm back).*
Я пошёл/пошла к врачу.	*I set out to the doctor (and I'm still away).*
Я ходил(а) в аптеку.	*I went to the pharmacy (and I'm back).*
Я пошёл/пошла в аптеку.	*I set out to the pharmacy (and I'm still away).*
Ты что-нибудь принимаешь от температуры?	*Are you taking anything for (your) fever/temperature?*
Нет, я ничего не принимаю.	*No, I'm not taking anything.*
Да, я что-то купил в аптеке.	*Yes, I bought something in the pharmacy.*
Ты никогда не болеешь.	*You're never sick.*
Одевайся теплее, а то ты простудишься.	*Dress warmer, or else you'll catch a cold.*
Я буду брать с тебя пример!	*I'll follow your example!*

NOTES

The aspect of the verb **измерил(а)** in the sentence **я измерил(а) температуру** *(I took my temperature)* is perfective because you took the temperature once, but also because taking the temperature was either a consequence of your getting sick or grounds for the next action, such as taking a medication. One way or another, the perfective verb belongs to a series of other actions plausible in this context. The imperfective **я мерил(а) температуру** would mean that you either took your temperature many times, as in **когда я болел(а), я мерил(а) температуру пять раз в день** *(when I was sick, I was taking my temperature five times a day),* or that you were taking your temperature continuously for a certain period of time, as in **я мерил(а) температуру пять минут** *(I was taking my temperature for five minutes).*

Keep in mind the multidirectional verb **ходить. Я ходил(а) к врачу** *(I went to the doctor)* implies two things at once: 1) that you went to the doctor, and 2) that you're back. On the other hand, **я пошёл/пошла к врачу** *(I went to the doctor)* means *I set out to the doctor's and I haven't been back.* The verb **пойти** is perfective, and it always denotes setting out and beginning of a new motion. Its vehicular counterpart is **поехать: Я поехал(а) в Москву** *(I set out for Moscow [by vehicle]).*

NUTS & BOLTS 1
SOMETHING AND ANYTHING

Now let's look at the sentence **Ты что-нибудь принимаешь от температуры?** *(Are you taking anything for the fever?).* You can add the indefinite, unstressed particle **-нибудь** to any Russian interrogative, and you will have an indefinite pronoun or adverb: **кто-нибудь, что-нибудь, как-нибудь, когда-нибудь, где-нибудь,** etc. For example, **что-нибудь** means either *anything* or *something.* The indefinite pronouns/adverbs with **-нибудь** are usually used in questions and/or in the future tense; they denote something indefinite.

Ты что-нибудь хочешь?

Do you want anything? (question)

Я что-нибудь куплю в аптеке.

I'll buy something in the pharmacy. (future tense)

When this *something* or *anything* is more definite (but still indeterminate), you should use the indefinite pronouns or adverbs with the particle -то: кто-то, что-то, как-то, когда-то, где-то, etc. These should normally be used in affirmative statements in the past or present tense.

Он что-то покупает в аптеке.

He's buying something in the pharmacy. (affirmative, present)

Он куда-то пошёл.

He went somewhere. (affirmative, past)

PRACTICE 1

Rephrase the following sentences using either **ходить** or **пойти** in the past tense. Remember to replace locations with direction!

1. Мой муж был у врача.

2. Мой муж сейчас у врача.

3. Они купили лекарства в аптеке утром.

4. Мы купили сегодня продукты в магазине.

5. Моя жена сейчас на работе.

NUTS & BOLTS 2
NEGATIVE PRONOUNS AND ADJECTIVES

And finally, as opposed to English, Russian indefinite pronouns and adjectives can't be used in the negative. Instead, you should replace them with the special negative pronouns/adverbs.

никто	*no one*
никак	*no how*
никогда	*never*
нигде	*nowhere*
ничего	*nothing* (rather than **ничто**)

These negative **ни-** pronouns/adverbs must be accompanied by the negative particle **не**. Technically, this is not a double negation, even if it may look so, because **ни-** is not a negation in Russian but merely a negative particle that must be used only in conjunction with the real negation the negative particle **не**.

Я ничего не принимаю.
I'm not taking anything.

Я ничего не хочу.
I don't want anything.

Ты никогда не болеешь.
You never get sick.

PRACTICE 2
Translate the following questions into Russian and then answer them in the positive and in the negative. Use indefinite pronouns or adverbs in your answers.

1. Did you *(infml.)* buy anything in the pharmacy?

2. Do you *(fml.)* take anything for a cough?

3. Did she live anywhere in Russia?

4. Do they want anything?

5. Will we go anywhere tonight?

SENTENCE LIST 2

Что вас беспокоит?	*What's bothering you?*
У меня тридцать восемь и пять по Цельсию.	*My (body) temperature is thirty-eight point five Celsius (101.3 F).*
Воспаления лёгких нет.	*No pneumonia.*
Мне больно кашлять.	*It hurts (me) to cough.*
Мне больно ходить.	*It hurts (me) to walk.*
Мне больно дышать.	*It hurts (me) to breathe.*
У вас, наверное, грипп.	*You probably have the flu.*
Сейчас многие болеют гриппом.	*Many are sick with the flu now.*
Через пять дней всё пройдёт.	*Everything will pass in five days.*
Дней через пять вы выздоровеете.	*You'll get well (recover) in about five days.*

Notes

Russians use the centigrade scale of temperature. Their temperature data is quoted **по Цельсию** *(according to the Celsius scale)* rather than **по Фаренгейту** *(according to the Fahrenheit scale)*. So, the normal body temperature is generally considered to be 36,6 C° (97.8 F). Notice that Russians write their decimal fractions with a comma rather than with a dot. So *36.6* is **36,6** in Russian. This is pronounced as **тридцать шесть и шесть,** where **и** *(and)* stands for the decimal point.

The preposition **через** + accusative means *after* or *in,* as in the phrase **через пять дней** *(in five days/five days after).* It denotes a gap in time after which something happens. The time period that follows this preposition is in the accusative if it's singular: **через неделю** *(in a week/a week later),* **через месяц** *(in a month/after a month).* If the phrase has a numeral, it should follow the Rule of Numbers: **через две недели** *(in two weeks),* **через пять недель** *(in five weeks),* etc. When you say **пять недель** *(five weeks),* you're being exact. One of the ways to express approximation in Russian is to flip the numeral and the noun around. For example, **недель пять** means *about five weeks* or *approximately five weeks*. Remember, if the phrase has a preposition, the preposition goes between the flipped noun and the numeral: **недель через пять** means *approximately in five weeks*.

NUTS & BOLTS 3
THE ACCUSATIVE OF PERSONAL PRONOUNS

The imperfective verb **беспокоить** is Conjugation II. It means *to trouble, to bother, to concern (lit., to disquiet*, since **бес-** is *without/dis-* in Russian and **покой** is *quiet*). The thing that bothers you is the grammatical subject of the sentence and must be in the nominative case.

Меня беспокоит моё здоровье.
My health is bothering me.

Его беспокоят зубы.
His teeth are bothering him.

Notice that the person who's being troubled is in the accusative case. However, the accusative coincides with the genitive for animate masculine singular nouns—that is, for the nouns denoting male human beings and animals, as well as all animate plurals (masculine and feminine). So, you should say **Ивана беспокоит горло** *(Ivan is bothered by his throat* or, literally, *his throat is bothering Ivan)*; **меня беспокоит кашель** *([this] cough is bothering me)*; **мою жену беспокоит насморк** *(nasal congestion is bothering my wife)*, etc.

The personal pronouns are the same in the accusative and genitive.

	Accusative	Genitive
я	меня	меня
ты	тебя	тебя

	Accusative	Genitive
он/оно	его	его
она	её	её
мы	нас	нас
вы	вас	вас
они	их	их

Что тебя беспокоит?

What's bothering you?

Её беспокоит высокая температура.

High fever/temperature is bothering her.

Нас беспокоит его здоровье.

His health concerns us.

The negated nouns need to be in the genitive of negation in Russian (see Unit 3). This is why **воспаления** in **воспаления лёгких нет** is in the genitive case. You should follow this rule whenever you negate anything.

У меня нет времени.

I don't have time.

У него нет жены.

He doesn't have a wife.

У неё нет денег.

She doesn't have money.

All the things you don't have should be in the genitive of negation. The past tense of **нет** is **не было**.

У меня не было времени.
I didn't have time.

У него не было жены.
He didn't have a wife.

У неё не было денег.
She didn't have money.

It is always fixed in the same singular neuter form **не было,** so it doesn't agree with anything else in the sentence. The future form of **нет** is **не будет;** it is equally fixed for all persons and things: **у меня не будет времени, у него не будет жены, у неё не будет денег.** In addition, remember that the personal pronouns **его, её,** and **их** add an **н-** in the genitive case after prepositions, such as **у: у него, у неё, у них.**

PRACTICE 3
Что вас беспокоит? *(What is bothering you?)* Say that these symptoms are bothering the following people. Remember to make the verb agree in number with the subject and to put the people in the animate accusative where necessary!

1. я—насморк

2. мой муж—высокая температура

3. моя сестра—больное горло

4. вы—больная нога

5. ты—зубы

PRACTICE 4
Restate the following sentences in the negative.

1. У неё была высокая температура.

2. У вас будет насморк.

3. У них есть время.

4. У тебя есть хорошее лекарство.

5. У него будет кашель.

Discovery activity

When was the last time you were sick? Describe your illness in Russian, mention as many symptoms as possible. Then imagine what the doctor might say in reply to your complaints.

ANSWERS

PRACTICE 1: 1. Мой муж ходил к врачу. **2.** Мой муж пошёл к врачу. **3.** Они ходили в аптеку утром (за лекарствами). **4.** Мы ходили сегодня в магазин. **5.** Моя жена пошла на работу.

PRACTICE 2: 1. Ты что-нибудь купил в аптеке? Да, я что-то купил в аптеке. Нет, я ничего не купил в аптеке. **2.** Вы принимаете что-нибудь от кашля? Да, я что-то принимаю от кашля. Нет, я ничего не принимаю от кашля. **3.** Она жила где-нибудь в России? Да, она жила где-то в России. Нет, она нигде не жила в России. **4.** Они хотят что-нибудь? Да, они что-то хотят. Нет, они ничего не хотят. **5.** Мы пойдём куда-нибудь сегодня вечером? Да, мы куда-нибудь пойдём сегодня вечером. Нет, мы никуда не пойдём сегодня вечером.

PRACTICE 3: 1. Меня беспокоит насморк. **2.** Моего мужа беспокоит высокая температура. **3.** Мою сестру беспокоит больное горло. **4.** Вас беспокоит больная нога. **5.** Тебя беспокоят зубы.

PRACTICE 4: 1. У неё не было высокой температуры. **2.** У вас не будет насморка. **3.** У них нет времени. **4.** У тебя нет хорошего лекарства. **5.** У него не будет кашля.

CONVERSATION 1

Sergey is not feeling well. He's talking about it to his girlfriend, Zhenya.

Женя:	**Привет, Серёжа! Как у тебя дела?**
Сергей:	**Всё нормально, только мне кажется, что я заболел. У меня с вечера болит голова и горло, и я себя плохо чувствую.**
Женя:	**У тебя есть температура?**
Сергей:	**Не знаю, я не мерил.**
Женя:	**А ты что-нибудь принимаешь?**
Сергей:	**Нет, ничего. Я ещё не ходил ни к врачу, ни в аптеку.**
Женя:	**Сходи на всякий случай. А сейчас иди домой, если можешь, и пей чай с мёдом.**
Сергей:	**Да, ты права. Мне лучше пойти домой.**
Женя:	**И одевайся теплее, а то ты ещё больше простудишься.**
Сергей:	**Хорошо. Вот ты, Жень, молодец! Ты никогда не болеешь!**
Женя:	**Это потому, что я занимаюсь спортом, по утрам делаю зарядку и плаваю.**
Сергей:	**Я последую твоему примеру!**

Zhenya:	*Hey, Seryozha! How are you?*
Sergey:	*Everything is alright, except that I perhaps (it seems to me) fell ill. I've had a headache and a sore throat since last night, and I'm not feeling well.*
Zhenya:	*Do you have a fever/temperature?*
Sergey:	*I don't know. I never took it.*
Zhenya:	*Are you taking anything?*
Sergey:	*Nothing. I haven't gone to the doctor's or the pharmacy yet.*

Zhenya: Go, just in case. And now, go home, if you can, and drink tea with honey.

Sergey: You're right. I'd better go home.

Zhenya: And dress up warmer, or else you'll get worse (you'll get even sicker).

Sergey: All right. But look at you, Zhenya! You never get sick!

Zhenya: This is because I play sports, exercise in the morning, and swim.

Sergey: I'll follow your example!

NOTES

Notice the verb **есть** in Zhenya's question **У тебя есть температура?** *(Do you have a fever/temperature?).* It's there because Sergey may or may not have a temperature. If the fact of Sergey's fever had already been established, and Zhenya inquired whether Sergey had a high fever or a moderate one, then there would be no **есть** in the question. It would be **У тебя высокая температура?** *(Do you have a high fever?)* (see Unit 2).

In the sentence **я ещё не ходил ни к врачу, ни в аптеку,** the conjunction **ни . . . ни** means *neither . . . nor.* Notice that, as with the negative pronouns **никто, ничего, никогда, нигде,** etc., the conjunction **ни** is usually not enough for the negation; it has to be coupled with the real negation, the negative particle **не: не ходил.**

Notice the agreement in the sentence **у меня с вечера болит голова и горло.** The verb **болит** is singular, because it agrees with the closest subject, the noun **голова,** which is singular. Alternatively, in more formal discourse, you could make the verb agree with both subjects, thus, making it plural: **У меня болят голова и горло.**

The verb **плавать** is another motion verb. It means *to swim* as well as *to sail.* This verb is multidirectional. This is why Zhenya uses it for the general action: **я плаваю** *(I swim).* Its unidirectional counterpart is **плыть**. Like the verb **жить** *(to live),* **плыть** is a Conjugation I verb with a в-stem: **я плыву, ты плывёшь, они плывут; он плыл, она плыла, они плыли. Я плыву** means *I'm swimming/sailing right now.*

NUTS & BOLTS 1
PERFECTIVE ASPECT IN NEGATIVE SENTENCES
By default, negative sentences in Russian require the imperfective aspect.

Я не мерил(а) температуру.
I didn't take my temperature.

Я не ходил(а) к врачу.
I didn't go to the doctor's.

However, this general rule is broken when the negated action frustrates one's expectations. The negative perfective would imply such a failure to complete an action.

Я не измерил(а) температуру.
I failed to have taken my temperature.

Я не пошёл/пошла к врачу.
I failed to have gone to the doctor's.

PRACTICE 1
Translate the following sentences into Russian. Don't translate the qualifications in brackets, they're meant to help you with your choice of aspect after negation!

1. I *(m.)* didn't go the doctor's *(why should I?).*

2. I *(f.)* didn't go to the doctor's *(although I knew that I should have).*

3. She didn't buy the medicine *(although I specifically had asked her to!).*

4. He wasn't sick for the entire winter *(he's a healthy guy)*.

5. He never fell sick *(although everybody around him was sick)*.

6. We didn't take any medication *(because we didn't have any)*.

CONVERSATION 2

Natalia has symptoms of the flu and goes to see the doctor. This is their conversation in the doctor's office.

> Доктор: Здравствуйте, проходите, садитесь! Что вас беспокоит?
>
> Наталья: Я уже два дня плохо себя чувствую. У меня высокая температура, 38,5.
>
> Доктор: Что у вас болит?
>
> Наталья: У меня сильный насморк и кашель и немного болит живот.
>
> Доктор: Откройте, пожалуйста, рот и скажите: «А-а».
>
> Наталья: «А-а . . . ».
>
> Доктор: Горло немного красное. Повернитесь, пожалуйста, спиной, я вас сейчас послушаю. Дышите . . . Не дышите . . . Так. Хорошо. Лёгкие чистые. Воспаления лёгких нет.
>
> Наталья: Да, но мне больно кашлять.
>
> Доктор: У вас, наверное, грипп. Сейчас многие болеют гриппом. Я вам выпишу рецепт. Вы принимайте лекарство два раза в день после еды. Дней через пять кашель пройдёт, и вы выздоровеете.
>
> Наталья: Большое спасибо. До свидания.
>
> Доктор: Всего хорошего, поправляйтесь.

> *Doctor:* Hello, come in, have a seat. What's bothering you?
>
> *Natalia:* I've felt bad for two days. I have a high temperature of 38.5 (Celsius).
>
> *Doctor:* What is hurting you?

Natalia:	I have a (severe) runny nose, a little cough, and stomach pain.
Doctor:	Open your mouth please, and say "Ah."
Natalia:	Ah . . .
Doctor:	Your throat is a little red. Turn over, please, I'll listen to you now. Breathe . . . don't breathe . . . So, okay. Your lungs are clear. No pneumonia.
Natalia:	Yes, but it hurts to cough.
Doctor:	You probably have the flu. Many are sick with the flu right now. I'll write you a prescription. Take the medication twice a day after meals. You'll have this cough for about five days, and then you'll be healthy.
Natalia:	Thank you so much. Good-bye.
Doctor:	All the best; get well.

NOTES

Culturally and grammatically, imperatives are much more common in Russian than in English. Instead of saying *would you please* or *will you please,* Russians use command forms—*do it* or *don't do it, please!* This is polite and culturally appropriate provided that you choose the correct imperative. In fact, the roundabout English requests may be considered too vague, disingenuous, and even impolite!

NUTS & BOLTS 2
IMPERATIVES

The imperative is used for commands, requests, and prohibitions. In order to form Russian imperatives, you need to follow a few simple rules. If you hear the sound "**й**" anywhere in the conjugation ending, stop right there—this is your basic imperative form. For example, in **я работаю,** you can hear (but can't see!) the sound "**й**" in the end of the stem before the grammatical ending: **работа[йу]=ю.** Consequently, your imperative is **работай** in the singular informal, and **работайте** in the plural or respectful form.

If the conjugated forms don't have the sound "й" before their endings, they will have a consonant. Look at the first person singular (я живу, я буду) and notice the difference in stress: я живу has an end stress, whereas я буду is stressed on the stem. This difference determines their imperatives. If the 1st person singular of a given verb has an end stress, its imperative will end with a stressed и: я живу > живи/живите *(live!)*; if the 1st person singular has stem stress, the imperative ends in the soft sign: я буду > будь/будьте *(be!* as in будь здоров, *be healthy/take care)*. Conjugation I verbs keep their mutation in the imperatives: я пишу; ты пишешь – пиши! Conjugation II verbs don't keep their mutations anywhere but in the first person singular; this goes for the imperatives as well: я люблю; ты любишь > люби!

One rare exception to the above: if the conjugation stem ends in two consonants, then the imperative ending is always an и regardless of the stress. For example, the verb *to remember* is помнить. The first person conjugation, я помню, has two consonants, м and н, in the end of the stem; consequently, the imperative is помни(те) regardless of its stem stress.

The reflexive endings, -ся and -сь, don't interfere with the above rules. You simply add them to the formed imperative. As always, add -ся after consonants (including the й) and -сь after vowels (поправляйся, поправляйтесь). Irregular verbs also have irregular imperatives.

Irregular verb	Imperative
дать	дай(те)
есть	ешь(те)

You'll learn more about the imperative of дать in Unit 6.

PRACTICE 2

Give singular and plural commands based on the following infinitive phrases.

1. не болеть
2. делать зарядку
3. принимать лекарство
4. выписать рецепт
5. заниматься спортом

6. любить меня
7. купить продукты
8. не покупать лекарства
9. измерить температуру
10. сказать правду

NUTS & BOLTS 3

IMPERFECTIVE AND PERFECTIVE ASPECT IN IMPERATIVES

You also need to consider the choice of aspect in the imperatives. Choose the imperfective imperatives when you presume that your command is expected. This will happen in polite invitations because they imply, *"Of course, you should know that you're welcome!"* For example, you say to a visitor, **Здравствуйте, проходите, садитесь!** *(Hello [lit., be healthy!], come in, have a seat!).* These imperatives clearly entail that the interlocutor should expect such a welcome. On the contrary, when you ask or command something, that the other person wasn't supposed to know or expect, you should use perfective imperatives. Only perfective imperatives are polite in the so-called real commands.

Пожалуйста, откройте окно!
Please open the window!

The perfective here implies that I realize that you weren't supposed to open the window without my explicit request.

Negative imperatives are almost always imperfective. The common exceptions to this general rule are **не забудь(те)** *(don't forget),* **не упади(те)** *(don't fall/watch your step),* **не скажи(те)** *(don't say that),* **не опоздай(те)** *(don't be late),* **не заболей(те)** *(don't get* *sick).* They usually follow the initial warning **смотри(те)!** *(watch out!/make sure you don't).*

Смотри(те) не забудь(те)!
Make sure you don't forget!

Смотри(те) не заболей(те)!
Make sure you don't get sick!

Смотри(те) не упади(те)!
Make sure you don't fall!

PRACTICE 3

Translate the following sentences into Russian. Pay attention to the choice of aspect in the imperatives. Make the imperatives formal where asked to.

1. Please buy me (some) tea! *(fml.)*
2. Don't take this medication!
3. Tell me what's your name?
4. Open your mouth please! *(fml.)*
5. Please come in! *(fml.)*
6. Get well! *(fml.)*
7. Follow my example!

Tip!

You may have noticed that Sergey in Conversation 1 called **Женя** "**Жень.**" This is the colloquial vocative form. The vocative case used to be the case of direct address. It no longer exists in Russian, except for a few idiomatic and very old expressions, such as **Боже мой!** *(My God!)* or **Господи!** *(Lord!/God!).* These are the vocative form of the nouns **Бог** *(God)* and **Господь** *(the Lord).* In colloquial speech, every Russian first name that ends in a vowel (male or female) can be shortened if you're addressing the person by his/her name directly. So, if your friend's name is **Женя,** you can directly call her or him **Жень, Миша** may be addressed as **Миш, Серёжа–Серёж, Лена–Лен, Таня–Тань, Ира–Ир,** etc. Remember that these vocative short forms are not nicknames and should be used only colloquially in the forms of direct address when you know a person well, as they imply a certain level of familiarity.

ANSWERS

PRACTICE 1: 1. Я не ходил к врачу. **2.** Я не пошёла к врачу. **3.** Она не купила лекарство. **4.** Он не болел всю зиму. **5.** Он не заболел. **6.** Мы не принимали лекарства.

PRACTICE 2: 1. Не болей(те)! **2.** Делай(те) зарядку! **3.** Принимай(те) лекарство! **4.** Выпиши(те) рецепт! **5.** Занимайся/занимайтесь спортом! **6.** Люби(те) меня! **7.** Купи(те) продукты! **8.** Не покупай(те) лекарства! **9.** Измерь(те) температуру! **10.** Скажи(те) правду!

PRACTICE 3: 1. Пожалуйста, купите мне чай! **2.** Не принимай это лекарство! **3.** Скажи мне, как тебя зовут? **4.** Откройте рот, пожалуйста! **5.** Пожалуйста, проходите! **6.** Поправляйтесь! **7.** Бери с меня пример!

UNIT 5 ESSENTIALS

Мне кажется, что я заболел(а).	*I must have gotten sick. (lit., It seems to me that I've gotten sick.)*
Я никогда не болею гриппом.	*I never have the flu. (lit., I'm never sick with the flu.)*
У меня с вечера болит голова и горло.	*I've had a headache and a sore throat since (last) night.*
Я плохо себя чувствую.	*I'm not feeling well. (lit., I'm feeling bad.)*
Я измерил(а) температуру.	*I took my temperature.*
У меня высокая температура—38,5.	*I have a high fever, 38.5.*
У меня нет температуры.	*I don't have a fever.*

Я ходил(а) к врачу.	*I went to the doctor's.*
Я был(а) у врача.	*I was at the doctor's.*
Врач мне выписал лекарство.	*The doctor prescribed me a medication.*
Я буду принимать лекарство два раза в день после еды/до еды/во время еды.	*I will take the medication twice a day after meals/before meals/with meals.*
Пожалуйста, проходите, садитесь!	*Please come in, have a seat!*
Вас что-нибудь беспокоит?	*Is anything bothering you?*
Он что-то купил в аптеке.	*He bought something in the pharmacy.*
Дней через пять всё пройдёт.	*Everything will pass in about five days.*
Поправляйтесь!	*Get well!*

Unit 6
Talking on the phone

In Unit 6, you'll learn to talk on the phone, whether you're calling an office or a private home. You'll learn Russian phone etiquette: how to ask for the people you need, leave messages for them, and make appointments. You'll continue expanding your Russian vocabulary and grammar. We'll cover more time expressions and imperatives, equip you with more rules and examples of Russian conjugation, aspect, and command forms. You'll start learning short adjectives and comparatives as well as the verbs and expressions commonly used in order to schedule a meeting with somebody.

--------------- Lesson 21 (Words) ---------------

WORD LIST 1

слушать *(imperf.; conj. I; -ай)*	to listen
слышать *(imperf.; conj. II; -а2)*	to hear
говорить *(imperf.; conj.II; -и)*	to speak
сказать *(perf.; conj. I; -а)*	to say
говорить по-русски/по-английски	to speak Russian/English
говорить по телефону	to speak on the phone
разговаривать *(imperf.; conj. I; -ай)*	to converse, to chat
разговор	conversation
договариваться *(conj. I)—* договориться *(conj. II)* (о чём?/с кем?)	to agree (mutually) (about what?/ with whom?)

встречать/ся *(conj. I)*— встретить/ся *(conj. II)* (кого?/с кем?)	*to meet (who?/with whom?)*
деловая встреча	*business meeting*
бизнес-ланч	*business lunch*
послезавтра	*the day after tomorrow*
позавчера	*the day before yesterday*

NOTES

The verbs **договариваться—договориться** mean *to agree mutually*. You should differentiate them from the verbs **соглашаться—согласиться** meaning *to consent*. For example, the sentence **они договорились встретиться вечером** means *they agreed to meet in the evening (and it was a mutual decision)*, as opposed to **она согласилась встретиться с ним вечером** which means *she consented to meet with him in the evening (because he insisted)*. It is common to use the perfective verb **договориться** in the past plural form **договорились** when you mean to say affirmatively *yes, okay, agreed*, or *done*.

You should also be careful to differentiate between the verbs **встречать(ся)—встретить(ся)** and **знакомить(ся)—познакоми ть (ся)**. Although all of them mean *to meet*, the second pair **знакомиться—познакомиться** stands for making one's acquaintance for the first time, while the first pair **встречаться—встретиться** is used for all other encounters. When these verbs are transitive, that is, when the action they denote is directed at another party, they drop the reflexive particle **-ся: я встретил вас у метро** *(I met you by the metro)*, **я познакомил вас с ним** *(I introduced you to him);* whereas **мы познакомились на работе** means *we met (became acquainted) at work*. In addition, the imperfective verb **встречаться** colloquially means *to date someone:* **они встречаются** *(they're dating)*.

NUTS & BOLTS 1

TO SPEAK AND TO LISTEN

Let's learn the three verbs for *to speak* in Russian: **говорить,** **сказать,** and **разговаривать.** The first one, **говорить,** is an imperfective Conjugation II verb with the stem ending in an–**и.** It has no mutations or stress shifts. Its past tense is also regular: **говорил, говорила, говорило, говорили.** This verb denotes a physical act of speaking. For example, you can speak **громко** *(loudly),* **быстро** *(fast),* or **тихо** *(softly).* You can also speak foreign languages. In this case, you need to add to the verb **говорить** an irregular adverb that literally means *in the manner of* a given language: **говорить по-русски** *(speak Russian),* or **говорить по-английски** *(speak English). To speak on the phone* is **говорить по телефону.**

Он говорит только по-русски.

He only speaks Russian

Я плохо говорю по-английски.

I speak English poorly.

Мы говорим по телефону.

We speak on the phone.

The Conjugation I verb **сказать** is perfective; it has the **a**-stem and the **з/ж** mutation throughout the entire future tense paradigm, as well as a stress shift. Its conjugation is similar to the verb **писать** *(to write),* except that **писать** has the **с/ш** mutation. The past tense of **сказать** is regular: **сказал, сказала, сказало, сказали.** This verb means *to say something specific and complete* rather than *to speak continuously.* When Russians ask for directions or any other information, they typically introduce their request with the following common phrase:

Скажите, пожалуйста...

Tell (me) please...

The third verb is **разговаривать**. It's imperfective, Conjugation I with the stem ending in **-ива(й)**. It conjugates exactly like **ай**-verbs, e.g., **работать**. The verb **разговаривать** means *to have a conversation*.

Они ужинали в ресторане и разговаривали.

They were having dinner in a restaurant and chatted/conversed.

The verbs **слушать** and **слышать** correspond to the English verbs *to listen* and *to hear*. Both are imperfective. **Слушать** is Conjugation I with the **ай**-stem (like **работать**); it takes a direct object in the accusative case.

Вы слушаете музыку?

Do you listen to music?

Слышать is Conjugation II and belongs to a special subtype. Its stem ends in an **-а** like in **писать,** but, as opposed to all **а**-type verbs which are Conjugation I, **слышать** is Conjugation II. So, its stem should be qualified as a_2-stem. Most verbs of this subtype have a husher before the last **-а** in their stems: **слы-ш-а-**. This is how they can be recognized and distinguished from regular **а**-verbs that belong to Conjugation I.

Before we go on, let's briefly summarize what you need to know about Conjugation II. Only three types of verbal stems belong to Conjugation II: **е**-verbs (e.g., **виде-ть**), **и**-verbs (e.g., **говори-ть**), and a_2-verbs with preceding hushers (e.g., **слыша-ть**). All other Russian stems are Conjugation I. If a Conjugation II verb has a mutation, it occurs only in the first person singular form: **я вижу, ты видишь, они видят,** etc. Conjugation II verbs have the endings **-ат/ят** in the third person plural. All Conjugation II forms (in the present/future tense) have an **и** in the ending except for the first person singular and third person plural forms.

PRACTICE 1

Как сказать по-русски? Translate the following sentences into Russian.

1. You *(fml.)* speak Russian too fast (слишком быстро).

2. What did you *(fml.)* say? I *(m.)* didn't hear.

3. They conversed in a restaurant.

4. He spoke on the phone with (his) wife.

5. I *(m.)* conversed with his daughter.

6. We agreed to meet the day after tomorrow, on Friday.

PRACTICE 2

Fill in the blanks choosing the right verb from **встречать, встречаться, встретить, встретиться, знакомить, знакомиться, познакомить, познакомиться.** Remember to make the verb agree with the rest of the subject.

1. Русские партнёры _____ американского бизнесмена в аэропорту вчера вечером.

2. –Откуда вы его знаете?–Мы _____ на деловой встрече прошлым летом.

3. Завтра все менеджеры _____ днём на бизнес ланче.

4. У тебя есть брат? Я хочу _____ с ним.

5. Приходи ко мне в гости. Я тебя _____ около метро.

6. После работы мы всегда _____ в этом кафе.

WORD LIST 2

к сожалению	*unfortunately*
знакомый/знакомая/ знакомые	*acquaintance (male/female/plural)*
друг/друзья	*(close) friend/friends*

звони́ть—позвони́ть *(conj. II; -и) (кому?)*	*to call/to make a phone call (to whom?)*
перезвони́ть *(кому?)*	*to call back (lit., re-call) (whom?)*
телефо́нный звоно́к	*phone call*
телефо́н	*phone, phone number*
но́мер телефо́на	*phone number*
но́мер гости́ницы	*hotel room*
дома́шний телефо́н	*home phone number*
моби́льный телефо́н	*mobile phone number*
спра́шивать *(conj. I; -ай)*— спроси́ть *(conj. II; -и)*	*to ask*

NOTES

The noun **телефо́н** denotes a *physical phone* or a *phone number*, so the phrase **какой у вас телефо́н** most often means *what's your phone number* (it can also be used to ask what brand of phone you have). The full Russian phrase for *phone number* is **телефо́нный но́мер** or **но́мер телефо́на**. The phrase **моби́льный телефо́н** means either *cell phone itself* or *cell phone number;* **дома́шний телефо́н** usually stands for *home phone number*. So it's common to say **перезвони́(те) мне на моби́льный/дома́шний телефо́н** *(call me back on my cell/home phone);* notice the use of the accusative case after the preposition **на** (**на дома́шний телефо́н/на рабо́ту/дом,** etc.). The colloquial or slang terms for *cell phone* in Russian are: **моби́льный, моби́льник, моби́ла, тру́бка, труба́.**

The verb **звони́ть—позвони́ть** belongs to Conjugation II; it has the **и**-stem without mutations or stress shifts. It means *to make/give a phone call.* Note that it takes the dative case (not the accusative): **позвони́(те) мне** *(call me).*

Перезвони́ть means to call back, literally *to re-call.* It's common to say **я перезвоню́ попо́зже** *(I'll call back later),* or **перезвони́(те) попо́зже** *([you] call back later).*

NUTS & BOLTS 2
EXPRESSING FRIENDSHIP IN RUSSIAN

The Russian word **друг** denotes a closer relationship than its English counterpart *friend*. **Друг** can be translated more accurately as *close friend*. Memorize the irregular plural **друзья** *(friends)*. Also, keep in mind that **друг** usually doesn't imply a romantic relationship.

The Russian language doesn't really have a standard neutral word for *boyfriend*. All of its possible equivalents are stylistically marked in Russian. For example, **молодой человек** *(lit., young man)* is somewhat euphemistic and old-fashioned—parents sometimes use this word to refer to boyfriends of their daughters; **парень** *(lit., guy)* is, on the contrary, folksy; **бойфренд** *(boyfriend)*, recently borrowed from English, is trendy and foreign.

The situation is slightly better for the word *girlfriend*. Russians do have a standard term, **девушка** *(lit., girl)* with the restriction that it applies only to young girls. Alternatively, there is also a new borrowing **гёрлфренд** *(girlfriend)*. Note that the phrase **это моя девушка** means *this is my girlfriend*, and not *this is my girl*. The Russian term **подруга** *(female friend)* usually refers to a female friend of a female and doesn't normally indicate a romantic relationship.

For a less close friendship, Russians use **знакомый,** the equivalent of the English *acquaintance*. As you can see, **знакомый** is a substantivized adjective; consequently, it has adjectival endings: **знакомая** for one *female friend,* and **знакомые** for the plural form.

Это мой друг.
This is my friend. This is my boyfriend.

Это моя девушка.
This is my girlfriend.

Это мой знакомый.
This is my acquaintance.

PRACTICE 3

Find the appropriate Russian term for the following definitions of your *friend*. Choose one of the following: **друг, подруга, знакомый, знакомая, девушка, бойфренд, гёрлфренд.**

1. You're a female and you have a good friend who's also a female.

2. You're a male and you have a good male friend.

3. Your acquaintance is a male.

4. You're a "trendy" female and you have a boyfriend.

5. You're a female and your acquaintance is a female.

6. You're a young male and you have a young girlfriend.

PRACTICE 4

Как сказать по-русски? Translate the following sentences into Russian.

1. Call *(infml.)* me on (my) cell phone.

2. This is my home phone number.

3. He called me back on my home phone number.

4. Her friends call me every day.

5. Your *(fml.)* acquaintances didn't call me back.

6. Call me back at work tomorrow after lunch.

Tip!

Use mnemonic devices for the words and expressions that are hard to remember or differentiate. It doesn't matter how silly or personal you make them. In fact, the sillier or more striking they are, the better you'll remember them! For example, to make a distinction between **слушать** *(to listen)* and **слышать** *(to hear)*, think of the phrase **слушать музыку** *(listen to music)* where you have an alliteration of three vowels **у**. This way, you'll remember that the

y in the root stands for music and for listening. Take time to create your own mnemonic devices that will help you remember so many Russian expressions and grammar points!

ANSWERS

PRACTICE 1: 1. Вы говорите по-русски слишком быстро. **2.** Что вы сказали? Я не слышал. **3.** Они разговаривали в ресторане. **4.** Он говорил по телефону с женой. **5.** Я разговаривал с его дочерью. **6.** Мы договорились встретиться послезавтра, в пятницу.

PRACTICE 2: 1. встречали/встретили; **2.** встретились/познакомились; **3.** встречаются/встретятся; **4.** познакомиться/встретиться; **5.** встречу; **6.** встречаемся

PRACTICE 3: 1. подруга; **2.** друг; **3.** знакомый; **4.** бойфренд; **5.** знакомая; **6.** девушка

PRACTICE 4: 1. Позвони мне на мобильный телефон. **2.** Это мой домашний телефон/телефонный номер. **3.** Он перезвонил мне на мой домашний телефон. **4.** Её друзья звонят мне каждый день. **5.** Ваши знакомые не перезвонили мне. **6.** Перезвони мне на работу завтра после обеда.

Lesson 22 (Phrases)

PHRASE LIST 1

договориться о встрече	*to set up a meeting (lit., agree about a meeting)*
главный офис фирмы	*main office of the firm/company*
дирекция фирмы	*firm's headquarters*
в прошлый понедельник	*last Monday*
на этой неделе	*this week*
в будущем/следующем месяце	*next month*

в будущем/следующем году	*next year*
в первой половине дня	*in the morning (lit., in the first half of the day)*
во второй половине дня	*in the afternoon (lit., in the second half of the day)*
в неформальной обстановке	*informally (lit., in the informal setting)*
у себя в кабинете	*at one's own office*
С приездом!	*Welcome! (lit., With arrival!)*
Как (вы) долетели?	*How was (your) flight?*

NOTES

When Russians make appointments, they often refer to the morning part of the day, before lunch, **первая половина дня**, literally, *the first half of the day.* The afternoon part of the work day is **вторая половина дня**, literally, *the second half of the day.* Remember that you need to use these time expressions with the prepositional case: **в первой половине дня, во второй половине дня.**

Notice the reflexive personal pronoun **себя** in the phrase: **у себя в кабинете** *(in his own office)*. This pronoun refers to the subject of the sentence. It stays in the same form regardless of the grammatical person of the subject. So you should say: **он у себя в кабинете, она у себя в кабинете, я у себя в кабинете,** etc. Literally, the phrase **он у себя в кабинете** means *he is at his (own) office;* this is the best idiomatic way of expressing this idea in Russian.

NUTS & BOLTS 1
RUSSIAN TIME EXPRESSIONS

When you need to set up a meeting (**договориться о встрече**), you need to use time expressions in order to say *when* (**когда**). Russian time expressions are different from the English ones, and you can't just translate them word by word. They also don't conform to one general rule. Yet they aren't random either. Let's notice certain patterns among Russian time expressions—they'll help you remember and use them properly. You already know how to say in the morning, in the afternoon, in the evening, and at night in Russian (see Unit 2); how to say on a given day of the week (see Unit 2); and how to say on a given date (see Unit 4). Now, consider the following rule of thumb:

1. if the time unit is less than a week, use the preposition **в** with the accusative case: **в пятницу** *(on Friday),* **в эту минуту** *(this minute),* **в этот день** *(this/that day),* etc;

2. if the time unit is a week, use the preposition **на** with the prepositional case: **на этой неделе** *(this week),* **на прошлой неделе** *(last week),* **на будущей неделе** *(next week),* etc;

3. if the time unit is more than a week, use the preposition **в** with the prepositional case: **в этом месяце** *(this month),* **в будущем году** *(next year),* **в прошлом веке** *(in the last century),* etc.

The adjectives **будущий** *(next),* **следующий** *(next or the next),* or **прошлый** *(last or past)* are commonly used with the above time expressions. But remember to agree them with the nouns they modify!

PRACTICE 1

Когда вы встретились или встретитесь с вашим другом? *(When did you meet or will you meet with your friend?).* Complete the sentences below with the time expressions in the parentheses.

1. Мы встречались два раза _____ (last year).

2. Вы встретитесь с директором _____ (this week).

3. Они встречаются на бизнес-ланч _____ (this Wednesday).

4. Я встречусь с вашим знакомым _____ (next week).

5. Ты с ним встречаешься _____ (next year).

6. Мы больше не будем встречаться _____ (this month).

NUTS & BOLTS 2
Irregular prepositional endings

Notice the irregular prepositional ending **y** in the phrase **в будущем году.** This ending occurs in a limited number of Russian masculine one syllable nouns in the prepositional case only after the prepositions denoting *location* (**в** or **на**). These nouns end in a hard consonant, and their locative ending **y** is always stressed. Look at the following chart.

берег (from **брег**)	**на берегу**	*shore, on the shore*
глаз	**в глазу**	*eye, in the eye*
год	**в году**	*year, in the year*
лес	**в лесу**	*forest/woods, in the woods*
мост	**на мосту**	*bridge, on the bridge*
нос	**на носу**	*nose, on the nose*
порт	**в порту**	*port, at the port*
ряд	**в ряду**	*row, in the row*
сад	**в саду**	*garden/orchard, in the garden*
угол	**в углу/на углу**	*corner, in the corner/at the corner*
час	**в часу**	*hour, in the hour*
шкаф	**в шкафу**	*cabinet/dresser/ cupboard, in the cabinet/dresser/ cupboard*

The phrase **в углу** means *in the corner (of a room)*; the phrase **на углу** means *at the corner (of a street)*.

PRACTICE 2
Как сказать по-русски? Translate the following sentences into Russian.

1. The director is in his office.

2. We arranged a meeting in an informal setting.

3. Welcome! How was your flight?

4. They will meet in the main office of the firm in the second half of the day.

5. I will meet you at the corner of the street.

PHRASE LIST 2

Алло!/Аллё!	*Hello (only when you pick up the phone)*
Откуда вы звоните?	*Where're you calling from?*
звонить—позвонить из гостиницы	*to call from a hotel*
останавливаться *(conj. I; -ай)*—**остановиться** *(conj. II; -и)* **в гостинице**	*to stay in a hotel*
уйти *(perf.)* **в магазин**	*to leave for a store*
прийти *(perf.)* **домой**	*to come home*
вернуться *(perf.; conj. I; -ну)* **домой**	*to come back/return home*
дайте мне, пожалуйста, ваш телефон	*give me your phone number please*
давать—дать *(irregular)*	*to give*
записывать—записать телефон	*to write down the phone number*
ждать—подождать *(conj. I; -а)* **звонка**	*to wait for a phone call*

Notes

The verbs **ждать—подождать** *(to wait for)* are regular. They belong to Conjugation I with the **a**-stem. However, as opposed to their English counterpart, the Russian verbs take the direct object in the accusative case: **я жду Аню** *(I'm waiting for Anya)*, **ты ждёшь директора** *(you're waiting for the director* [notice the animate form!]), **они подождут меня** *(they will wait for me)*, etc. Also remember that the imperative form of this verb is usually perfective in Russian: **подожди(те) меня** *(wait for me)*. The genitive **звонка** in the phrase **ждать звонка** is idiomatic; it means *waiting for a phone call* as opposed to *waiting for a more specific phone call:* **ждать звонок**. By and large, this distinction is not very strong in modern Russian, and both forms are fully interchangeable.

NUTS & BOLTS 3

THE PERFECTIVE MOTION VERBS уйти AND прийти.

Let's look at the perfective motion verbs **уйти** and **прийти**. Both denote a pedestrian action rather than a vehicular one. The verb **уйти** means *to leave a place on foot;* the verb **прийти** means *to arrive on foot*. Both verbs can also denote a movement within the city limits (even including vehicular ones!) when the mode of transport is irrelevant, but it's important that the activity is a local one. Thus, the sentence **они придут ко мне в гости** *(they will come over to my house)* doesn't necessarily mean that they will walk. It merely implies that we live in the same city, and they'll visit me locally; the mode of their transport stays unidentified and irrelevant. Remember that, since both verbs are perfective, they don't have a present tense. This is how these verbs are conjugated in the future tense.

уйти *(to leave a place on foot)*

я уйду	мы уйдём
ты уйдёшь	вы уйдёте
он/она/оно уйдёт	они уйдут

прийти *(to arrive on foot)*

я приду	мы придём
ты придёшь	вы придёте
он/она/оно придёт	они придут

The prefix **у-** means *away from;* the prefix **при-** means *to.* Notice how the stem **ид-** in the verb **идти** mutates when these prefixes are added to it: **у-йд-у** and **при-д-у;** and in the infinitives: **у-й-ти** and **при-д-ти.**

These verbs need to be contrasted with the verbs **выйти** *(to leave, to exit)* and **войти** *(to enter).* The latter two describe shorter movements, the ones that emphasize a physical exiting and entering rather than just leaving a place or arriving at it. The verb **выйти** is often used when a specific time of leaving is mentioned, and when the person is expected to be back. For example, you should say **я вышел/вышла) из дома в восемь часов утра** *(I left home at eight o'clock in the morning),* because the action happened at a specific time, and I also will be back by the end of the day.

The verb **уйти** denotes *to leave* as a more radical departure, such as *for the day* or *for good.* For example, you should say **он ушёл с работы в пять часов вечера** *(he left work at five p.m.),* regardless of the specific time **в пять часов** *(five p.m)* being mentioned, but because he *left for the day.* Moreover, the phrase **он ушёл с работы** can mean in another context *he quit his job.*

The past tense forms of these verbs are predictable if you remember the past tense of the verb **идти** (**шёл, шла, шло, шли**): **ушёл/ушла, пришёл/пришла, вышел/вышла** (the prefix **вы-** is always stressed in perfective verbs!), etc.

The phrases **прийти домой** *(come back home)* and **вернуться домой** *(return home)* are synonymous. Notice that, because of the movement toward home, the adverb **домой** is in the directional form **(домой)** rather than its locative form **(дома)**.

PRACTICE 3
Fill in the blanks using the correct form of the motion verb given in the parenthesis. Pay attention to the conjugation, agreement, and tense!

1. Я _____ (left/exited) из дома в девять часов утра.

2. Она _____ (will come) домой после работы вечером.

3. Сегодня я _____ (will leave) с работы в шесть часов вечера.

4. Мы _____ (exited) из такси и _____ (entered) в главный офис фирмы.

5. Я перезвонил ей, когда она _____ (came) на работу.

NUTS & BOLTS 4
THE VERBS давать–дать *(to give)*
The verbs **давать** *(to give)* are irregular in both the imperfective and perfective forms.

давать *(to give, imperfective)*

я даю	мы даём
ты даёшь	вы даёте
он/она/оно даёт	они дают

Past: **давал, давала, давало, давали**

дать *(to give, perfective)*

я дам	мы дадим
ты дашь	вы дадите
он/она/оно даст	они дадут

Past: дал, дала, дало, дали

The past tenses are regular for both verbs: **давал, давала, давало, давали** and **дал, дала, дало, дали** (notice the feminine/neuter stress shift for **дала/дало**). **Давай(те)** is the imperfective imperative; the perfective imperative is **дай(те)**.

Давать/дать take the accusative case for direct object and the dative for indirect object (the recipient of the action).

Дайте мне *(dat.)*, **пожалуйста, ваш телефон** *(acc.)*.
Give me your telephone number, please.

PRACTICE 4
Give Russian equivalents to the following English sentences.

1. I'll call you *(fml.)* from the hotel.

2. Give *(infml.)* me please your phone number. I'll write it down.

3. Wait *(pl.)* for him! He'll come in a minute.

4. We'll stay in a hotel in the center of the city.

5. When will you *(fml.)* come back home?

Culture note

Cell phone service is more expensive in Russia than in the U.S. Unlimited calling is rare; so are monthly plans and yearly contracts. Most cell phones are prepaid. Consequently, Russians usually keep their cell phone conversations to a minimum and use text messaging as much as possible. Calls from a cell phone to a cell phone are usually cheaper than those between a cell phone and a land line. Therefore, it's generally considered impolite to call someone's cell phone from a land line. Keep this in mind when you are in Russia!

ANSWERS

PRACTICE 1: 1. в прошлом году; **2.** на этой неделе; **3.** в эту среду; **4.** на следующей/будущей неделе; **5.** в следующем/будущем году; **6.** в этом месяце

PRACTICE 2: 1. Директор у себя в кабинете. **2.** Мы договорились о встрече в неформальной обстановке. **3.** С приездом! Как вы долетели? **4.** Они встретятся в главном офисе фирмы во второй половине дня. **5.** Я вас встречу на углу улицы

PRACTICE 3: 1. вышел; **2.** придёт; **3.** уйду; **4.** вышли, вошли; **5.** пришла

PRACTICE 4: 1. Я позвоню вам из гостиницы. **2.** Дай мне, пожалуйста, твой телефон. Я запишу его. **3.** Подождите его! Он придёт через минуту. **4.** Мы остановимся в гостинице в центре города. **5.** Когда вы вернётесь/придёте домой?

Lesson 23 (Sentences)

SENTENCE LIST 1

Я вас слушаю.   *I'm listening to you. (fml., used instead of hello when talking on the phone)*

Здравствуйте, это говорит Иван Петров.	*Hello, this is Ivan Petrov speaking.*
Вас беспокоит Иван Петров.	*Ivan Petrov calling (formal; lit., Ivan Petrov is disturbing you).*
Соедините меня, пожалуйста, с Александром Васильевичем.	*Connect me please with Aleksandr Vasilievich.*
Подождите, пожалуйста, одну минуту.	*Just a minute please (lit., Wait please for one minute).*
Одну минуточку/минутку.	*One minute.*
Я звоню, чтобы договориться о нашей встрече.	*I'm calling in order to set up our meeting (lit., to agree about our meeting).*
Я вас буду ждать завтра у себя в кабинете.	*I'll wait for you tomorrow in my office.*
Мы можем встретиться завтра в любое время.	*We can meet any time tomorrow.*
Давайте встретимся в пятницу, в десять часов утра.	*Let's meet on Friday, at 10 a.m.*
Давайте вместе пойдём на ланч.	*Let's go have lunch together. (the word* **ланч/бизнес-ланч** *is mostly used for a business lunch in Russian, and* **обед** *for a more traditional midday meal)*
Давайте продолжим разговор в неформальной обстановке.	*Let's continue (this) conversation in an informal setting.*

NOTES

The Russian **чтобы** + *infinitive* is equivalent to the English expression *in order to* + *infinitive*. The sentence **я звоню, чтобы договориться о нашей встрече** means *I'm calling in order to set up our meeting*. As in English, both clauses refer to the same subject: I'm calling and I'm trying to set up a meeting. So just as in English, you can leave out **чтобы** *(in order to)* in colloquial speech and simply say **я звоню договориться о нашей встрече** *(I'm calling to set up our meeting)*. The following infinitive is often perfective because you do something *in order to* accomplish it.

Здравствуйте, это говорит + *nominative,* **Вас беспокоит** + *nominative,* or **соедините меня, пожалуйста, с** + *instrumental* are more formal expressions in Russian phone etiquette. It's not customary to introduce oneself when calling someone at home. However, people do so in formal situations.

The elliptic phrases **одну минуту** or **одну минуточку/минутку** are in the accusative case because the imperative **подожди(те)** *(wait for)* is implied. So the full sentence would be: **Пожалуйста, подождите одну минуту!** *(Please wait for one minute)*. It's common and idiomatic to leave out **подождите, пожалуйста** in the situations when you ask somebody to wait for a moment. You can also replace the noun **минута** in the accusative case with other nouns in the accusative that denote intervals of time: **минуточка/минутка** *(little minute),* **секунда** *(second)/***секундочка** *(little second),* etc. So you can equally say: **одну минуту** or **одну минуточку, одну секунду** or **одну секундочку.**

NUTS & BOLTS 1
Давай(те) *(LET'S)*
Now, let's learn one more way of expressing commands in Russian. Besides standard imperatives, you can also use the inclusive command that starts with *let's.* It consists of two parts: first, the imperative **давай(те),** and then, either the imperfective infinitive or the 1st person plural form of a perfective verb. If what you're suggesting is an expected, continuous, or recurrent action, you should use the imperfective infinitive after **давай(те).**

Давайте обедать!
Let's have dinner! (i.e., let's go ahead and have dinner, the one you've been expecting to have).

Давай всегда встречаться в центре!

Let's always meet downtown! (**всегда** *marks a recurrent action and calls for the imperfective aspect*)

However, if what you're suggesting is a perfective singular action—the one that requires a change of state and is relatively new to the context—you need to have the perfective verb in the first person plural.

Давайте встретимся в центре!

Let's meet downtown! (i.e., let's this time do something different and meet downtown)

Давай пойдём в кино!

Let's go to the movies! (i.e., let's get out of the house, let's change this state and go to the movies instead)

The expression **пойдём** *(let's go)*, which you learned in Unit 1, is an elliptic command; **давайте пойдём** *(let's go)* is a full expression. Notice that for the elliptic form—and only for this elliptic command *(let's) go (on foot)*—there exists the plural elliptic form: **Пойдёмте!** (see Unit 1).

PRACTICE 1

Fill in the blanks with the appropriate Russian forms of the English verbs given in the parentheses.

1. Давайте _____ (go) в театр сегодня вечером.

2. Давайте завтра _____ (meet) с директором в главном офисе фирмы.

3. Давай всегда _____ (wait for) её после работы.

4. Не уходи! Давай _____ (wait for) наших друзей.

5. Давайте иногда _____ (have dinner) в этом ресторане.

6. Он ещё не пришёл?! Давайте _____ (call) ему.

PRACTICE 2

Как сказать по-русски? Translate the following sentences into Russian.

1. –Hello, this is Mike speaking. Please connect me with the director.–Just a minute.

2. Let's continue this conversation in the restaurant. *(fml.)*

3. Let's set up a meeting. *(infml.)*

4. I'm waiting for you in my office. *(fml.)*

5. Will you wait for me? We'll go have lunch together. *(infml.)*

SENTENCE LIST 2

Здравствуйте! Позовите, пожалуйста, Ивана.	*Hello! May I speak to Ivan please?*
К сожалению его нет дома.	*Unfortunately, he's not home.*
Кто его спрашивает?	*(May I ask) who's calling? (lit., Who is asking for him?)*
Куда вы звоните?	*Where're you calling?*
Вы не туда попали.	*You have the wrong number. (lit., You didn't hit there. You missed.)*
Вы ошиблись номером.	*You have the wrong number. (lit., You made a mistake in the phone number.)*
Что ему передать?	*May I take a message? (lit., What [should I] pass to him?)*
Передайте, пожалуйста, что звонил Иван.	*Tell (him) please that Ivan called.*
Обязательно передам.	*I certainly will (tell him that).*
Он вам перезвонит с мобильного телефона.	*He'll call you back from (his) cell phone.*
Он вам перезвонит, когда вернётся домой.	*He'll call you back when he returns.*

Позови(те), пожалуйста, + *name in the accusative/animate case* is the most common way of asking for a person on the phone. The shorter expression **можно Николая** is often considered too casual and familiar. Don't hesitate to use imperatives for requests in Russian as in **Позови(те), пожалуйста!** They are perfectly courteous when you choose the right aspect!

There are two ways of saying *you have the wrong number* in Russian. You can say **вы не туда попали,** which literally means *you didn't hit there,* or you can say **вы ошиблись номером,** which literally means *you made a mistake in the phone number.* Both are equally idiomatic and you can use them interchangeably.

NUTS & BOLTS 2
SUBJECTLESS GENITIVE OF NEGATION
Notice the genitive of negation in the seemingly simple sentence **его нет дома** *(he's not home).* As opposed to its English counterpart, this sentence is subjectless in Russian. It reads literally *it's none of him at home.* Consequently, the missing person needs to be put in the genitive case—the genitive of negation. **Нет** in the past tense becomes **не было;** it always stays the same in the past because it agrees with the implied subject *it.*

Его не было дома.
He wasn't home.

Её не было дома.
She wasn't home.

Их не было дома.
They weren't home.

Similarly, the future form is always **не будет.**

Его не будет дома.
He won't be home.

Её не будет дома.
She won't be home.

Их не будет дома.
They won't be home.

PRACTICE 3

Кого нет дома? *(Who is not home?)* Say that the following people aren't, weren't, and won't be at the given locations at the given times. Remember to use the genitive of negation!

1. директор (tomorrow; in the main office)

2. она (now; at home)

3. я (yesterday; at work)

4. наш американский партнёр (next week; in Moscow)

5. мы (yesterday; at the meeting)

6. твой знакомый (now; at home)

NUTS & BOLTS 3

TELEPHONE GRAMMAR

If you call a person, you should use the dative case (**кому?** *to whom?*) after the Russian verb **звонить:**

Я звоню Ивану.
I'm calling Ivan.

Кому вы звоните?
Who are you calling?

But if you call an office, a company, or any other organization, you should use the accusative of direction (**куда?** *where to?*) with the appropriate preposition **в** or **на:**

Я звоню в университет.
I'm calling the university.

Я звоню на почту.

I'm calling the post office.

Куда вы звоните?

Where are you calling?

In order to *take a message* or *leave a message,* Russians use one verb **передать,** which literally means *to pass* or *to give.*

Что ему передать?

May I take a message?

When you want someone to take a message, simply use the perfective imperative.

Передайте, пожалуйста, что звонил Иван.

Tell [him/her] that Ivan called please.

Notice that the subject **Иван** in the subordinate clause is in the end of the clause. However, if this subject is a pronoun, you should place it before the verb.

Передайте, пожалуйста, что я звонил(а).

Tell [him/her] that I called please.

PRACTICE 4

Как сказать по-русски? Rewrite the following conversation in Russian.

1. Hello! May I speak to Natasha?

2. Hello! Unfortunately, she's not home.

3. (May I ask) who's calling?

4. This is her friend (друг), Mike.

5. May I take a message?

6. Please tell her I called.

7. She'll call you back when she returns.

Discovery activity

Imagine that you need to get in touch with your Russian friend over the phone. You're calling him or her at home, but he or she is not there. Someone else picks up the phone. What happens next? Act out a possible conversation. Be creative and talkative!

ANSWERS

PRACTICE 1: 1. пойдём; **2.** встретимся; **3.** ждать; **4.** подождём; **5.** ужинать; **6.** позвоним

PRACTICE 2: 1.—Здравствуйте, это говорит Майк. Соедините меня, пожалуйста, с директором.—Одну минуточку. **2.** Давайте продолжим этот разговор в ресторане. **3.** Давай договоримся о встрече. **4.** Я жду вас у себя в кабинете. **5.** Ты подождёшь меня? Мы вместе пойдём на ланч.

PRACTICE 3: 1. Директора завтра не будет в главном офисе. **2.** Её сейчас нет дома. **3.** Меня вчера не было на работе. **4.** Нашего американского партнёра не будет в Москве на следующей неделе. **5.** Нас вчера не было на встрече. **6.** Твоего знакомого сейчас нет дома.

PRACTICE 4: 1. Здравствуйте! Позовите, пожалуйста, Наташу. **2.** Здравствуйте! К сожалению её нет дома. **3.** Кто её спрашивает? **4.** Это говорит её друг (знакомый), Майк. **5.** Что ей передать? **6.** Передайте, пожалуйста, что я звонил. **7.** Она вам перезвонит, когда вернётся.

CONVERSATION 1

Kim Brighton, an American businessperson, is calling her business partner, the director of a Russian company GosEnergo Aleksandr Vasilievich Rubliov. She is calling his Moscow office in order to make an appointment with him. First, she speaks with his office assistant who then connects her with the director.

Секретарь:	Дирекция фирмы «ГосЭнерго» слушает.
Г-жа Брайтон:	Здравствуйте. Это говорит Ким Брайтон, американский партнёр вашей фирмы. Соедините меня, пожалуйста, с Александром Васильевичем.
Секретарь:	Здравствуйте, госпожа Брайтон. Вы очень хорошо говорите по-русски. Вы звоните из Америки?
Г-жа Брайтон:	Нет, я сейчас в Москве.
Секретарь:	Одну минуточку. Я вас сейчас соединю с директором.
Г-н Рублёв:	Я вас слушаю.
Г-жа Брайтон:	Здравствуйте, господин Рублёв. Вас беспокоит Ким Брайтон. Я уже в Москве.
Г-н Рублёв:	Здравствуйте, госпожа Брайтон. Рад вас слышать! С приездом! Как вы устроились?
Г-жа Брайтон:	Спасибо. Я прекрасно устроилась. Я звоню, чтобы договориться о нашей встрече. Когда у вас будет время на этой неделе?
Г-н Рублёв:	Мы можем встретиться завтра в любое время после обеда. Я также свободен в пятницу в первой половине дня. Когда вам удобнее?
Г-жа Брайтон:	Давайте встретимся в пятницу, в 10 часов утра, в главном офисе вашей фирмы на Цветном бульваре.
Г-н Рублёв:	Очень хорошо. А после деловой встречи давайте вместе пойдём на ланч и продолжим разговор в неформальной обстановке.

Г-жа Брайтон:	Договорились. До встречи.
Г-н Рублёв:	Всего хорошего. Я буду вас ждать у себя в кабинете послезавтра, в пятницу, в десять.

Secretary:	*The management office of GosEnergo (lit., is listening).*
Ms. Brighton:	*Hello. This is Kim Brighton speaking, an American partner of your company.*
Secretary:	*Hello, Ms. Brighton. You speak very good Russian. Are you calling from America?*
Ms. Brighton:	*No, I'm in Moscow now.*
Secretary:	*Just a minute. I'll connect you with the director.*
Mr. Rubliov:	*Hello (lit., I'm listening).*
Ms. Brighton:	*Hello, Mr. Rubliov. Kim Brighton's speaking (lit., disturbing you). I'm already in Moscow.*
Mr. Rubliov:	*Hello, Ms. Brighton. Glad to hear (from) you! Welcome! Are you well settled?*
Ms. Brighton:	*Thank you. I'm very comfortable (lit., I'm very well settled). I'm calling in order to set up our meeting. When will you have time this week?*
Mr. Rubliov:	*We can meet any time tomorrow after lunch. I'm also free on Friday in the morning (lit., in the first half of the day).*
Ms. Brighton:	*Let's meet on Friday at 10 a.m. in the main office of your company on Tsvetnoy Boulevard.*
Mr. Rubliov:	*Very well. And after the business meeting, let's have lunch together and continue our conversation in an informal setting.*
Ms. Brighton:	*Agreed. See you then (lit., until the meeting).*
Mr. Rubliov:	*All the best. I'll be waiting for you in my office the day after tomorrow, on Friday at ten.*

NOTES

The English adverb *also* has three equivalents in Russian: **тоже, также,** and **ещё.** You already know two of them (see Unit 1). **Тоже** means *too,* when one subject is compared to another: **Мой друг любит оперу, и я тоже люблю оперу.** *(My friend likes opera, and I like opera too.)* Here, **тоже** *(also/too)* means *as compared to* my friend or *likewise*. **Ещё** means *in addition to,* when it introduces a new item to the list of things. For example, if you say **я люблю оперу, и ещё я люблю балет** (*I like opera and also I like ballet*), it's understood that the same subject likes opera and **ещё**, *in addition* to it, ballet. But there's one more possibility. Notice how Mr. Rubliov says in the conversation: **Я также свободен в пятницу** (*I'm also free on Friday*). **Также** doesn't differentiate between the two meanings above and stands for *in addition to* as well as for *likewise*. **Также** is characteristic of more formal speech, so you shouldn't use it when speaking with friends. Mr. Rubliov is being formal with his American partner; therefore, his choice of **также** instead of **ещё** is well justified.

NUTS & BOLTS 1
SHORT PARTICIPLES

Notice the short adjective **рад** in the following sentence:

Я рад вас слышать.
I'm glad to hear you.

Short adjectives and participles are used as predicates only. They need to match the gender of their subjects. Masculine subjects require the masculine (zero) ending in their predicates (**он рад**); feminine subjects require the feminine **-а/я** ending (**она рада**); plural subjects should be matched with the plural ending **-ы/и** (**они рады**). As always, the verb *to be* is left out in the present tense. In the past and future, it reappears in appropriate forms: **он был рад/он будет рад, она была рада/она будет рада, они были рады/они будут рады.**

Let's look at another example.

Я свободен/свободна в пятницу.
I'm free on Friday.

Here, **свободен/свободна** is a short participle. **свободен** is a short participle. Participles are somewhat more complicated hybrids between verbs and adjectives. You should study them at a more advanced level. For now, just remember that short participles function the same way as short adjectives. So you should say: **он свободен, она свободна, они свободны, он был свободен, он будет свободен,** etc. Notice the fleeting **е** before all vowel endings. The short adjective **занят** *(busy)* works the same way as **рад: он занят, она занята, оно занято, они заняты.**

PRACTICE 1
Restate the following sentences in the past and in the future tense.

1. Он рад меня видеть.

2. Вы свободны в пятницу после обеда?

3. Она занята в первой половине дня.

4. Я свободен в пять часов вечера.

5. Мои друзья рады пойти со мной на ланч.

NUTS & BOLTS 2
COMPARATIVES
Now, let's learn how to form Russian comparatives. **Удобнее** *(more convenient/comfortable)* is an example of a standard Russian comparative adjective, the one that ends in **-ее.** Take a look at a few common standard comparatives below.

Adjective	English	Comparative	English
новый	*new*	**новее**	*newer*
старый	*old*	**старее**	*older*
красивый	*pretty*	**красивее**	*prettier*
интересный	*interesting*	**интереснее**	*more interesting*
холодный	*cold*	**холоднее**	*colder*

Some comparatives have only one **-e** in the end preceded by a mutated consonant. Learn the following common comparatives of this type.

Adjective	English	Comparative	English
большой	*big*	**больше**	*bigger*
маленький	*small*	**меньше**	*smaller*
дорогой	*expensive*	**дороже**	*more expensive*
дешёвый	*cheap*	**дешевле**	*cheaper*
близкий	*close*	**ближе**	*closer*

Like in English, the Russian adjectives **хороший** *(good)* and **плохой** *(bad)* have irregular comparative forms **лучше** *(better)* and **хуже** *(worse)*.

If you have trouble remembering the correct comparative form (or if this form doesn't exist), you can always use a compound comparative which consists of **более** *(more)* or **менее** *(less)* and a regular adjective. So, instead of saying **новее** *(newer)*, you can say **более новый** *(more new)* and, by analogy, **менее новый** *(less new)*.

And finally, Russian comparatives can be used in the adverbial function, that is, they can modify actions.

Он живёт ближе.

He lives closer.

However, as opposed to English, Russian simple comparatives can't function as adjectives—they can't modify nouns! For example, you can say in English *I live in a newer house;* in order to say it in Russian, you need to use a compound comparative, that is, an adjective with the comparative word *more*.

Я живу в более новом доме.
I live in a newer house.

We'll come back to the question of comparatives in the following unit.

PRACTICE 2
Restate the following sentences using comparatives.

1. Эта книга интересная.

2. Мне удобно с вами встретиться после обеда.

3. Он жил близко от работы.

4. Продукты в этом магазине дорогие.

5. Мы остановились в новой гостинице.

6. Он хорошо говорит по-русски.

7. Этот ресторан был дешёвый.

CONVERSATION 2
Kelly McCann, an American visitor to Russia, is trying to reach her Russian acquaintance, Nastya Larina. Unfortunately, Nastya isn't home. Her husband, Vasilii, picks up the phone and talks to Kelly.

Василий: Аллё!

Келли: Здравствуйте! Позовите, пожалуйста, Настю.

Василий: Здравствуйте! К сожалению, её нет дома. А кто её спрашивает?

Келли: Это говорит её американская знакомая Келли. Я сейчас в России и звоню из гостиницы. Когда она будет дома?

Василий:	Настя ушла в магазин, но уже скоро должна прийти.
Келли:	Хорошо. Передайте ей, пожалуйста, что я звонила.
Василий:	Обязательно передам. Или вот что, дайте мне, пожалуйста, ваш телефон в гостинице. Настя перезвонит вам или с мобильного телефона, или когда вернётся домой.
Келли:	Хорошо. Записывайте. Телефон гостиницы 137–77–91. Я остановилась в номере 1017.
Василий:	Спасибо. Я всё записал.
Келли:	До свидания. Я буду ждать её звонка.
Василий:	Всего хорошего.

Vasilii:	*Hello!*
Kelly:	*Hello! May I speak to Nastya?*
Vasilii:	*Hi! Unfortunately, she's not home. May I ask who is calling?*
Kelly:	*This is her American acquaintance, Kelly, calling. I'm in Russia now, and I'm calling from the hotel. When will she be back?*
Vasilii:	*Nastya went to the store, but she should come back rather soon.*
Kelly:	*Okay. Please let her know that I called.*
Vasilii:	*Certainly, I will. Or, you know what, give me your phone number in the hotel. Nastya will call you back either from her cell phone or when she comes back home.*
Kelly:	*Okay. Write it down. The hotel phone number is 137–77–91. I am in room 1017.*
Vasilii:	*Thank you. I wrote everything down.*
Kelly:	*Good-bye. I'll be waiting for her phone call.*
Vasilii:	*Take care.*

NOTES

Notice that Vasilii says **аллё** when he first picks up the phone. Although it sounds like a hello, this is not a greeting of any kind that you might use on the street; it's just a signal that he answered the phone, and the person on the other line can speak up. **Аллё** or **алло** are equivalent to the more formal **я слушаю,** as in conversation 1. They are the most common ways of answering the phone. The actual greeting follows in the next two lines. Kelly says **здравствуйте** *(hello),* and Vasilii responds with his own greeting. The caller is considered polite when he or she begins with an actual greeting: **здравствуйте.**

NUTS & BOLTS 3
THE MODAL WORD ДОЛЖЕН

Она скоро должна прийти.
She should be back soon.

The modal word **должен** is a short adjective. You should use it on two occasions. First, when you need to express *necessity,*

Я должен/должна договориться о встрече.
I have to set up a meeting.

In this case, **должен** (as opposed to other modal words) implies a deeply felt necessity. Second, when you need to express *probability,*

Она должна помнить вас.
She must remember you.

The phrase **она скоро должна прийти** is of the second kind.

PRACTICE 3
Что вы должны сделать? *(What do you have to do?)* Express a necessity to do the following things. Use the subjects and the prompts below. Then restate the same sentences in the past tense.

1. мы—позвонить в главный офис

2. моя дочь—вернуться домой после обеда

---

3. моя жена—передать им привет

4. мой знакомый—перезвонить вам на домашний телефон

5. мои друзья—ждать вашего звонка

NUTS & BOLTS 4
ASPECT AND CONTEXT

Notice the imperfective aspect of **звонила** in the sentence **передайте ей, пожалуйста, что я звонила.** Regardless of the fact that Kelly called once and got through (at least to Nastya's husband), the aspect of **звонила** is still imperfective, because it denotes an action taken out of the immediate context, out of causes and consequences, and, in a way, out of temporality. It becomes a mere statement of fact. In other words, it's irrelevant when exactly she called, or what her phone call was supposed to mean. She just happened to have called.

Let's consider another example. If you say that you read *War and Peace* in the past, what aspect should you use? You can say either **я читал/а «Войну и мир»** or **я прочитал/а «Войну и мир»**. It's crucial to understand that in both situations you read it once and to the end. However, the decision depends on the connection of this statement with the greater context. The perfective statement **я прочитал «Войну и мир»** implies that I was supposed to have read it (let's say, it was on my syllabus at school), and I did. The imperfective **я читал «Войну и мир»** doesn't imply any prior obligation (I just happened to have read it at one point of time), so it becomes a mere statement of the fact. Sometimes, such statements of facts can be translated into English in the present perfect tense as *I've read* War and Peace, *I've seen this movie, I've done this before,* etc.

Я читал(а) «Войну и мир».

I read War and Peace.

Я прочитал(а) «Войну и мир».

I have read War and Peace.

Notice also the imperfective aspect of the imperative **записывайте**. It is imperfective because it doesn't introduce a new notion into the context: Kelly knows that Vasilii wants to have her phone number (he just said so), so she gives him the go ahead to write it down. Therefore, her imperative is imperfective. However, when he originally asked for her phone number, he used the perfective aspect.

Дайте мне ваш телефон в гостинице.

Give me your number at the hotel.

Here, he is suggesting something radically new to the context. Remember that Russian imperatives are perfective when they command a totally new action, a change of state. On the other hand, most invitations are imperfective in Russian because they imply the generally shared understanding of a welcome.

Пожалуйста, приходите в гости!

Please come to see us!

Садитесь.

Have a seat.

Ешьте!

Eat! (go ahead and have food)

Пейте!

Drink! (please have a drink)

PRACTICE 4
Translate the following sentences into Russian. Pay attention to your choice of aspect, but don't translate the clues in brackets.

1. I've stayed in this hotel *(at one point in time)*.

2. Give *(fml.)* me please your phone number.

3. Call me back from your cell phone.

4. Do you *(fml.)* want to make a phone call? (Go ahead), call!

5. May I speak to Natasha?

6. Do you *(infml.)* want to write down my cell phone number? (Go ahead), write (it) down!

Language link

Russian phone numbers function much like American ones: the first three numbers are the area code, the following seven numbers are the actual local phone number. However, when you write your phone number in Russian, it's customary to group the digits in a slightly different manner than in the U.S. This is how people normally write their phone numbers in Russia: (812) 137-77-91. As of recently, you may also see some Russian businesses imitate the American style of grouping the last four digits together and writing their phone number as this: (812) 137-7791. Keep in mind that Russians usually pronounce their phone numbers not as individual digits, but as three- and two-digit numerals. For example, the above phone number should be pronounced as follows: **восемьсот семнадцать-сто тридцать семь-семьдесят семь-девяносто один.** The country code for Russia is 7 **(код России)**; it's often preceded by a plus (+7), which you can dial only from your cell phone. Now, find out the area codes **(код города)** of Moscow, St. Petersburg, Novosibirsk, and Vladivostok over the internet. You can do so by going to www.telecode.ru.

ANSWERS

PRACTICE 1: 1. Он был рад меня видеть. Он будет рад меня видеть. **2.** Вы были свободны в пятницу после обеда? Вы будете свободны в пятницу после обеда? **3.** Она была занята в первой половине дня. Она будет занята в первой половине дня. **4.** Я был свободен в пять часов вечера. Я буду свободен в пять часов вечера. **5.** Мои друзья были рады пойти со мной на ланч. Мои друзья будут рады пойти со мной на ланч.

PRACTICE 2: 1. Эта книга интереснее/более интересная. **2.** Мне удобнее/более удобно с вами встретиться после обеда. **3.** Он жил близко от работы. **4.** Продукты в этом магазине дороже/более дорогие. **5.** Мы остановились в более новой гостинице. **6.** Он лучше говорит по-русски. **7.** Этот ресторан был дешевле/более дешевый.

PRACTICE 3: 1. Мы должны позвонить в главный офис. Мы должны были позвонить в главный офис. **2.** Моя дочь должна вернуться домой после обеда. Моя дочь должна была вернуться домой после обеда. **3.** Моя жена должна передать им привет. Моя жена должна была передать им привет. **4.** Мой знакомый должен перезвонить вам на домашний телефон. Мой знакомый должен был перезвонить вам на домашний телефон. **5.** Мои друзья должны ждать вашего звонка. Мои друзья должны были ждать вашего звонка.

PRACTICE 4: 1. Я останавливался/останавливалась в этой гостинице. **2.** Дайте мне, пожалуйста, ваш телефонный номер (телефон). **3.** Перезвоните мне с вашего мобильного телефона. **4.** Вы хотите позвонить? Звоните! **5.** Позовите, пожалуйста, Наташу. **6.** Ты хочешь записать номер моего мобильного телефона? Записывай!

UNIT 6 ESSENTIALS

Здравствуйте, это говорит + *пот.*	*Hi, this is . . . speaking.*
Позовите, пожалуйста, + *асс.*	*May I speak to . . . (lit., Invite please . . .)*
Одну минуточку!	*Just a minute.*
Рад вас слышать.	*Glad to hear (from) you.*
К сожалению, её нет дома.	*Unfortunately, she's not home.*
Я звоню вам, чтобы договориться о встрече.	*I'm calling (you) in order to set up a meeting.*
Мне удобнее встретиться на этой неделе.	*It's more convenient for me to meet this week.*

Я свободен/свободна в первой половине дня.	*I'm free in the first half of the day.*
Давайте продолжим разговор в неформальной обстановке.	*Let's continue (our) conversation in an informal setting.*
Я буду вас ждать у себя в кабинете.	*I'll wait for you in my office.*
Она скоро должна вернуться.	*She should be back soon.*
Передайте ей, что я звонил(а).	*Tell her that I called.*
Я вам перезвоню с мобильного телефона.	*I'll call you back from a cell phone.*
Дайте мне ваш домашний телефон.	*Give me your home phone number.*
Я остановился/ остановилась в гостинице.	*I have been staying (lit., stopped) in a hotel.*

UNIT 7
Getting around town

In Unit 7, you'll learn to ask and understand directions in Russian, when you walk or go by public transportation. You will expand your knowledge of Russian motion verbs both with prefixes and without them, modal verbs, comparatives, and short adjectives, as well as the general vocabulary of urban orientation. The idiomatic expressions and grammar in this unit will help you get your bearings in an unfamiliar Russian city.

———————— Lesson 25 (Words) ————————

WORD LIST 1

Большой театр	*the Bolshoi Theater (lit., the Big Theater)*
Красная площадь	*Red Square*
москвич *(m.)*/**москвичка** *(f.)*/ **москвичи** *(pl.)*	*Muscovite(s) (resident of Moscow)*
переодевать(ся) *(conj. I; -ай)*—**переодеться** *(conj. I; -н)*	*to change (clothes)*
переходить *(conj. II; -и)*—**перейти** *(conj. II; -л)*	*to cross, to go across*
перейти на другую станцию/линию	*change stations/lines (lit., to pass from one metro station/line to another)*
пересесть на другой автобус	*to transfer to another bus*
переезжать *(conj. I; -ай)*—**переехать** *(conj. I; -д)*	*to move*
садиться *(conj. II; -и)*—**сесть** *(conj. I; -д)* **на** + *acc.*	*to get on (to take a means of transportation)*
выходить *(conj. II; -и)*—**выйти** *(conj. I; -д)* **из** + *gen.*	*to get off (a bus, etc.)*

сходить *(conj. II; -и)*—**сойти**   *to get off (a bus, etc.)*
(conj. I; -д) **с + gen.**

любой   *any (kind)*

NOTES

Getting out of a bus (or any other means of transportation including a car) is **выходить—выйти из** + genitive, and *getting off a bus*
(or any other means of transportation, but a car) is **сходить—
сойти с** + genitive in Russian. The prefix **вы-** means *out* (you remember that it's always stressed in perfective verbs!). The prefix
с- means *down*. So, **выйти из автобуса** literally means *to go out of
the bus*, whereas **сойти с автобуса** means *to step down from the bus*.
They are fully interchangeable.

NUTS & BOLTS 1
THE PREFIX пере-

The prefix **пере-** occurs in many Russian verbs. It usually adds
the meaning of change, such as *across, over, trans,* or *re-*. *Going by
vehicle* is **ездить** (**-езжать** with prefixes), or **ехать** in Russian;
consequently, **переезжать** or **переехать** means *to move*, literally,
to go from one place to another by vehicle.

Now, remember the following important aspect rule for prefixed
motion verbs: when you add any prefix to a multidirectional verb
(except for the prefix **по-**), this verb remains imperfective; when
you add a prefix to a unidirectional verb, it becomes perfective.
For example, **переходить** is an imperfective verb because **ходить**
is multidirectional; but **перейти** is perfective because **идти** is unidirectional. Once you've determined the aspect of the prefixed
motion verb, you should use it as any other perfective or imperfective Russian verb. In other words, you no longer apply the
mutli-/unidirectional rules (the ones we covered in Unit 4) to prefixed motion verbs.

The verbs **переходить** and **перейти** work the same way. They
generally mean *to cross over*. You can use them in the following
contexts:

1) going across a square or street: **перейти площадь/улицу** (without a preposition), or **перейти через площадь/улицу** (with an optional preposition **через** which is used in order to emphasize difficulty of crossing over);

2) changing trains/lines in the metro: **перейти на другую станцию, перейти на другую линию;**

3) changing jobs and such: **перейти на другую работу** *(job)*, **перейти на другую должность** *(position)*.

Он перешёл на другую работу.
He changed jobs.

The verbs **пересесть** and **переодеться** aren't motion verbs, but the meaning of their prefix is still the same. **Пересаживаться—пересесть** mean *to change seats/to re-sit*, or *to change buses, trains,* etc. For example, you should say **пересесть на другой автобус,** or **пересесть на другое место** *(seat)*. **Пересаживаться** is a standard imperfective Conjugation I verb with the stem ending in **-ай**. **Пересесть** is a perfective Conjugation I verb with the stem ending in the consonant **-д**, which stays before all vowel endings, but disappears before consonant endings, that is, in the past tense or in the infinitives: **я пересяду, ты пересядешь, они пересядут; он пересел, она пересела,** etc.

Здес пересайте на другой автобус.
Change here for another bus.

Without the prefix **пере-**, this verb means either *to sit/to take a seat* or *to get on a bus* (or any other means of public transportation).

Он сел на автобус.
He took a bus.

Переодеваться—переодеться mean *to change clothes*. The imperfective **переодеваться** verb is Conjugation I with the stem ending in **-ай**; the perfective **переодеться** is Conjugation I with the stem ending in **-н** (like all verbs with consonant stems, this verb conjugates in the same way as **пересесть** above): **я переоденусь, ты переоденешься, они переоденутся; он переоделся, она переоделась,** etc. Notice that these verbs are reflexive when you're changing clothes yourself. However, when you're changing the clothes of another person, for example, a child, the verb becomes transitive: **переодеть ребёнка** (*change clothes of a child*).

PRACTICE 1
Translate the following sentences into English and determine the aspect of the prefixed motion verbs.

1. Вы выходите на следующей остановке?

2. Я вышла на станции «Площадь Революции».

3. Они переехали в Москву в прошлом году.

4. Он всегда здесь переходил улицу.

5. Мы сошли на этой остановке.

PRACTICE 2
Fill in the blanks using the correct form of the verbs given in the parentheses.

1. Мы должны _____ (to change clothes), чтобы вечером идти в Большой театр.

2. Он _____ (got out) из метро и _____ (took) на автобус, чтобы ехать в центр.

3. В следующем месяце мы _____ (are moving) на другую квартиру.

4. На следующей остановке вы должны _____ (to transfer to) на любой другой автобус.

5. Туристы _____ (crossed) Красную площадь и вошли в Кремль.

WORD LIST 2

направо	*to the right (direction)*
налево	*to the left (direction)*
справа	*on the right (location)*
слева	*on the left (location)*
прямо	*straight ahead*
дальше	*further/farther*
всё время	*all the time*
проходить *(conj. II; -и)—* пройти *(conj. I; -д)*	*to go by (on foot)*
проезжать *(conj. I; -ай)—* проехать *(conj. II; -д)*	*to go by (by vehicle)*
прогуливаться *(conj. I; -ай)—* прогуляться *(conj. I, -ай)*	*to go for a walk*
находиться	*to be situated, to be located, to be*
река	*river*

Notes

You should use the adverbs **направо** and **налево** only when you're referring to a movement *to the right* or *to the left*. Their stationary counterparts are **справа** *(on the right)* and **слева** *(on the left)*. For example: **идите направо** *(go to the right)*; **вы увидите Большой театр справа** *(you'll see the Bolshoi Theater on the right hand side)*.

NUTS & BOLTS 2
The prefix про-

The prefix **про-** means *by* or *through*. When added to motion verbs, it usually means *covering a distance*, *passing by*, or *coming/going through*. For example, you can use **проходить—пройти** with or without the following prepositions in the following contexts:

1) **пройти два километра** *(walk/cover two kilometers);*

Он прошёл два километра.
He walked two kilometers.

2) **пройти Казанский собор** *(walk by Kazan Cathedral* [accusative]/*pass by it* or, possibly, *miss it by accident);*

Она прошла Казанский собор.
She walked by Kazan Cathedral.

3) **пройти мимо Казанского собора** *(walk by Kazan Cathedral* [**мимо** + genitive], *walk by it deliberately);*

Мы прошли мимо Казанского собора.
We walked by Kazan Cathedral.

4) **пройти в дом** *(enter, come into the house,* see Unit 5).

Проходете в дом.
Come into the house.

The verbs **проезжать–проехать** work exactly the same way as the ones above, except that they denote a vehicular movement.

Прогуливаться–прогуляться are the conversational variants of the verb **гулять** (see Unit 2). They designate essentially the same action of *going for a walk* or *strolling,* perhaps, with the additional connotation of walking *back and forth.*

PRACTICE 3
Fill in the blanks with the appropriate adverb given in the parentheses. Remember the distinction between directional and stationary adverbs!

1. Посмотрите _____ (to the right)—мы проезжаем мимо Казанского собора.

2. Эрмитаж находится _____ (on the right); Адмиралтейство— _____ (on the left).

3. Идите _____ (straight ahead) по Невскому проспекту, и _____ (on the left) вы увидите большой магазин.

4. Станция метро находится _____ (farther on) по Невскому проспекту.

5. Пройдите два дома _____ (to the left), и вы увидите вашу гостиницу.

PRACTICE 4

Как сказать по-русски? Translate the following sentences into Russian.

1. We went by Kazan Cathedral on the bus.

2. Where's the Hermitage (Эрмитаж) located?

3. I'd like (I want) to go for a walk tonight.

4. My hotel is on Nevsky Prospect, on the right.

5. She walked by (прошла) the Hermitage and saw the river.

Culture note

The following types of public transportation are common in Russian cities: **метро** (*metro*), **автобус** (*bus*), **троллейбус** (*trolleybus*, which is a trackless electric bus with two poles connected to the wires overhead), and **трамвай** (*streetcar*, which is an electrically powered vehicle on tracks). There are also privately owned and operated buses that work just like the municipal ones, except that they are newer, less crowded, and more expensive. There are also minivans called **маршрутки;** like buses, they have specific routes, but you can get on and off them at any point of each route. *Route* is **маршрут** in Russian; hence, the name of this type of transport. Taxi companies are usually privately owned. Nevertheless, it's common to avoid **такси** (*taxicabs*) and hitch a ride from any willing driver in the city for a fee that is either negotiated beforehand or mutually understood as fair. The great majority of Russians prefer these unofficial cabs to more expensive official ones. Yet, unofficial cabs may be challenging for a foreign visitor both in terms of safety and comfort.

ANSWERS

PRACTICE 1: 1. Are you getting off at the next stop? (imperfective) **2.** I got off at the *Revolution Square* station. (perfective) **3.** They moved to Moscow last year. (perfective) **4.** He always crossed the street here. (imperfective) **5.** We got off at this stop. (perfective)

PRACTICE 2: 1. переодеться; **2.** вышел, сел; **3.** переезжаем; **4.** пересесть; **5.** перешли

PRACTICE 3: 1. направо; **2.** справа, слева; **3.** прямо, слева; **4.** дальше; **5.** налево

PRACTICE 4: 1. Мы проехали мимо Казанского собора на автобусе. **2.** Где находится Эрмитаж? **3.** Я хочу прогуляться сегодня вечером. **4.** Моя гостиница (находится) на Невском проспекте, справа. **5.** Она прошла Эрмитаж и увидела реку.

—————————— Lesson 26 (Phrases) ——————————

PHRASE LIST 1

на другую сторону + *gen.*	*to the other side of*
через одну остановку	*at the following stop*
через две остановки	*two stops later*
на следующей (остановке)	*next stop*
ехать без пересадки	*to go directly (lit., go without a transfer)*
ехать с пересадкой	*to go with a transfer*
по прямой *(adv.)*	*on the direct line (in the metro)*
терять *(conj. I; -ай)—* потерять *(conj. I; -ай)* + *acc.*	*to lose*
если ты потеряешься	*if you get lost*
находить—найти + *acc.*	*to find*
спросить у кого-нибудь, как пройти/проехать (куда?)	*to ask anyone how to get to (where?)*

показывать—показать +	to show
dat. + acc.	
на любом автобусе	by any bus
билет	ticket

Notes

Although the verbs **находить—найти** aren't motion verbs (they mean *to find*), they have the motion verbs **ходить—идти** at their foundation. So you should conjugate them accordingly: **нахожу, находишь, находят**, etc.; **найду, найдёшь, найдут**, etc.

You can use the verbs **терять—потерять** *(to lose)* in their transitive form, in this case, they take the direct object in the accusative case: **он потерял билет** *(he lost [his] ticket)*. If you use them with the reflexive particle **теряться—потеряться**, they acquire the meaning of *getting lost:* **мы потерялись в городе** *(we got lost in the city)*.

The adverbial expressions **без пересадки** *(without a transfer)* and **по прямой** (directly) are synonymous. They mainly refer to traveling directly, on one metro/bus/etc. line.

NUTS & BOLTS 1
THE NOUN сторона (*SIDE*)

The feminine noun **сторона** means *side* (be careful to distinguish it from **страна** [*country*]). Consequently, *the other side of the street* is **другая сторона улицы**. As all Russian expressions of place, this one can be used as direction or location.

Она перешла на другую сторону улицы.

She crossed over to the other side of the street.

Станция метро находится на другой стороне улицы.

The metro station is located on the other side of the street.

Equally, you should say: **на правую сторону** or **на левую сторону** in the directional mode, but **с правой стороны** or **с левой стороны** in the locative one.

PRACTICE 1

Fill in the blanks using the prompts in the parentheses. Remember the difference between location and direction.

1. Перейдите улицу на _____ . (the other side)

2. Я живу на _____ улицы. (the other side)

3. Вход в метро на _____ . (the left side)

4. Остановка такси находится на _____ проспекта. (the right side)

5. Мы перешли на _____ площади. (the other side)

Culture note

Navigating a crowded transportation system sometimes requires some special language. The phrase **как пройти** or **как проехать** is customarily used to ask for directions.

Скажите, пожалуйста, как пройти в центр?
Could you tell me please how to get downtown?

На следующей *(at the next one)* is a common phrase that refers to the next stop, when you travel by any means of public transportation. If you need to get off a bus or train at the next stop, but people in front of you block the exit, you should ask them:

Вы выходите на следующей?
Are you getting off at the next one?

You can also simply say **Вы выходите?** If they do, they will say so and you will be able to get off after them; if they don't, they will understand your question as a request to let you pass by them to the exit door. This is the most standard and polite way of getting through a crowded bus to the exit.

NUTS & BOLTS 2
Expressing consecutiveness
Notice the grammar in the following expressions:

через одну (остановку)
one stop later

через две (остановки)
after two stops

The following three expressions designate three consecutive stops, when you're traveling by any means of public transportation:

на следующей
at the following

через одну
at the second from now

через две
at the third from now

As you already know, the preposition **через** takes the accusative case. You can see it when the following noun is singular: **через одну остановку**. However, when it's in any number different from one (and from those that end in one: 21, 31, 101, etc.), then the rule of numbers takes over the accusative case (see Unit 3). In accordance with this rule, you put the following noun in the genitive singular after the numerals 2, 3, and 4, and in the genitive plural after the numerals from 5 to 9: **через две остановки, через шесть остановок**.

PRACTICE 2
Как сказать по-русски? Translate the following sentences into Russian.

1. We got lost in the city and couldn't find the museum.

2. They asked a waiter directions downtown.

3. We couldn't find our tickets. Perhaps we lost them.

4. Are you getting off at the next stop?

5. No, I'm getting off at the one after it.

PHRASE LIST 2

идти по улице	*to go along (down) the street*
идти до улицы	*to go up to the street*
идти к метро	*to go in the direction of/toward the metro*
поворачивать *(conj. I; -ай)—* поверну́ть *(conj. I; -ну)* напра́во/нале́во	*to turn right/left*
дово́льно далеко́	*rather far*
на такси́	*by taxi*
на авто́бусе	*by bus*
на метро́	*by metro*
вы уви́дите Дворцо́вую пло́щадь	*you'll see Palace Square*
рад помо́чь *(perf.)*	*glad to help*

NOTES

The verbs **поворачивать—повернуть** mean *to turn* when you go on foot or in a vehicle. Their conjugations are regular; the suffix **-ну-** in **повернуть** stays in the past tense: **он повернул, она повернула, они повернули.**

The perfective verb **увидеть** conjugates like its imperfective counterpart **видеть** (see Units 2, 4, 6). You should use the perfective verb in the future tense when you refer to a single act of seeing.

Вы увидите Дворцовую площадь.
You'll see (catch sight of) Palace Square.

However, in the past tense it is normally imperfective, even when it denotes a single act.

Я видел моего друга, когда я был в Москве.
I saw my friend when I was in Moscow.

You should use the perfective **увидеть** in the past tense only when you locate this singular act in a sequence of other actions, or when you see something suddenly.

Я увидел его и поздоровался.
I saw him and said hello. (sequence)

Я вдруг увидел его.
I suddenly saw him.

NUTS & BOLTS 3
THE PREPOSITIONS ПО, ДО, AND К

The prepositions **по** *(along)*, **до** *(up to)*, and **к** *(toward)* are commonly used with motion verbs when one gives directions.

Идите по улице Герцена.
Go along Hertzen Street.

Идите до Садовой улицы.
Go up to Sadovaya Street.

Идите к Невскому проспекту.
Go toward Nevsky Prospect.

The preposition **до** is often coupled with the motion verbs that have the prefix **до-** *(up to)*.

Мы дошли до станции метро.
We walked up to the metro station.

In order to designate any particular type of transportation, Russians usually use the preposition **на** + the means of transportation in the prepositional case, as in **ехать на автобусе** *(go by bus)*, **на троллейбусе** *(by trolleybus)*, **на трамвае** *(by tram/streetcar)*, **на метро** *(by the metro)*, **на поезде** *(by train)*, **на такси** *(by taxi)*, **на машине** *(by car)*, **на электричке** *(by commuter train)*, etc. However, you should say **идти пешком/пешком** for traveling *on foot* (see Unit 4).

PRACTICE 3

На чём вы едете? *(How do you get there? lit., What are you riding in?)* Fill in the blanks using the prompts in the parentheses.

1. Я езжу на работу на _____. (метро)

2. Мы поедем из Петербурга в Москву на _____ . (поезд)

3. Если будет поздно, я поеду на _____ . (такси)

4. Удобнее всего ехать на _____ . (автобус)

5. Давай поедем на _____ . (трамвай)

PRACTICE 4

Как сказать по-русски? Give Russian equivalents to the following English sentences.

1. Turn left and you'll see Palace Square.

2. This is quite far. Let's take the metro.

3. We walked down Nevsky Prospect up to the metro station "Mayakovskaya."

4. She turned right and went toward the bridge.

5. I'm always glad to help you.

Tip!

When you study Russian motion verbs, don't translate them into English simply as *come* or *go*, because this way you would gloss over the important differences. You need to distinguish among various subtypes of *coming* and *going* in Russian. Each time you deal with a motion verb, specify for yourself exactly what type of movement it designates by highlighting its distinctive characteristics. Hence, **поехал** is s*et out by vehicle* (rather than simply *went*), **пришёл** is *arrived on foot* (and not just *came*), **вошёл** is *entered on foot*, etc. This will help you get accustomed to the complicated system of motion verbs in Russian.

ANSWERS

PRACTICE 1: 1. на другую сторону; **2.** на другой стороне; **3.** на левой стороне; **4.** на правой стороне; **5.** на другую сторону

PRACTICE 2: 1. Мы потерялись в городе и не могли найти музей. **2.** Они спросили официанта, как доехать до центра. **3.** Мы не могли найти наши билеты. Может быть, мы потеряли их. **4.** Вы выходите на следующей? **5.** Нет, я выхожу через одну.

PRACTICE 3: 1. на метро; **2.** на поезде; **3.** на такси; **4.** на автобусе; **5.** на трамвае

PRACTICE 4: 1. Поверните налево, и вы увидите Дворцовую площадь. **2.** Это довольно далеко. Давай(те) поедем на метро. **3.** Мы шли по Невскому проспекту до станции метро «Маяковская». **4.** Она повернула направо и пошла в сторону моста. **5.** Я всегда рад помочь вам.

--- Lesson 27 (Sentences) ---

SENTENCE LIST 1

Вы не знаете, как мне лучше доехать до центра?	*Would you know the best way downtown (for me)?*

Сколько времени ехать *(imperfective; duration)* в центр?	*How long does it take to get downtown?*
Сколько идти *(imperfective; duration)* до метро?	*How long does it take to walk to the metro?*
До метро идти *(imperfective; duration)* минут пять.	*It takes about five minutes to walk to the metro.*
Вам выходить на следующей.	*You need to get off at the next stop.*
Откуда вы поедете?	*Where will you go from?*
Садитесь/сядьте на любой автобус на этой остановке.	*Take any bus at this bus stop.*
Поезжайте на метро до станции «Новокузнецкая».	*Go by metro up to Novokuznetzkaya station.*
До «Новокузнецкой» ехать без пересадки/по прямой.	*There's a direct line up to Novokuznetzkaya.*
На какой станции делать пересадку?	*At what station (should I) change trains?*
На метро ехать быстрее, чем на автобусе.	*It's faster to go by metro than by bus.*
Ехать на метро лучше всего.	*It's best to go by metro.*

NUTS & BOLTS 1
More on asking directions

The Russian language doesn't have an adequate grammatical equivalent of the English *would* as in *would you know?*, and other polite requests. For this purpose, Russians put their questions/requests in the negative form. So instead of *would you happen to know*, you should literally say *don't you know* (**Вы не знаете . . . ?**) It's common to turn to a passerby with this phrase when you ask directions in Russian. The negation here implies that it's perfectly fine, if you don't happen to know what I'm about to ask.

When you ask or give directions in Russian, it's customary to use the infinitive form for the verb of motion: **ехать, проехать, доехать, дойти, пройти, идти,** etc., and the dative case for the person who's about to travel.

Вы не знаете...?

Do you know...?

Как мне доехать до центра?

How do I get downtown? (lit., How is it possible for me to reach downtown by vehicle?)

Как мне дойти до дома?

How do I get home? (lit., How is it possible for me to reach home by foot?)

If you leave the personal pronoun out, then your sentence becomes more general.

До метро идти пять минут.

It takes five minutes to walk to the metro.

Сколько времени ехать в центр?

How long does it take to get downtown (by vehicle)?

The adjective **любой** means *any kind at all, it doesn't matter which one.*

Садитесь на любой автобус.

Get on any bus.

PRACTICE 1

Как сказать по-русски? Translate the following sentences into Russian.

1. Would you know how to get (by vehicle) to the hotel?

2. How long does it take to walk up to the museum?

3. It's best of all to go by metro.

4. At what station (should one) make a transfer?

5. It takes about ten minutes to walk up to the theater.

NUTS & BOLTS 2
MORE ON COMPARATIVES

Russian comparatives (see Unit 6), such as **лучше** *(better)* or **быстрее** *(faster)*, often have the compared item (the one introduced in English by the conjunction *than*) either in the genitive case without any conjunction, or in any other appropriate case preceded by the conjunction **чем** *(than)*. For example, the comparative statement *Moscow is bigger than Petersburg* can be rendered in Russian in two ways:

1. **Москва больше Петербурга** *(m., gen.)*.

2. **Москва больше, чем Петербург.**

Note that the first option is possible only if the compared items are nouns, pronouns, or adjectives in the nominative or accusative case. Thus, *it's warmer in Moscow than in Petersburg* can be translated into Russian only with the conjunction **чем: в Москве теплее, чем в Петербурге** because **в Москве** is in the prepositional case.

Here are more imperatives to expand on those you learned in Unit 6.

Adjective	English	Comparative	English
удобный	*convenient*	**удобнее**	*more convenient*
быстрый	*fast*	**быстрее**	*faster*
далёкий	*far*	**дальше**	*farther, further*
новый	*new*	**новее**	*newer*

красивый	*beautiful*	красивее	*more beautiful*
интересный	*interesting*	интереснее	*more interesting*
богатый	*rich*	богаче	*richer*
молодой	*young*	моложе	*younger*
старый	*old*	старше	*older*
высокий	*high*	выше	*higher*

PRACTICE 2

Compare the following items using the prompts below, stating that the first item is better, bigger, or older, etc., than the second, using both the genitive case and **чем**.

1. метро—удобнее—автобус

2. Москва—старше—Петербург

3. ехать на такси—быстрее—идти пешком

4. такси—дороже—метро

5. Большой театр—дальше—Исторический музей

6. моя сестра—моложе—я

7. эта книга—интереснее—фильм

SENTENCE LIST 2

Извините, вы не подскажете, как пройти к Эрмитажу?	*Excuse me, could you tell me how to get to the Hermitage?*
Я хочу прогуляться по городу.	*I'd like to take a walk around the city.*

Идите прямо по Невскому проспекту до Садовой улицы.	Go straight down Nevsky Prospect up to Sadovaya Street.
На следующем углу поверните направо.	Turn right at the next corner.
Идите дальше всё время прямо.	Go on straight ahead all the way.
Перейдите большую площадь.	Cross over the big square.
Перейдите улицу по подземному переходу.	Cross the street underground (through the underground crossing).
Вы пройдёте мимо Казанского собора.	You'll walk by the Kazan Cathedral.
Идите к реке.	Walk toward the river.
Справа вы увидите Дворцовую площадь.	You'll see the Palace Square on the right.

Notes

Вы не подскажете, как пройти/проехать к + *dative*/**в** + *accusative* is another common expression for asking directions. **Подсказать** is a more conversational form of the verb **сказать** *(to say, to tell)*.

NUTS & BOLTS 3
Review of imperatives

Now, let's look at the imperatives of motion verbs, which Russians commonly use when giving directions.

идти *(to go)*	иди(те)!
пойти *(to begin)*	пойди(те)!
пройти *(to go by)*	пройди(те)!
перейти *(to cross)*	перейди(те)!

дойти *(to arrive)*	дойди(те)!
ехать *(to go)*	едь(те)!
поехать *(to go, to drive)*	поезжай(те)!
повернуть *(to turn)*	поверни(те)!

PRACTICE 3
Restate the following statements as directions using imperatives.

1. Ты идёшь прямо по Невскому проспекту.

2. Вы едете в центр по Московскому проспекту.

3. Они дойдут до следующего угла.

4. Ты повернёшь направо на углу.

5. Вы идёте к реке.

6. Вы перейдёте через Невский проспект по подземному переходу.

NUTS & BOLTS 4
THE PREPOSITION ПО + *DATIVE*

The preposition **по** + *dative* often denotes a movement *along, down,* and *up* as in **идти по улице,** or *around* in the sense of everywhere within (not circumventing) as in **гулять по городу,** or **ходить по парку.** The expression **ходить по магазинам** means *to go shopping,* because it literally means *going around all of the shops.*

Я ходил(а) по магазинам.
I went around all of the shops.

Переход is *a street crossing* in Russian. Two types of crossings are common in big cities in Russia: street level crossing, much like in the U.S., and underground crossing known as **подземный переход. Подземный переход** is often not a part of the metro system but is built separately to insure a safe crossing without affecting the street traffic. Use the preposition **по** + *dative* when you mention a crossing as a means for crossing the street: **переходить улицу по переходу/подземному переходу**.

Я переходил(а) улицу по переходу.
I crossed the street at the crosswalk.

PRACTICE 4
Как сказать по-русски? Translate the following conversation in Russian.

1. –Excuse me please, could you tell me where the Hermitage is?

2. –Gladly. Go straight ahead down Nevsky Prospect, cross over it at the next underground crossing, turn right, and walk along the river Moika for five minutes. You'll see the Hermitage on your left.

3. –Thank you very much for (your) help.

Discovery activity

Look at the interactive map of Moscow (**карта Москвы**) at *http://maps.yandex.ru/moscow_sputnik*. Locate Red Square and the Tretiakov Gallery on it. Now, ask a passerby how to get from one to the other. It's only twenty minutes away, so you should probably walk. Play out both parts of this imaginary conversation.

ANSWERS
PRACTICE 1: 1. Вы не знаете, как доехать до гостиницы? **2.** Сколько времени идти до музея? **3.** Лучше всего ехать на метро. **4.** На какой станции делать пересадку? **5.** Идти до театра минут десять.

PRACTICE 2: 1. Метро удобнее автобуса/, чем автобус.
2. Москва старше Петербурга/, чем Петербург. **3.** Ехать на такси быстрее, чем идти пешком. **4.** Такси дороже метро/, чем метро. **5.** Большой театра дальше Исторического музея/, чем Исторический музей. **6.** Моя сестра моложе меня/, чем я. **7.** Эта книга интереснее фильма/, чем фильм.

PRACTICE 3: 1. Иди прямо по Невскому проспекту.
2. Поезжайте в центр по Московскому проспекту.
3. Дойдите до следующего угла. **4.** Поверни направо на углу. **5.** Идите к реке. **6.** Перейдите через Невский проспект по подземному переходу.

PRACTICE 4: 1. Извините, пожалуйста, вы не подскажете, где Эрмитаж? **2.** С удовольствием. Идите прямо по Невскому проспекту, перейдите его по подземному переходу, поверните направо и идите по реке Мойке пять минут. Вы увидите Эрмитаж слева. **3.** Большое спасибо за помощь.

─────────── **Lesson 28 (Conversations)** ───────────

CONVERSATION 1

Brian Moore is staying at the Sputnik hotel in Moscow. He's asking his Russian friend, Svetlana Ilyina, for directions to the Bolshoi Theater.

Брайан:	**Света, я сегодня вечером иду в Большой театр на балет. Ты не знаешь, как мне лучше доехать до него?**
Света:	**Конечно, знаю. Я же москвичка! Откуда ты поедешь, из гостиницы?**
Брайан:	**Да, из гостиницы. Мне ведь нужно будет переодеться перед театром.**
Света:	**Хорошо, когда выйдешь из гостиницы, перейди на другую сторону Ленинского проспекта и сядь на любой автобус или троллейбус.**

Брайан: Чтобы ехать в центр?

Света: Да, в центр. Но через две остановки выходи, это будет метро «Ленинский проспект». На метро ехать быстрее, чем на автобусе. Поэтому садись на метро и поезжай до станции «Новокузнецкая».

Брайан: Это без пересадки?

Света: До «Новокузнецкой» по прямой, а там перейдёшь на станцию «Третьяковская» и проедешь ещё одну остановку до «Площади Революции».

Брайан: Да, я знаю, где это. Это в самом центре, около Красной площади и Исторического музея.

Света: Да, это именно там. Когда ты выйдешь из метро, ты сразу же увидишь Большой театр. Тебе нужно будет только перейти Театральную площадь.

Брайан: Огромное спасибо! Я уверен, что найду его.

Света: Да, так ехать лучше всего. Удачи!

Brian: Sveta, I'm going to the ballet at the Bolshoi Theater tonight. Would you happen to know how to get there best?

Sveta: Of course I would. I'm a Muscovite, after all. Where will you be coming from? From the hotel?

Brian: Yes, from the hotel. You know, I need to change before the theater.

Sveta: Okay, when you come out of the hotel, cross over to the other side of Leninsky Prospect and get on any bus or trolleybus.

Brian: Going downtown?

Sveta: Yes, downtown. But get off two stops later, it will be Leninsky Prospect station. It's faster to go by the metro than by bus. Therefore, get on the metro and go up to Novokuznetskaya station.

Brian: Is this a direct line?

> Sveta: *Direct up to Novokuznetskaya, then you'll make a*
> *transfer to Tretiakovskaya station, and go one more*
> *stop to Revolution Square.*
> Brian: *Okay, I know where it is. It's in the very center, by the*
> *Red Square and the Historical Museum.*
> Sveta: *Yes, it's exactly there. When you come out of the metro,*
> *you'll see the Bolshoi Theater right away.*
> Brian: *Thank you so much! I'm sure I'll find it.*
> Sveta: *Yes, this is the best way to go. Good luck!*

NOTES

Notice the Russian word for *resident of Moscow*—**москвич**. There isn't one single formula for such derivatives in Russian; in fact, many Russians don't know what residents of smaller and lesser-known cities are properly called. Nevertheless, the names for residents of Moscow and St. Petersburg are familiar to all.

City	Male singular	Female singular	Plural
Москва	**москвич**	**москвичка**	**москвичи**
Петербург	**петербуржец**	**петербурженка**	**петсрбуржцы**

Remember that the derivatives of proper names are not capitalized in Russian.

When Sveta says in the conversation **я же москвичка** *(I'm a Muscovite, after all)*, she's using an emphatic particle **же**. This particle has a certain function: it appeals to the interlocutor's understanding of the point you're making in your statement. It is used to mean *don't you know it* or *after all*.

Another common emphatic particle is **ведь**. Brian is using it when he says that he needs to change before going to the theater: **Мне ведь нужно будет переодеться перед театром.** This particle is similar to the one above except that, instead of appealing to the interlocutor's understanding, it introduces the reason after the consequence has already been mentioned. Brian will go to the theater from his hotel, not from any other place downtown. Why? Because he needs to change first. The consequence *(going to the hotel first)* is given before the reason *(he needs to change)*. The Russian particle **ведь** justifies this logical inversion.

NUTS & BOLTS 1
EXPRESSING NEED WITH нужно AND надо
In addition to the modal verb **должен** (see Unit 6), there's another modal expression in Russian that consists of the subject in the dative case (the person in need), the short adjective **нужно** in the neuter form, and the infinitive (for the needed action). In other words, when you're saying that *you need to go by bus,* you should use the following construction: *dative* + **нужно** + *infinitive* as in **вам нужно ехать на автобусе.**

The modal word **нужно** is synonymous with another short adjective—**надо.** Remember that they are fully interchangeable only when followed by infinitives.

Мне нужно поехать в центр.
I need to go downtown.

Мне надо поехать в центр.
I need to go downtown.

Both mean exactly the same thing.

When whatever you need is an object (not an action), you cannot use **надо.** You have to use the form of **нужно** that agrees in gender and number with the object (a noun or pronoun) you need.

Мне нужен (*m.*) **телефон.**	*I need a phone.*
Мне нужна (*f.*) **ручка.**	*I need a pen.*
Мне нужно (*n.*) **метро.**	*I need the metro.*
Мне нужны (*pl.*) **билеты.**	*I need tickets.*

Notice that **нужно** for neuter nouns and pronouns coincides with **нужно** for infinitives.

To express the same necessity in the past or future, you should add the verb **быть** (*to be*), in the past or future tense: **был, была, было, были,** or **буду, будешь, будет, будем, будете, будут.** Remember that the needed object is the grammatical subject of the sentence; it governs the number, gender, and person of the verb **быть.** For example, you should say: **мне была нужна ручка, ему были нужны деньги, нам будет нужно такси, вам будут нужны билеты,** etc.

Мне была нужна ручка.
I needed a pen.

Ему были нужны деньги.
He needed money.

Нам будет нужно такси.
We'll need a taxi.

Вам будут нужны билеты.
You'll need tickets.

Consider one more grammatical subtlety. You may often hear Russians say: **мне нужно сыр** (instead of **мне нужен сыр**), **мне нужно ручку** (instead of **мне нужна ручка**), etc. These colloquial constructions don't break the above rule that you can't use **нужно** with feminine, masculine, or plural nouns. They're simply elliptic: they leave out the infinitive understood by the context. For example, instead of saying **мне нужно купить сыр** *(I need to buy cheese)*, you can leave out *to buy* in colloquial Russian and say **мне нужно (купить) сыр** *(I need [to buy] cheese)*, which is not the same as **мне нужен сыр** *(I need cheese)*.

Мне нужно купить сыр.

I need to buy cheese.

Мне нужно сыр.

I need (to buy) cheese.

Мне нужен сыр.

I need cheese.

The differences between the modal word **должен** and **нужно/надо** are quite subtle. You can use both more or less interchangeably, though some basic idea of how they work will help you use the right one. The modal **должен** *(one ought to/should)* more often expresses internal moral obligation, whereas when necessity is more of an external obstacle, you should use **нужно/надо** *(one needs to/has to)*. If your friend is in trouble and you need to help, you should use **должен.**

Я должен ему помочь.

I (m.) need to help him.

Я должна ему помочь.

I (f.) need to help him.

On the other hand, if you'd like to go to the movies with your friends, but you need to study instead, you should excuse yourself by using **нужно,** implying that you'd like to go with your friends, but you can't because of an external commitment.

Мне нужно заниматься.

I need to study.

PRACTICE 1

Say what the following people need. Use the modal word **нужно** and the prompts below. Then restate the same sentences in the past and future.

1. мы—идти прямо

2. Маргарита—ехать на метро

3. я—билеты на балет

4. вы—перейти на другую сторону

5. она—другой автобус

PRACTICE 2

Как сказать по-русски? Give the Russian equivalents of the following sentences.

1. We have to help him. Would you *(infml.)* happen to know where he lives?

2. Of course, we'll go by taxi. After all, we don't have time!

3. You *(fml.)* need to cross over to the other side of the street in order to go (by vehicle) downtown.

4. You'll *(fml.)* get lost if you go by bus. *(Watch the tense!)*

5. Muscovites go to work by metro.

CONVERSATION 2

Margaret Rutherford just arrived in St. Petersburg, Russia. A taxi took her to her hotel *Oktyabrskaya*. She checked in to the hotel, left her things in the room, and went out for a walk. She wanted to take a walk down the famous Nevsky Prospect to the Hermitage. She remembered passing them in the taxi. However, as soon as Margaret walks out of the hotel, she realizes that she doesn't know which way to go. She approaches a police officer **(милиционер)** on the street and asks him for directions.

Маргарита:	Извините, пожалуйста, вы не подскажете, как пройти к Эрмитажу.
Милиционер:	Пешком—это довольно далеко.
Маргарита:	Ничего, я с удовольствием прогуляюсь по городу.
Милиционер:	Тогда идите прямо по улице Восстания до большой площади. Это будет площадь Восстания. На углу поверните направо, и вы окажитесь на Невском проспекте.
Маргарита:	Очень хорошо! Я помню, как я проезжала по Невскому на такси.
Милиционер:	Дальше идите по Невскому к Неве минут сорок.
Маргарита:	Всё время по Невскому?
Милиционер:	Да, идите всё время прямо. Сначала, вы перейдёте реку Фонтанку по Аничкову мосту, потом канал Грибоедова, пройдёте мимо Казанского собора с другой стороны, перейдёте реку Мойку и дальше, справа, вы увидите Дворцовую площадь и Эрмитаж.
Маргарита:	Спасибо за помощь. Теперь всё ясно. Если я потеряюсь, я спрошу у кого-нибудь ещё раз.
Милиционер:	Конечно, все вам будут рады помочь. Хорошего дня!

Margaret:	Excuse me, could you please tell me how to get (walk) to the Hermitage?
Police officer:	It's rather far on foot.
Margaret:	That's okay. I'll be happy to take a walk around the city.
Police officer:	Then, go straight ahead along Vosstaniya Street up to a big square. This will be Vosstaniya Square. Turn right at the corner, and you'll find yourself on Nevsky Prospect.
Margaret:	Very well! I remember driving on Nevsky (Prospect) in a taxi.
Police officer:	Go further down Nevsky toward the Neva (river) for about forty minutes.

Margaret:	*All the time down Nevsky?*
Police officer:	*Yes, go straight all the time. First, you'll cross the Fontanka river over the Anichkov Bridge, then, the Giboedov Canal, (you'll) walk by Kazan Cathedral on the other side, cross the Moika river, and then, you'll see the Palace Square and the Hermitage on the right.*
Margaret:	*Thank you for (your) help. It's all clear now. If I get lost, I'll ask someone again.*
Police officer:	*Of course, everybody will (would) be glad to help you. Have a good day!*

NOTES

You should use the Russian words **полиция** and **полицейский** only for non-Russian police forces and police officers, or for the Russian ones before the Revolution of 1917. Soon after the Revolution, the people's militia replaced the old police force of the Russian Empire, and the name **милиция** and **милиционер** became the new Soviet equivalents of *police force* and *police officer*.

Notice the Russian syntax in Margaret's sentence **я помню, как я проезжала по Невскому на такси** *(I remember driving on Nevsky in a taxi)*. Although you normally have one clause in English *(I remember driving)*, in Russian you should break it into two clauses connected with the conjunction **как: Я помню, как я проезжала.** You may also leave **как** out in colloquial speech, and say **я помню, я проезжала.** In other words, always replace English gerunds or infinitives after the verbs of perception (**помнить, видеть, слышать, чувствовать,** etc.) with Russian subordinate clauses.

Notice also that it's common to use imperatives when you give directions in Russian. Use the conjugated future tense only when you want your interlocutor to imagine the exact details of your directions. Thus, the police officer in the conversation uses the imperative, when he says to Margaret **идите прямо** *(go straight ahead);* then, however, as he describes the exact landmarks in his directions, he chooses the future tense: **Вы перейдёте реку,**

пройдёте мимо собора, etc. *(You'll cross the river, pass by the cathedral,* etc.)

NUTS & BOLTS 2
THE VERB оказаться
The phrase **вы окажитесь на Невском проспекте** means *you'll find yourself on Nevsky Prospect, you'll be on Nevsky Prospect,* or *you'll turn up on Nevsky Prospect.*

The verb **оказаться** doesn't have an exact equivalent in English, but it's very common in Russian. It means *to be,* with an element of surprise. Consequently, it's often translated as *turn out to be.* It's a reflexive perfective Conjugation I verb with the **a**-stem, the **з/ж** mutation, and the 1st person singular stress shift: **окажусь, окажешься, окажутся.** The past tense is regular: **оказался, оказалась, оказалось, оказались.**

Как ты здесь оказался?
What are you doing here? (lit., How did it happen that you turned up here?)

Я не знаю, как я здесь оказалась.
I don't know how I ended up here.

Он оказался хорошим врачом.
He turned out to be a good doctor.

Notice the instrumental case in **оказаться врачом.**

PRACTICE 3
Как сказать по-русски? Translate the following sentences into Russian.

1. They turned out to be from Petersburg.

2. I saw him walk down Nevsky Prospect.

3. How did you *(infml.)* happen to be here?

4. The policeman was glad to help Brian.

5. If you walk *(Watch the tense!)* straight all the way, you'll find yourself on the Palace Square.

6. If you *(fml.)* get lost, ask somebody.

7. Now it's all clear to me.

NUTS & BOLTS 3
SUBJECTLESS SENTENCES

It's common to use adverbs as predicates in subjectless sentences in Russian. These sentences have the implied subject *it,* which is left out of the Russian sentence.

Ясно.

It is clear.

Ясно is a full sentence, where *it* and *is* are omitted. If you want to mention a person who is experiencing the state of being described by an adverb, such as **холодно** *(cold),* **жарко** *(hot),* **тепло** *(warm),* **весело** *(fun),* **смешно** *(funny),* **скучно** *(boring),* etc., you add this person in the dative case. So **мне холодно** *(I am cold)* is literally *it is cold to me.* Notice that the semantic subject in the dative **мне** usually comes first, in place of the omitted grammatical nominative subject *it.*

Ивану весело.

It's fun for Ivan.

Ей жарко

She's hot.

Нам смешно.

It's funny to us.

If you want to restate the same sentences in the past or future, you need to add the verb *to be.* But remember to agree it with the omitted grammatical subject *it* (singular and neuter), not with the semantic dative subject! So, regardless of the number or gender of the people who, let's say, were cold, you should always say:

Мне было холодно.

I was cold.

Нам было холодно.

We were cold.

Ему будет холодно.

He will be cold.

Им будет холодно.

They will be cold.

Notice also the future tense of the verb **потеряюсь** *(will get lost)* in the Russian conditional clause **если я потеряюсь.** This is radically different from English, where the future tense is not used in conditional clauses with the conjunction *if*: *if I get lost* and never *if I will get lost.* This English language rule doesn't apply to Russian! So, don't hesitate to use the future tense in Russian conditional sentences when they refer to a future action.

Если будет холодно, . . .

If it is (lit., will be) cold, . . .

Если ты будешь в Москве, . . .

If you are (lit., will be) in Moscow, . . .

Если ты поедешь в центр, . . .

If you go (lit., will go) downtown, . . .

PRACTICE 4

Compose full sentences in the present tense using the words below. Then, restate them in the past and future.

1. мы—холодно

2. я—всё ясно

3. Наши гости—удобно

4. вы—интересно

5. Виктор—очень смешно

Culture note

Until recently, it was impossible in a simple way to wish someone a good day, good weekend, etc., in Russian. It wasn't common to wish someone all these things on a regular basis, as is done in many other languages, including English. When Russians needed to say anything of the kind, they used cumbersome and formal expressions similar to the following: **Желаю вам хорошо провести выходные** (*I'm wishing that you spend your weekend well*), or **Поздравляю с началом каникул** (*I congratulate you on the beginning of the break/vacation*), etc. This situation has changed. Now, you may often hear such loan translations from English as **хорошего дня** (*have a good day*), **хороших выходных** (*have a good weekend*), etc. The genitive case there implies the omitted verb **желать** (*to wish* + genitive). For a lot of Russians, these calques still sound foreign and artificial, yet many use them on a daily basis. It's easy to predict that very soon they will become a standard part of the Russian language.

ANSWERS

PRACTICE 1: 1. Нам нужно идти прямо. Нам нужно было идти прямо. Нам нужно будет идти прямо. **2.** Маргарите нужно ехать на метро. Маргарите нужно было ехать на метро. Маргарите нужно будет ехать на метро. **3.** Мне нужны билеты на балет. Мне нужны были билеты на балет. Мне нужны будут билеты на балет. **4.** Вам нужно перейти на другую сторону. Вам нужно было перейти на другую сторону. Вам нужно будет перейти на другую сторону. **5.** Ей нужен другой автобус. Ей нужен был другой автобус. Ей нужен будет другой автобус.

PRACTICE 2: 1. Мы должны помочь ему. Ты не знаешь, где он живёт? **2.** Конечно, мы поедем на такси. У нас ведь нет времени! **3.** Вам нужно перейти на другую сторону улицы, чтобы ехать в центр. **4.** Вы потеряетесь, если вы поедете на автобусе. **5.** Москвичи ездят (or едут) на работу на метро.

PRACTICE 3: 1. Они оказались из Петербурга. **2.** Я видел, как он шёл по Невскому проспекту. **3.** Как ты здесь оказался? **4.** Милиционер был рад помочь Брайану. **5.** Если вы пойдёте всё время прямо, вы окажитесь на Дворцовой площади. **6.** Если вы потеряетесь, спросите у кого-нибудь. **7.** Теперь мне всё ясно.

PRACTICE 4: 1. Нам холодно. Нам было холодно. Нам будет холодно. **2.** Мне всё ясно. Мне было всё ясно. Мне будет всё ясно. **3.** Нашим гостям удобно. Нашим гостям было удобно. Нашим гостям будет удобно. **4.** Вам интересно. Вам было интересно. Вам будет интересно. **5.** Виктору очень смешно. Виктору было очень смешно. Виктору будет очень смешно.

UNIT 7 ESSENTIALS

Вы не знаете, как доехать до (+ *gen.*) . . . ?	*Would you know how to get to . . . ?*
Вы не подскажете, как пройти к (+ *dat.*) . . . ?	*Could you show me the way to . . . ?*
Мне нужно переодеться.	*I need to change (clothes).*
Вам нужно перейти на другую сторону улицы.	*You need to cross over to the other side of the street.*
Сядьте на любой автобус.	*Take any bus.*
Поезжайте до станции метро.	*Go (by means of transportation) until you get to the metro station.*
Вы выходите на следующей остановке?	*Are you getting off at the next stop?*
Сделайте пересадку.	*Make a transfer.*
На метро ехать быстрее, чем на автобусе.	*It's faster to go by metro than by bus.*
Я с удовольствием прогуляюсь по городу.	*I'll gladly take a walk around the city.*
Идите прямо по Невскому проспекту.	*Go (by foot) straight down Nevsky Prospect.*

Поверните направо/налево на углу.	*Turn right/left at the corner.*
Собор находится справа/ слева.	*The cathedral is located on the right/left.*
Мне всё ясно.	*It's all clear to me.*

UNIT 8
Shopping

In Unit 8, you will learn how to shop in a Russian department store and at a souvenir market. We'll provide you with the Russian vocabulary for items of clothing, colors, patterns, and sizes, as well as other useful shopping and buying expressions. Many grammatical points covered in this unit will help you form proper and adequate sentences in Russian that can be used while shopping and in other situations.

—————————— Lesson 29 (Words) ——————————

WORD LIST 1

свой/своя/своё/свои	*one's own*
рубашка	*shirt*
галстук	*tie*
одежда *(sg.)*	*clothing, clothes*
отдел	*department*
универмаг	*department store*
торговый центр	*shopping mall*
цвет/цвета *(pl.)*	*color, colors*
голубой	*light blue*
синий	*dark blue, navy blue*
касса	*cash register*
кредитная карточка/кредитка *(coll.)*	*credit card*
наличные (деньги) *(pl.)*	*cash*
брюки *(pl.)*	*pants, trousers*
джинсы *(pl.)*	*jeans*
мужские ботинки *(pl.)*	*men's shoes*

женские туфли *(pl.)*	*women's shoes*
кроссовки *(pl.)*	*sneakers*
майка	*T-shirt*
платье	*dress*
юбка	*skirt*
свитер	*sweater*
куртка	*outdoor jacket, short coat*
пиджак	*suit jacket*
пальто *(n., indecl.)*	*overcoat*

NOTES

Универмаг is the common Russian word for *department store*. It's the contraction of two words: **универсальный (универ-)** and **магазин (маг-)**—literally, *universal store*. One department in such a store is called an **отдел**. So, there are an **отдел мужской одежды** *(men's department)*, an **отдел женской одежды** *(women's department)*, etc.

Note that the Russian word **цвет** *(color)* has an irregular plural form **цвета** (cf. **дом–дома**).

Notice that Russian has two different words for *blue:* **голубой** *(light blue)* and **синий** *(dark blue, navy blue)*. **Синий** is a soft adjective; this is somewhat unusual because most Russian adjectives are hard.

NUTS & BOLTS 1
THE UNIVERSAL POSSESSIVE PRONOUN

Besides the possessive pronouns introduced in Unit 2, Russian has a universal possessive pronoun **свой**. It's universal because it denotes the subject's possession regardless of its person. It effectively means *one's own*. Like any other possessive pronoun, it agrees in number, gender, and case with the noun it modifies. It declines like the pronoun **мой/моя/моё/мои: мой–свой, мою– свою, моём–своём, моей–своей**, etc.

Мы любим нашу работу.

We like our job.

Мы любим свою работу.

We like our (own) job.

The two sentences have the same meaning; **свой** refers back to the subject of the sentence **мы**.

It's optional to use **свой** for the first and second persons, but it is obligatory to use it for the third person subjects, because **свой** and its third person possessive counterparts **его, её,** and **их** refer to different possessors.

Николай дал ей свои деньги.

Nikolai gave her his (own) money.

Николай дал ей его деньги.

Nikolai gave her his (somebody else's) money.

Note that both sentences sound the same in English: *Nikolai gave her his money.* Russian doesn't allow this ambiguity and requires the above differentiation.

It's also important to remember that **свой** refers only to the subject of the same clause.

Вася знает, что Иван дал ей свои деньги.

Vasya knows that Ivan gave her his own (Ivan's) money.

Вася знает, что Иван дал ей его деньги.

Vasya knows that Ivan gave her his (Vasya's) money.

In the first example, **свои деньги** refers to Ivan (the subject of the same clause) and not to Vasya in the principal clause. In the second example, it is clear that the money belongs to Vasya.

PRACTICE 1

Fill in the blanks using the universal possessive pronoun **свой** where possible. Remember to make it agree in number, gender, and case with the noun it modifies.

1. Вы любите _____ работу?

2. Ты купишь _____ сыну рубашку в универмаге.

3. Он хороший муж. Он очень любит _____ жену.

4. Мой друг просил вас позвонить ему. Я вам дам сейчас номер _____ телефона.

5. Петербуржцы очень любят _____ город.

6. Дайте мне, пожалуйста, _____ кредитную карточку.

7. Мы живём в _____ доме.

PRACTICE 2

Translate the following sentences into Russian.

1. He bought a light blue shirt and a navy blue jacket in a new department store.

2. I don't like this color. Please show me another sweater.

3. This department has only men's clothes.

4. She didn't have a credit card, but he had cash.

5. These shoes are pretty (beautiful). Your husband will like them.

WORD LIST 2

продавец *(m.)*	*seller, vendor, shop assistant (male)*
продавщица *(f.)*	*seller, vendor, shop assistant (female)*
продавцы *(pl.)*	*sellers, vendors, shop assistants*
покупатель *(m.)*	*buyer, customer (male/female)*
брать *(conj. I; -a)*—взять *(conj. I; irregular)* + *acc.*	*to take*

посмотреть *(conj. II; -е)—* посмотреть на + *acc.*	*to take a look at*
продавать—продать	*to sell*
продаваться—продаться	*to be for sale*
платить за—заплатить *(conj. I; -и)* за + *acc.*	*to pay for*
цена	*price*
рубль *(m.)*	*ruble*
в рублях	*in rubles*
доллар	*dollar*
в долларах	*in dollars*
евро	*euro*
в евро	*in euros*
сдача	*change (money)*

NOTES

The noun **покупатель** *(buyer)* is derived from the imperfective verb **покупать** with the help of the agentive suffix **-тель** similar to the English *-er*. Many Russian words follow the same pattern of formation. For example: **читать—читатель** *(reader)* is the person who reads, **писать—писатель** *(writer)*, **учить—учитель** *(teacher)*, **строить—строитель** *(builder)*, etc. Keep in mind that the nouns with this suffix are masculine.

Цена is the Russian for *price;* **цены** *(prices)* is the plural form. It's common to say **в этом магазине высокие цены** *(prices are high in this store)* or **низкие цены** *(low prices)*. All prices are officially quoted **в рублях** *(in rubles)* in Russia.

NUTS & BOLTS 2

THE VERBS **взять**, **продавать—продать**, AND **платить—заплатить**

The conjugation of the perfective verb **взять** *(to take)* is irregular.

взять (*to take*)

я возьму	мы возьмём
ты возьмёшь	вы возьмёте
он/она/оно возьмёт	они возьмут

The past tense of this verb is regular: **взял, взяла, взяло, взяли** with the feminine stress shift.

The verb **продавать—продать** (*to sell*) consists of the familiar verb **давать—дать** (see Unit 6) and the prefix **про-**. The conjugation of **продавать—продать** is exactly like **давать—дать**.

Once you add a reflexive ending, **-ся/-сь,** the verb means *to be available for sale* or *to be sold.*

Вы не знаете, где продаются билеты?
Would you know where tickets are sold?

This is the idiomatic way of asking in Russian: Where can I buy something?

The verb *to pay* is **платить—заплатить** in Russian. This is a Conjugation II verb with the **-и** stem, the **т/ч** mutation in the first person singular, and the present/future stress shift: **за/плачу, за/платишь, за/платят,** etc. The past tense is regular: **за/платил, за/платила, за/платили.** This verb takes the accusative case for the amount of money you pay, but the rule of numbers (see Unit 3) always overrides the accusative: **он заплатил один доллар/два доллара/пять долларов.** In addition, this verb can take the preposition **за** + *accusative* for the item(s) you purchased. For example, you can say **он заплатил доллар за билет** (*he paid a dollar for the ticket*).

PRACTICE 3

Где продаются эти вещи? *(lit., Where are these things sold?)* Say where one can buy the following items. Use the verb **продаваться** and the prompts below.

1. билеты в музей—касса

2. мужская одежда—универмаг; второй этаж

3. галстуки—другой отдел

4. эта книга—книжный магазин

5. женские туфли—торговый центр

NUTS & BOLTS 3

ASKING PERMISSION

When you'd like to take a look at a particular item in a store, you should ask the shop assistant: **можно посмотреть** + *acc. (may I take a look at)* or **разрешите посмотреть** + *acc. (permit [me] to take a look at)*.

Можно посмотреть вот эту матрёшку?

May I take a look at this matryoshka doll?

Notice that Russians usually leave out the personal pronoun **мне** *(me)*. You also shouldn't use the preposition **на** in this situation. **Смотреть на** + *acc.* usually means *turning your attention to* or *looking at something from a distance.*

Посмотри на эту машину!

Look at that car (over there)!

PRACTICE 4

Give the Russian equivalents of the following sentences.

1. We paid two hundred rubles for this T-shirt.

2. The shop assistant *(male)* gave me the change.

3. May I see this tie?

4. Are these prices in rubles or in dollars?

5. I like these jeans. I'll take them.

> ### *Culture note*
>
> Many vendors in Russia consider it the responsibility of the buyer to have the exact or small change when buying something like ice cream or a bottle of water. Consequently, you may often hear from them the following: **У меня нет сдачи** (*I don't have change*); **У кого есть без сдачи?** (*Who [in the line] has the exact change?*); **Давайте без сдачи** (*give [me] the exact change*), etc. Vendors often say this in a rather assertive tone. Whether you agree with their business approach or not, it's a good idea not to take this personally and carry smaller bills instead. This way you'll avoid frustration on both ends.

ANSWERS
PRACTICE 1: **1.** свою; **2.** своему; **3.** свою; **4.** его; **5.** свой; **6.** свою; **7.** своём

PRACTICE 2: **1.** Он купил голубую рубашку и синий пиджак в универмаге. **2.** Мне не нравится этот цвет. Покажите мне, пожалуйста, другой свитер. **3.** В этом отделе только мужская одежда. **4.** У неё не было кредитной карточки, но у него были наличные. **5.** Эти ботинки/туфли красивые. Твоему мужу они понравятся.

PRACTICE 3: **1.** Билеты в музей продаются в кассе. **2.** Мужская одежда продаётся в универмаге на втором этаже. **3.** Галстуки продаются в другом отделе. **4.** Эта книга продаётся в книжном магазине. **5.** Женские туфли продаются в торговом центре.

PRACTICE 4: **1.** Мы заплатили двести рублей за эту майку. **2.** Продавец дал мне сдачу. **3.** Можно посмотреть этот галстук? **4.** Эти цены в рублях или в долларах? **5.** Мне нравятся эти джинсы. Я возьму их.

PHRASE LIST 1

подарок + *dat.*	*present/gift for (somebody)*
подарок на день рожденья	*birthday present*
Что ты ему подаришь на день рожденья?	*What will you give him for (his) birthday?*
рубашка в полоску	*striped shirt*
рубашка в клетку	*checkered shirt*
Какого цвета . . . ?	*What color . . . ?*
Сколько стоит . . . ?	*How much does/do (something) cost?*
платить в кассу	*to pay at the cash register*
nom. + идёт + *dat.*	*(something) looks good (on someone)*
nom. + идёт/подходит — подойдёт к + *dat.*	*(something) matches/looks good with (something)*
цена на этикетке	*price on the tag*

Notes

The noun **подарок** means *gift* or *present*. It has a fleeting **o** before all endings: **подарка, подарком, подарки,** etc. The dative case without preposition **(кому?)** denotes the receiver of the gift: **подарок моей жене** *(a gift for my wife),* **подарок моему мужу** *(a gift for my husband).* The accusative case with the preposition **на (что?)** refers to the occasion for this gift: **подарок на день рождения** *(birthday present);* **подарок на Новый Год** *(New Year's present);* **подарок на Рождество** *(Christmas present);* **подарок на свадьбу** *(wedding present),* etc. The verbs **дарить/подарить** are derived from the same root and mean *to give as a gift.* So the question **Что ты ему/ей подаришь на день рождения?** means *What will you give him/her for (his/her) birthday?*

Сколько стоит + *nominative* is the standard way of asking *how much* something costs. The item in question is the grammatical subject of the sentence; it governs the number of the imperfective verb **стоить** *(to cost).* This verb is Conjugation II with the и-stem: **стою, стоишь, стоит, стоим, стоите, стоят.** The past tense is also regular: **стоил, стоила, стоило, стоили.**

NUTS & BOLTS 1
DESCRIBING COLOR
Какого цвета эта рубашка? is the proper way of asking *What color is this shirt?* You can answer this question in two ways.

Эта рубашка голубого цвета.
This shirt is of light-blue color.

Эта рубашка голубая.
This shirt is light-blue.

Now, let's learn the names for the following common colors in Russian (in addition to **голубой** and **синий,** covered in the previous lesson).

белый	*white*
чёрный	*black*
красный	*red*
зелёный	*green*
жёлтый	*yellow*

The phrases **в полоску** *(striped)* and **в клетку** *(checkered)* describe the common fabric patterns. Use them after the noun in question to say: **галстук в полоску** *(tie with stripes),* **рубашка в клетку** *(checkered shirt),* etc. Alternatively, you can use the adjectives **полосатый** *(striped)* and **клетчатый** *(checkered).*

PRACTICE 1

Какого цвета эти вещи? *(What color are these things?)* Answer the question using the noun **цвет** and the prompts below. Then, ask how much the items cost.

1. галстук–красный
2. брюки–синие
3. рубашка–белая

4. ботинки–чёрные
5. пальто–жёлтое

NUTS & BOLTS 2

The expressions *NOMINATIVE* + ИДЁТ **AND** ПОДХОДИТ К + *DATIVE*

When one piece of clothing matches the other, you should use the following pattern: *nominative* + **идёт** and **подходит к** + *dative (lit., goes to/with)*.

Этот галстук идёт к этой рубашке.
This tie matches/goes with this shirt.

Эта рубашка подходит к этому пиджаку.
This shirt matches/goes with this jacket.

However, when you want to compliment someone on his or her outfit, you should use **идёт** without the preposition **к**.

Этот галстук идёт тебе.
This tie looks good on you.

Эти туфли идут вам.
These shoes look good on you.

Literally, this expression means *(something) is becoming to you* or *(something) suits you well.*

PRACTICE 2
Say that the items below either go well together or look good on a person. Use the following prompts.

1. белые брюки—синий пиджак

2. красный галстук—Николай

3. белая рубашка—Наталья

4. белый свитер—зелёная юбка

5. чёрные туфли—жёлтые брюки

6. голубая майка—ты

PRACTICE 3
Give the Russian equivalents of the following sentences.

1. What will you give your husband for his birthday? *(infml.)*

2. I'll give him a white shirt with stripes.

3. These shoes look good on your sister. *(infml.)*

4. How much is this coat? I don't see the price on the tag.

5. Now you should pay at the cash register. *(infml.)*

PHRASE LIST 2

магазин сувениров	*souvenir shop*
киоск с сувенирами	*kiosk with souvenirs*
рынок	*market*
на рынке	*at the market*
матрёшка	*matryoshka (traditional Russian wooden nesting doll)*
ручная работа	*handmade*
торговаться *(conj. I; -ова)* + inst.	*to bargain, to haggle with*
побольше	*somewhat bigger, a little bigger*

поменьше	*somewhat smaller, a little smaller*
по-моему	*in my opinion*
Подешевле не продадите?	*Would you be willing to sell it for a little less?*
взять/купить за + *acc.*	*to buy for (a certain amount of money)*
платить—заплатить в рублях	*to pay in rubles*
сдача с тысячи	*change for a thousand*

Notes

Матрёшка is a traditional Russian wooden cylindrical nesting doll. It opens up in the middle and contains within itself another one of a slightly smaller size, which in turn has one a bit smaller, and so on until the very last one, which doesn't open up. A good **матрёшка** can have more than ten smaller **матрёшки** nested one inside the other. Most of them are hand-painted **(ручной работы;** notice the genitive case). Their price largely depends on the quality of the work and the size.

When you buy **сувениры** *(souvenirs)* at street kiosks or at a souvenir market, rather than from a store, it's perfectly acceptable **торговаться** *(to bargain for a better price)*. The original **цена на этикетке** *(price on the tag)* is rarely the one the item **продаётся** *(is sold for)*. So, you can ask if the **продавец** *(salesman)* or **продавщица** *(saleswoman)* would be willing to sell the item for less: **А подешевле не продадите?**

Сдача *(change for a particular bill)* takes the preposition **с** with the genitive case. **Сдача с тысячи** means *change for a thousand ruble bill*. When you're paying with a larger bill, it's common to ask: **У вас есть/будет сдача с тысячи, с пятисот рублей, со ста рублей?** *(Do (will) you have change for 1,000 rubles, for 500 rubles, for 100 rubles?)* Notice that the above numerals are in the genitive case.

NUTS & BOLTS 3
The prefix по- with comparatives
Many Russian comparatives (see Units 6 and 7) can be used with the prefix **по-,** which adds to them the somewhat colloquial connotation *a little bit.*

побольше
a little bigger

подешевле
a little cheaper

Remember that, although these comparatives are highly common, they are colloquial and should be avoided in formal discourse.

The expressions **по-моему, по-твоему, по-нашему,** and **по-вашему** mean *in my opinion, in your (infml.) opinion, in our opinion,* and *in your (fml.) opinion* respectively. They are more conversational in Russian than in English, so they sound more like *I think, you think,* etc.

PRACTICE 4
Fill in the blanks below. Remember to make sure the words and expressions in the parentheses agree with the rest of the sentence.

1. _____ (In my opinion) много интересных _____ (souvenirs) продаётся _____ (at the market) или _____ (in kiosks) на улице.

2. Покажите, пожалуйста, матрёшку _____ (a little bigger).

3. У меня нет _____ (change) с тысячи.

4. Я возьму матрёшку _____ (a little smaller) _____ (for five hundred) рублей.

5. Можно _____ (to bargain) со многими продавцами на улице, но не в магазине.

6. В магазинах нужно всегда _____ (to pay in rubles).

7. Он никогда не _____ (bargains) и всегда платит больше.

ANSWERS

PRACTICE 1: 1. Этот галстук красного цвета. Сколько он стоит? **2.** Эти брюки синего цвета. Сколько они стоят? **3.** Эта рубашка белого цвета. Сколько она стоит? **4.** Эти ботинки чёрного цвета. Сколько они стоят? **5.** Это пальто жёлтого цвета. Сколько оно стоит?

PRACTICE 2: 1. Белые брюки идут/подходят к синему пиджаку. **2.** Красный галстук идёт Николаю. **3.** Белая рубашка идёт Наталье. **4.** Белый свитер идёт/подходит к зелёной юбке. **5.** Чёрные туфли идут/подходят к жёлтым брюкам. **6.** Голубая майка идёт тебе.

PRACTICE 3: 1. Что ты подаришь своему мужу на день рождения? **2.** Я подарю ему белую рубашку в полоску. **3.** Эти туфли идут твоей сестре. **4.** Сколько стоит это пальто? Я не вижу цену на этикетке. **5.** Сейчас ты должен заплатить в кассу.

PRACTICE 4: 1. по-моему, сувениров, на рынке, в киосках; **2.** побольше; **3.** сдачи; **4.** поменьше, за пятьсот; **5.** торговаться; **6.** платить в рублях; **7.** торгуется

—————— Lesson 31 (Sentences) ——————

SENTENCE LIST 1

Он обычно носит белые рубашки.	*He usually wears white shirts.*
Он был вчера в белой рубашке.	*He wore a white shirt yesterday.*
Какой у него размер?	*What's his size?*
Мне нужна рубашка сорок четвёртого размера.	*I need a size 44 shirt.*
Можно померить эти ботинки?	*May I try these boots/shoes on?*
Эти ботинки мне велики.	*These boots/shoes are too big for me.*
Этот свитер мне мал.	*This sweater is too small for me.*
Это пальто мне как раз.	*This coat fits me just right.*
Мне кажется, что красный галстук подходит к этой рубашке.	*It seems to me (I think) (that this) red tie matches this shirt.*
Где я могу заплатить?	*Where can I pay?*
Вам нужно платить в кассу.	*You need to pay at the cash register.*

NUTS & BOLTS 1

THE EXPRESSIONS носить + *ACCUSATIVE* AND быть в + *PREPOSITIONAL*

Notice that there are two expressions for *wearing clothes* in Russian. One is **носить** + *acc.;* it's used only when you describe one's habit of wearing something on a regular basis.

Он обычно носит галстук.
He usually wears a tie.

Он обычно носит очки
He usually wears glasses.

Он обычно носит пиджак.
He usually wears a jacket.

Он обычно носит джинсы.
He usually wears jeans.

The other, **быть в** + *prep.*, refers to wearing an item on a specific day.

Он был в белой рубашке (вчера).
He wore a white shirt (yesterday).

Она будет в юбке (завтра).
She'll wear a skirt (tomorrow).

Он сейчас в очках.
He's wearing glasses now.

PRACTICE 1

What do these people wear? Make up correct Russian sentences using the appropriate Russian verb for *wearing* and the prompts below.

1. он всегда—красивые галстуки

2. она вчера—чёрная юбка

3. я зимой—это пальто

4. летом студенты—джинсы и майки

5. обычно он—свитер, но вчера он—пиджак

NUTS & BOLTS 2
EXPRESSING SIZE

The Russian word for *size* is **размер.** When you need to say that an item is a certain size, you should follow the same pattern as you learned for colors.

Какого размера эта куртка?

What size is this jacket?

Эта куртка маленького размера.

This jacket is the small size.

If you have a particular number for size, this number becomes an ordinal numeral, and you should decline it as an adjective (see Unit 4).

Эта рубашка сорок четвёртого размера.

This shirt is size 44.

Keep in mind that Russian sizes are different from American sizes, yet most shop assistants in Russia should be able to help you with conversion if necessary.

If you'd like to try any article of clothing on, you should ask a shop assistant: **Можно померить** + *acc.?*

Можно померить эти ботинки?

May I try these shoes on?

Мерить—померить are Conjugation II verbs with the **и**-stem and stable stress. They literally mean *to size, to measure up.*

When something you try on is too big or too small, you should use special short adjectives: **велик, велика, велико, велики** (for *too big*) and **мал, мала, мало, малы** (for *too small*). The gender/number of the short adjective used as a predicate depends on the gender/number of the subject: **ботинки малы, рубашка велика, пальто велико,** etc. **Как раз** is a colloquial expression meaning *a perfect fit.*

PRACTICE 2

Какого размера эти вещи? *(What size are these things?)* Ask what size the following things are. Then, answer the question using the prompts below and add whether they are too big, too small, or just right for you. Remember that ordinal numerals are declined like adjectives.

1. jeans—34—too small

2. outdoor jacket—48—too big

3. men's shoes—42—just right

4. trousers—38—too big

5. shirt—46—just right

SENTENCE LIST 2

Молодой человек, покажите, пожалуйста, эту матрёшку.	Sir (lit., young man), show me this matryoshka, please.
Девушка, можно посмотреть эту майку.	Ma'am/Miss (lit., young lady), may I see this T-shirt?
Пятьсот рублей—это очень дорого!	Five hundred rubles—this is too expensive!
Я готов уступить.	I can (lit., am prepared) make it less (lit., to yield, let you have your way).
Я готов взять две за восемьсот.	I can buy (lit., am prepared to take) two for eight hundred.
Сколько с меня?/Сколько я вам должен?	How much do I owe you? (lit., How much is it from me?)
С вас восемьсот рублей.	You owe eight hundred rubles. (lit., From you, eight hundred rubles.)
Вам завернуть?	Would you like me to wrap it for you?
Заверните, пожалуйста.	Please wrap it up.
Мне её далеко везти.	I (need) to carry it far.
Пожалуйста, пожалуйста!	No problem. (lit., Please, please!)

NOTES

The verbs уступать—уступить generally mean *to yield, let one pass, let one have his or her way.* You can *yield your seat on a bus to an older person* (уступить место в автобусе), *yield the way to traffic* (уступить дорогу), or *yield while negotiating a price at a market place* (уступить в цене). So, the sentence **Я вам уступлю за восемьсот** means *I will give (yield) it to you for eight hundred*. **Уступать** is a Conjugation I verb with an **-ай** stem and stable stress: **уступаю, уступаешь, уступают; уступал, уступала, уступали. Уступить** is Conjugation II, **и**-stem, with an **л**-mutation and the stress shift in the first person singular: **уступлю, уступишь, уступят; уступил, уступила, уступили.** Both perfective and imperfective verbs take the direct object in the accusative case.

The short adjective **готов/готова/готово/готовы** (cf. **рад, рада, рады** in Unit 6) means *ready* or *prepared*. It agrees in gender and number with the subject, the person who's ready. So, you should say: **он готов** *(he's ready)*, **она готова** *(she's ready)*, **мы готовы** *(we're ready)*. The past and future tenses will require the verbs **был, была, было, были,** and **будет, будут,** etc.

When you want to ask how much you owe, you should use the following expression in Russian: **Сколько с меня?** Literally, it means *How much is it from me?* **Сколько я вам должен/должна?** is also a perfectly acceptable way of expressing the same idea in Russian. Possible answers that you may often hear in restaurants, stores, and shops are: **с вас сто рублей** *(you owe one hundred rubles)*, **с меня двести рублей сдачи** *(I owe you two hundred rubles)*, etc.

The verb **возить** *(conj. II; -и)*—**везти** *(conj. I; -з)* means *to carry by vehicle* of any kind: a car, a plane, a truck, a cart, a stroller, etc. **Возить/везти** conjugates as follows: **вожу, возишь, возят; возил, возила, возили** and **везу, везёшь, везёт; вёз, везла, везли. Возить** and **везти** are motion verbs and constitute a multidirectional-unidirectional pair (see Unit 6).

When in colloquial speech **пожалуйста** is repeated twice **пожалуйста–пожалуйста,** it means *no problem, I don't mind,* or *as you wish.*

Addressing strangers

The Russian language doesn't have uniform words similar to the English *Sir, Ma'am,* or *Miss* for addressing directly the people one doesn't know. The Russian terms **молодой человек** and **девушка** are obviously restricted by gender and age (the latter being somewhat generous and relative). In addition, it may be inappropriate for a young man to address another man of more or less his age as **молодой человек,** whereas it's perfectly acceptable for a young woman to address another unfamiliar young woman as **девушка.** These restrictions mean that on many occasions there's no standard and neutral way of addressing a person you don't know. So, one often has to attract attention by saying: **извините, пожалуйста** *(excuse me please),* **будьте добры** *(be so kind),* etc.

NUTS & BOLTS 3
ELLIPTIC SENTENCES WITH *DATIVE* + *INFINITIVE*

Завёртывать *(conj. I; -ай)*—**завернуть** *(conj. I; -ну)* is *to wrap, wrap up.* The perfective imperative **заверните, пожалуйста** is a common request at the end of a purchase.

Вам завернуть?

Would you like me to wrap it for you?

This is an elliptic way of asking if the other person would like you to do something; the grammatical construction *dative* + *infinitive* implies the missing modal word **нужно/надо.**

Вам помочь?

Would you like me to help you?

Вам показать?

Would you like me to show (it to you)?

Мне её далеко везти.

I need to carry it far (by vehicle).

This ellipsis of the modal verb of necessity **нужно/надо** in this type of expression *(dative + infinitive)* is common in Russian.

PRACTICE 3
Give the Russian equivalents of the following sentences.

1. –How much do I owe you?–You owe me two hundred rubles. *(fml.)*

2. She was ready to help me.

3. We're prepared (can) to pay eight hundred rubles for two matryoshka dolls.

4. –Please wrap this matryoshka up. I need to carry it far.–No problem. *(fml.)*

5. (Would you like me) to show these souvenirs to you? *(fml.)*

Tip!

We discussed basic stress patterns in the past tense in the Tip! section of Unit 2. Now, let's consider the basic stress shifts in the imperfective present or perfective future tense. If stress shifts in the present/future conjugation, it normally does so in one way: from the end of the first person singular form back to the stem in the remaining five forms of the paradigm—for example: **пишу, пишешь, пишет, пишем, пишете, пишут; напишу, напишешь, напишет, напишем, напишите, напишут.** This is the only standard stress shift in the present/future tense. Other present/future stress patterns include stable stress (but not a stress shift!) either on the stem or on the ending. Remember that stress shifts in the present/future and past are normally mutually exclusive.

ANSWERS
PRACTICE 1: 1. Он всегда носит красивые галстуки. **2.** Она вчера была в чёрной юбке. **3.** Я зимой ношу пальто. **4.** Летом студенты носят джинсы и майки. **5.** Обычно он носит свитер, но вчера он был в пиджаке.

PRACTICE 2: 1. Какого размера эти джинсы? Эти джинсы тридцать четвёртого размера. Они мне малы. **2.** Какого размера эта куртка? Эта куртка сорок восьмого размера. Она мне велика. **3.** Какого размера эти ботинки? Эти ботинки сорок второго размера. Они мне как раз. **4.** Какого размера эти брюки? Эти брюки тридцать восьмого размера. Они мне велики. **5.** Какого размера эта рубашка? Эта рубашка сорок шестого размера. Она мне как раз.

PRACTICE 3: 1. Сколько с меня?—С вас двести рублей. (Сколько я вам должен?—Вы мне должны двести рублей). **2.** Она была готова мне помочь. **3.** Мы готовы заплатить восемьсот рублей за две матрёшки. **4.** Заверните, пожалуйста, эту матрёшку. Мне её далеко везти.— Пожалуйста, пожалуйста! **5.** Вам показать эти сувениры?

―――――― Lesson 32 (Conversations) ――――――

CONVERSATION 1

Larisa Gerasimova is shopping in a Moscow department store for a birthday gift for her husband. Her American friend, Charley Morison, came along.

Чарли:	**Что ты хочешь купить своему мужу на день рожденья?**
Лариса:	**Не знаю точно, может быть, рубашку и галстук?**
Чарли:	**Посмотри, рубашки продаются вон в том отделе. Какую рубашку ты хочешь купить? Белую рубашку или в полоску? А вот есть ещё в клетку.**
Лариса:	**Нет, только нс в полоску и не в клетку. Он обычно носит однотонные рубашки. Посмотри, тебе нравится вот эта, голубая?**
Чарли:	**Да, очень красивая. Какой у него размер?**

Лариса:	Обычно сорок четвёртый. Вот как раз есть одна сорок четвёртого размера.
Чарли:	А вот и галстуки. Как ты думаешь, какого цвета галстук подойдёт к этой рубашке?
Лариса:	Мне кажется, синий с красным подходит лучше всех.
Чарли:	По-моему, тоже. Сколько он стоит? Посмотри на этикетке.
Лариса:	Восемьсот рублей. Это, наверное, дорого?
Чарли:	Да, но галстук очень красивый. Твоему мужу он должен понравиться. Пойдём теперь платить в кассу.
Лариса:	Надеюсь, что здесь принимают кредитные карточки. А то у меня мало наличных.
Чарли:	Не волнуйся. Если тебе не хватит наличных, я одолжу тебе.

Charley:	What would you like to buy your husband for his birthday?
Larisa:	I don't know exactly, maybe a shirt and a tie?
Charley:	Look, shirts are sold in the department over there. What shirt would you like to buy? A white shirt or with stripes? Here are also checkered ones.
Larisa:	No, not with stripes or checkered. He usually wears shirts without a pattern. Look, do you like this blue one?
Charley:	Yes, it's very nice. What size does he wear?
Larisa:	Forty-four, usually. Here's one, size forty-four.
Charley:	And the ties are here. What do you think; what color tie would match this shirt?
Larisa:	I think (lit., it seems to me) the red and blue one goes well with it.
Charley:	I think so too. How much does it cost? Look at the tag.
Larisa:	Eight hundred rubles. This is probably a lot?
Charley:	Yes, but the tie is very nice. Your husband will like it. Let's go pay at the cash register.

> Larisa: *I hope they accept credit cards. Otherwise, I have little cash.*
>
> Charley: *Don't worry. If you don't have enough cash, I'll lend you (some).*

NOTES

Notice how Larisa says to Charley: **Вот как раз есть одна сорок четвёртого размера** *(here's one, size forty-four)*. It's hard to translate **как раз** into English here. In an earlier lesson, you learned that **как раз** meant *a perfect fit*. **Как раз** on its own is a common exclamation of serendipity that means something like *what a nice coincidence* or *in the nick of time*. Here are more examples: if you'd like to have lunch, and we happen to be standing in front of a restaurant, your friend can turn to you and say **Посмотри, вот как раз ресторан!** *(Look, here's a restaurant!)* **Как раз** here means *by chance*. The sentence **Я как раз хотел тебе сказать** means *I was just going to tell you.*

Как ты думаешь? is the idiomatic way of asking *What do you think?* in Russian. Notice that Russians say *how* instead of the English *what:* **Как ты думаешь, какого цвета галстук подойдёт к этой рубашке?** *(What do you think; what color tie would match this shirt?)*

Notice the compound conjunction **а то** in Larisa's last words in the conversation 1. It generally means *or else, otherwise,* or *if not so, then.* Larisa hopes that the store accepts credit cards; **а то** *(if they don't),* she may not have enough cash.

NUTS & BOLTS 1
DEMONSTRATIVES вот AND вон
If you need to say *here it is* in Russian, *here* should be rendered as **вот.**

Где магазин?

Where's the store?

Вот он.

Here it is.

If the object in question is far away, you should replace **вот** *(here)* with **вон** *(over there)*.

Вон он.

It's over there.

Рубашки продаются вон в том отделе.

Shirts are sold in the department over there.

В том *(in that)* as opposed to **в этом** *(in this)* corresponds to the idea of distance expressed by **вон** as opposed to **вот**.

PRACTICE 1

Как сказать по-русски? Give the Russian equivalents of the following sentences.

1. The mall is over there.

2. Where are the men's shirts? Over there.

3. –You don't happen to know where the department store is, do you?–I'll show you. I just happen to be going there. *(fml.)*

4. Pants are sold in the department over there.

5. –Where are my glasses?–Here they are.

NUTS & BOLTS 2

Making general statements

Notice the syntax in the clause **здесь принимают кредитные карточки.** This clause is technically subjectless, because the implied subject **они** *(they)* is missing. It should be translated either as *one accepts credit cards here, they accept credit cards here,* or *credit cards are accepted here.* When making general statements in Russian, it's common to put the verb in the third person plural form, but leave the subject **они** *(they)* out.

Так говорят по-русски.
This is how they say it in Russian.

Интересные вещи пишут в газетах.
They write interesting things in newspapers.

Сейчас в Москве строят много новых зданий.
They're building many new buildings in Moscow now.

Keep in mind that, once you take the subject **они** out, you normally shouldn't start the subjectless sentence with the verb. You need to fill the void left from the missing subject with any other word in the sentence as in all of the examples above.

PRACTICE 2
Restate the following sentences in the general subjectless form. Remember to fill the void at the beginning of the sentence!

1. Мы говорим так по-русски.

2. Вы здесь принимаете кредитные карточки?

3. Бутики *(boutiques)* продают модную *(fashionable)* одежду в Гостином дворе.

4. Покупатели в универмаге обычно платят в кассу.

5. Он обычно носит галстук с пиджаком.

NUTS & BOLTS 3
EXPRESSING *TO HAVE ENOUGH, TO BORROW,* AND *TO LEND*
In order to say *to have enough* or *not to have enough* in Russian, you need to use the following construction: *dative* + **(не) хватает— хватит** + *genitive*. The dative case denotes the person or the persons who do or don't have enough of anything; the genitive denotes the sufficient or insufficient thing; and the verb **хватать** *(conj. I; -ай)*—**хватить** *(conj. II; -и)* means *to be enough.* **Мне хватит наличных** or **мне не хватит наличных** are subjectless sentences; they imply the subject *it,* and literally mean *(It)*

will/won't be enough cash for me. Consequently, the verb is always in the third person singular form, since it agrees with the implied subject *it*. The past tense works exactly the same way.

Ей хватило денег.

She had enough money.

Нам никогда раньше не хватало денег.

We never used to have enough money.

You should use the imperfective verb **хватать** only when you describe the state of affairs rather than saying exactly what happened or will happen.

The verb pair **одалживать** *(conj. I; -ай)*—**одолжить** *(conj. II; -и; stress shift in future)* means *to borrow* or *to lend*. As well as the word **должен,** it comes from the noun **долг** *(debt)*. The verb takes the accusative case for whatever you borrow or lend, and the dative for the person you lend to. So, you should say: **Я одолжу тебе наличные** *(I will lend you some cash)*. However, if you borrow from a person, you should use the preposition **у** + *genitive* in Russian.

Я одолжил(а) деньги у моего друга.

I borrowed money from my friend. (lit., I borrowed money at my friend's.)

If you are borrowing money from an organization such as a bank, don't use this expression; instead you should use the preposition **в** + *prepositional:* **Она одолжила деньги в банке.** You should use the two different verbs **одалживать—одолжить** and **занимать—занять** in direct correspondence with the English *lend* and *borrow,* in order to avoid confusion resulting from using one verb **одолжить** in both meanings.

PRACTICE 3

Чего вам не хватит? *(What don't you have enough of?)* Say what won't be enough for you. Then, restate the same sentences in the past tense. Use the prompts below.

1. я—наличные
2. ты—время
3. студенты—деньги

4. ваш друг—место в автобусе
5. мы—билеты в театр

CONVERSATION 2

Paul Jackson is shopping for gifts at a souvenir market in St. Petersburg. A stand with matryoshka dolls, fur hats, and old Soviet pins attracts his attention. The seller notices Paul's interest and approaches him.

Продавщица:	Покупайте сувениры! Отличные сувениры и недорого! Молодой человек, вам что-нибудь показать?
Пол:	Можно посмотреть вот эту матрёшку?
Продавщица:	Да, пожалуйста. Это ручная работа.
Пол:	Сколько она стоит?
Продавщица:	Та, что у вас в руках, стоит пятьсот рублей, а вот эти, поменьше, отдам за четыреста.
Пол:	Пятьсот рублей?! Это очень дорого. Подешевле не продадите?
Продавщица:	Если купите две, я готова уступить. Возьмёте две за восемьсот?
Пол:	Одну большую и одну маленькую. Договорились?
Продавщица:	Договорились. Будете платить в рублях?
Пол:	Да, в рублях. У вас будет сдача с тысячи?
Продавщица:	Да, с меня двести рублей сдачи. Вам завернуть?
Пол:	Да, будьте добры, заверните, пожалуйста. Мне их далеко везти.

Продавщица: Пожалуйста, пожалуйста. Вот, возьмите. Благодарю за покупку. Хорошего вам дня!

Пол: Вам спасибо! Всего хорошего.

Seller: Buy souvenirs here! Great souvenirs, and inexpensive! Sir, would you like me to show you anything?

Paul: May I take a look at this matryoshka doll?

Seller: Yes, please. It's handmade.

Paul: How much does it cost?

Seller: The one in your hands costs five hundred rubles, but these ones, a bit smaller, I'd sell to you for four hundred.

Paul: Five hundred rubles? This is too expensive. Would you be willing to sell it for a little less?

Seller: I would if you buy two. Would you take two for eight hundred?

Paul: One big and one small. Agreed?

Seller: Agreed. Will you pay in rubles?

Paul: Yes, in rubles. Will you have change for a thousand?

Seller: Yes, I owe you two hundred in change. Would you like me to wrap (them) up for you?

Paul: Yes, please wrap them up. I have a long way to go.

Seller: No problem. Here you are. Thank you for your purchase. Have a good day!

Paul: Thank you! Have a good one too!

NOTES

The demonstrative pronoun **та** in the sentence **та, что у вас в руках, стоит пятьсот рублей** is singular and feminine, because it substitutes for the singular feminine noun **матрёшка**. It means *the one, the one you're holding*. Its other forms in the nominative case are: **тот** *(m.)*, **то** *(n.)*, and **те** *(pl.)*. These pronouns can also change according to the case. The following conjunction **что** *(that)* stands for the inanimate object *the one that;* **кто** *(who)* would substitute for a person: **тот, кто пришёл** *(the one, who came)*.

Notice the accusative case in the sentence: **Одну большую и одну маленькую** *(one big and one small)*. It is so because this short sentence is elliptic–it leaves out **я возьму** from the sentence above which takes the accusative case.

NUTS & BOLTS 4
THE PREPOSITION у + PERSONAL PRONOUN IN THE GENITIVE
Look at the following phrase:

у вас в руках
in your hands

Notice the use of **у** + *personal pronoun in the genitive* instead of the simple possessive pronoun **в ваших руках** as you would say in English. This substitution is idiomatic in Russian. The possessive pronoun **в ваших** would sound emphatic in Russian–*in your hands* as opposed to someone else's. Similarly, it's more neutral and standard to say in Russian: **у вас в городе** *(in your city)*, **у меня дома** *(in my house)*, **у нас на работе** *(at our work)*, etc. instead of saying **в вашем доме, в моём доме, на нашей работе** respectively. Follow this tendency and replace possessive pronouns in the prepositional case with personal pronouns in the genitive preceded by the preposition **у**.

PRACTICE 4
Change the sentences below using the possessive phrases **у** + *genitive* instead of the possessive pronouns.

1. В нашем магазине продаются хорошие сувениры.

2. Что это в ваших руках?

3. В его киоске есть красивые матрёшки ручной работы.

4. В моей квартире четыре комнаты.

5. Я купил матрёшку на вашем рынке.

NUTS & BOLTS 5
FUTURE TENSE IN THE CONDITIONAL

Notice the use of the future tense in the conditional clause **если купите две** *(if you buy two)*. See the analogous sentences in conversation 1 above and in conversation 1 in Unit 7. As it was explained in Unit 7, you need to use the future tense after *if* in Russian when the condition refers to the future.

Если тебе понравится этот галстук, я куплю его тебе.

If you like (will like) this tie, I'll buy it for you.

Если тебе не хватит денег, я одолжу тебе.

If you run (will run) out of money, I will lend you (some).

Always keep this rule in mind and don't blindly follow English every time you have to say **если** *(if)* in Russian.

PRACTICE 5

Translate the following sentences into Russian. Remember to use the appropriate tense in the conditional clauses after **если**.

1. If they don't have change for a thousand, I'll pay with a credit card.

2. If we buy two matryoshkas, he will sell them for eight hundred rubles.

3. I'll buy you this souvenir if you liked it so much. *(infml.)*

4. If they don't have enough money tomorrow, I'll lend them some.

5. I'll go to the mall alone if you tell me where it is located. *(fml.)*

Discovery activity

Что вам нужно купить в большом торговом центре? *(What do you need to buy in a mall (lit., big shopping center)?)* Make a shopping list of things you need to buy in a mall for yourself, as well as gifts for your friends and family. Say how much they would cost, and where they are available. Give good reasons why you or they really need them. Imagine possible conversations with the salespeople in the mall and/or with your shopping partner. Use the new expressions and grammar as much as possible and have fun shopping!

ANSWERS

PRACTICE 1: 1. Торговый центр вон там. **2.** Где мужские рубашки? Вон они. **3.** —Вы не знаете, где универмаг? —Я покажу вам. Я как раз иду туда. **4.** Брюки продаются вон в том отделе. **5.** —Где мои очки? —Вот они.

PRACTICE 2: 1. Так говорят по-русски. **2.** Здесь принимают кредитные карточки? **3.** Модную одежду продают в Гостином дворе/в бутиках. **4.** В универмаге обычно платят в кассу. **5.** Галстук обычно носят с пиджаком.

PRACTICE 3: 1. Мне не хватит наличных. Мне не хватило наличных. **2.** Тебе не хватит времени. Тебе не хватило времени. **3.** Студентам не хватит денег. Студентам не хватило денег. **4.** Вашему другу не хватит места в автобусе. Вашему другу не хватило места в автобусе. **5.** Нам не хватит билетов в театр. Нам не хватило билетов в театр.

PRACTICE 4: 1. У нас в магазине продаются хорошие сувениры. **2.** Что это у вас в руках? **3.** У него в киоске есть красивые матрёшки ручной работы. **4.** У меня в квартире четыре комнаты. **5.** Я купил матрёшку у вас на рынке.

PRACTICE 5: 1. Если у них не будет сдачи, я заплачу кредитной карточкой. **2.** Если мы купим две матрёшки, он продаст их за восемьсот рублей. **3.** Я куплю тебе этот сувенир, если он так тебе понравился. **4.** Если у них не будет денег завтра, я одолжу им. **5.** Я пойду в торговый центр один (одна), если вы скажете мне, где он находится.

UNIT 8 ESSENTIALS

купить подарок своему мужу на день рожденья	*to buy a birthday present for one's own husband*
мужская/женская одежда продаётся в этом торговом центре/универмаге	*men's/women's clothing is sold in this mall/department store*
Какого размера ботинки он носит?	*What size shoes does he wear?*
Какого цвета у него пальто?	*What color is his coat?*
Вчера она была в юбке в клетку.	*She wore a checkered skirt yesterday.*
Этот галстук подходит к этому пиджаку.	*This tie matches this jacket.*
Вам это идёт.	*It looks nice on you.*
Вам нужно платить в кассу.	*You need to pay at the cash register.*
Здесь принимают кредитные карточки?	*Do they take credit cards here?*
Если тебе не хватит наличных, я одолжу тебе.	*If you don't have enough cash, I'll lend you (some).*
Девушка, покажите, пожалуйста, эту матрёшку.	*Miss, would you show me this matryoshka please?*
Молодой человек, сколько с меня?	*Sir (lit., young man), how much do I owe you?*
У вас будет сдача с тысячи рублей?	*Would you have change for a thousand rubles?*
Сколько стоят эти джинсы?	*How much do these jeans cost?*
Благодарю за покупку.	*Thank you for your purchase.*

UNIT 9
At the restaurant

In Unit 9, you will learn Russian restaurant etiquette. You will find out how to order meals, talk to the waiter or waitress, and make restaurant reservations. You'll expand your knowledge of the food vocabulary covered in Unit 2. In addition to food items, names of typical Russian dishes, and specific restaurant expressions, we'll also cover such topics of Russian grammar as the expressions of quantity, wishing, and the subjunctive mood.

-------------------- Lesson 33 (Words) --------------------

WORD LIST 1

выбирать *(conj. I; -ай)—* выбрать *(conj. I; irreg.)*	*to choose*
заказывать *(conj. I; -ай)—* заказать *(conj. I; -а)* + *acc.*	*to order*
официант/официантка	*waiter, waitress*
почти	*almost*
варёный	*cooked, boiled*
жареный	*fried*
на гриле	*grilled (lit., on the grill)*
запечённый	*baked*
огурец	*cucumber*
соль, солёный	*salt, salty (or pickled)*
сахар, сладкий	*sugar, sweet*
оливки, оливковое масло	*olives, olive oil*
уксус	*vinegar*
брынза	*feta cheese*

курица	chicken
куриный *(adj.)*	chicken
шашлык	*shish kebab*

NUTS & BOLTS 1

THE VERBS выбирать–выбрать AND заказывать–заказать

The Russian verb pair **выбирать–выбрать** is used in situations similar to when the English verb *to choose* would be used. You can choose dishes on the menu, the restaurant, etc. All of the things you choose should be in the accusative case. **Выбирать–выбрать из** *(to choose from)* takes the genitive case: **выбрать из меню** *(choose from the menu)*. The imperfective **выбирать** is Conjugation I, **ай**-stem, regular, with the stable stress. Its perfective counterpart **выбрать** is also Conjugation I, but it's irregular: it largely conjugates as an **a**-stem verb, except for the fleeting vowel **e** in the infinitive and the past tense: **выберу, выберешь, выберут; выбрал, выбрала, выбрали** (remember that the prefix **вы-** is always stressed in perfective verbs).

Что они выбрали на обед?

What did they choose for lunch?

The verb **заказывать–заказать** *(to order)* takes the direct object in the accusative case. **Заказывать** is a Conjugation I **ай**-stem verb; **заказать** is also Conjugation I, but **a**-stem with the **з/ж** mutation and the future tense stress shift: **закажу, закажешь, закажет; заказал, заказала, заказали.** Besides ordering things in a restaurant, you can order them **по каталогу** *(from a catalogue)* and **по интернету** *(over the internet)*. However, keep in mind that, when you order meals in a restaurant, it's more idiomatic to say **я буду** + *accusative (I'll have)* rather than using the verb above.

Она заказала по интернету.

She ordered over the internet.

PRACTICE 1

Что они выбрали на обед? *(What did they choose for lunch?)* Make up Russian sentences using the prompts below. State them in the past tense first, and then restate them in the future.

1. туристы—салат с оливковым маслом и уксусом

2. я—куриный суп

3. моя жена—овощи с мясом

4. вы—шашлык из курицы

5. гости—жареную курицу

PRACTICE 2

Как сказать по-русски? Give the Russian equivalents of the following sentences.

1. They ordered a salad with olive oil and vinegar.

2. I'll have feta cheese with olives and tomatoes.

3. Order grilled chicken! *(infml.)*

4. Do you like pickles (say: pickled cucumbers)? *(infml.)*

5. I always order shish kebab in this restaurant.

WORD LIST 2

возможно	*possible*
невозможно	*impossible*
обсуждать *(conj. I; -ай)—* обсудить *(conj. I; -и)* + *acc.*	*to discuss*
блин	*thin pancake (crepe)*
блины	*thin pancakes (crepes)*
копчёная рыба	*smoked fish*
чёрная икра	*caviar*
красная икра	*red caviar (salmon roe)*
зелень	*greens*

пирожки с мясом	*small pies with meat*
пирожки с капустой	*small pies with cabbage*
бутылка	*bottle*
сухое вино	*dry wine*
минеральная вода	*mineral water*
всё равно	*all the same, doesn't matter*
счёт	*check (in a restaurant), bill*

NOTES

The adverb **возможно** *(possible)* and its negative counterpart **невозможно** *(impossible)* are immediately related to the adverb **можно.** However, **можно** is usually followed by the infinitive, meaning it's possible to do something: **можно войти, можно заказать, можно купить,** etc.; whereas **возможно** is typically used as a qualifying predicate by itself, meaning something is possible or impossible: **это возможно, это невозможно** *(it's possible, it's impossible).* Notice that the negative form of **можно** is **нельзя;** it requires the imperfective infinitive when referring to a general prohibition: **нельзя входить** *(do not enter),* **нельзя курить** *(no smoking),* etc.

The verbs **обсуждать—обсудить** *(to discuss)* take the accusative case. The imperfective **обсуждать** is Conjugation I, **ай-**stem, with no mutations or stress shifts; the perfective **обсудить** is Conjugation II, **и-**stem, with the **д/ж** mutation in the first person singular, and the stress shift in the future tense. You can **обсуждать—обсудить меню** *(discuss the menu),* or **планы на вечер** *(plans for the night),* etc.

Caviar is **чёрная икра** *(lit., black caviar)* in Russian. What most Russians refer to as **красная икра** *(red caviar)* is *salmon roe.* Although both are referred to by the name **икра** in Russian, the former is approximately ten times more expensive than the latter.

The noun **зелень** *(lit., greens)* is feminine and always singular in Russian. It collectively denotes all fresh green herbs, such as укроп *(dill)*, петрушка *(parsley)*, кинза *(cilantro)*, etc. Sometimes, зелень may include other vegetables often used in salads, such as зелёный лук *(green onions)*, салат *(lettuce)*, even огурцы *(cucumbers)* and помидоры *(tomatoes)*. It's common to lay out such зелень on a separate plate on the table and eat it raw with other dishes without making a salad.

The expression всё равно *(all the same)* functions as an adverb in Russian. So, you can say: мне всё равно *(it's all the same to me)*, мне было всё равно *(it was all the same to me)*, etc. If someone is asking you to choose, but you don't really care whether it's one choice or another, it's appropriate to answer with this expression.

Какую минеральную воду вы хотите?
What kind of mineral water would you like?

Всё равно какую.
It doesn't matter what kind.

You can also simply say: Всё равно.

NUTS & BOLTS 2
More on the instrumental case
Пирожки (пирожок in the singular) are, literally, *little pies* the size of a donut that come in all kinds of shapes with all kinds of stuffing: meat, cabbage, eggs, mushrooms, fish, cheese, jams, fruits, etc. The specific stuffing of пирожок is usually put in the instrumental case with the preposition с, so you have: пирожки с мясом *(with meat)*, пирожки с капустой и яйцами *(with cabbage and eggs)*, пирожки с грибами *(with mushrooms)*, etc. People eat them as appetizers, with soups, for snacks, and even for dessert with coffee or tea. Russian блины *(thin pancakes* or *crepes)* often have stuffing too, for which you should also use the instrumental case with the preposition с: блины с икрой *(pancakes with caviar)*.

PRACTICE 3

С чем у вас пирожки? *(With what stuffing are your* **пирожки?)** Answer this question by putting the following food items in the instrumental case with the preposition **с.**

1. мясо и зелень

2. капуста и лук

3. копчёная рыба

4. красная икра

5. картошка и грибы

PRACTICE 4

Как сказать по-русски? Give the Russian equivalents of the following sentences.

1. They discussed the menu yesterday on the phone.

2. We ordered white wine and mineral water.

3. I don't like caviar.

4. Pancakes with soup? That's impossible!

5. It's prohibited to smoke in this restaurant.

6. May I buy a bottle of wine?

Culture note

Although most restaurants in Russia are similar to the restaurants in the U.S., there are certain cultural differences you need to be aware of when you go there. First of all, you may not be offered drinks and bread while you're looking at the menu. Many servers expect you to order the whole meal first, including the drinks, and then they bring everything to you at once. This often makes your wait feel longer than what you're used to. On the other hand, there are restaurants with the Western style of management where waiters and waitresses follow the familiar protocol. Second, most soft drinks are served chilled but without ice even when the restaurant has plenty. If you prefer to have ice in your drink, you should say so to your server and, perhaps, show explicitly how much ice you'd like to have, or else you'll be given one or two cubes. And finally, tips in Russia are about 10%, if you're satisfied with the service. If you're paying with a credit card, include the tip in the total amount of your check before you give your card to the server or, better, leave it in cash. It's uncommon to add tip to your check after you've already signed it, as it's normally done in the U.S. Apart from these minor cultural differences, the service in Russian restaurants is friendly and efficient, especially when you use your Russian!

ANSWERS

PRACTICE 1: 1. Туристы выбрали/выберут салат с оливковым маслом и уксусом. **2.** Я выбрал(а)/выберу куриный суп. **3.** Моя жена выбрала/выберет овощи с мясом. **4.** Вы выбрали/выберете шашлык из курицы. **5.** Гости выбрали/выберут жареную курицу.

PRACTICE 2: 1. Они заказали салат с оливковым маслом и уксусом. **2.** Я буду брынзу с оливками и помидорами. **3.** Закажи курицу на гриле! **4.** Ты любишь солёные огурцы? **5.** Я всегда заказываю шашлык в этом ресторане.

PRACTICE 3: 1. пирожки с мясом и зеленью; **2.** пирожки с капустой и луком; **3.** пирожки с копчёной рыбой; **4.** пирожки с красной икрой; **5.** пирожки с картошкой и грибами

PRACTICE 4: 1. Они обсуждали/обсудили меню вчера по телефону. **2.** Мы заказали белое вино и минеральную воду. **3.** Я не люблю чёрную икру. **4.** Блины с супом? Это невозможно! **5.** В этом ресторане нельзя курить. **6.** Можно мне купить бутылку вина?

PHRASE LIST 1

несколько вопросов	*a few questions*
салат из свежих овощей	*salad made of fresh vegetables*
салат из варёных овощей	*salad made of cooked vegetables*
большая порция	*big portion*
маленькая порция	*small portion*
гарнир	*side dish*
закуска	*appetizer*
на закуску	*for an appetizer*
первое *(n., decl. as an adj.)*	*soup (lit., first course)*
на первое	*for a soup*
второе *(n., decl. as an adj.)*	*entrée (lit., second course)*
на второе	*for an entrée*
десерт	*dessert*
на десерт	*for dessert*
борщ со сметаной	*borscht (beet soup) with sour cream*
вода без газа	*plain water*
вода с газом	*sparkling water*
лёд	*ice*
со льдом	*with ice*
безо льда	*without ice*
побольше льда	*more ice*
поменьше льда	*less ice*
с лимоном	*with lemon*
без лимона	*without lemon*
с майонезом	*with mayonnaise*
без майонеза	*without mayonnaise*
капуччино *(m., indecl.)* с сахаром	*cappuccino with sugar*
капуччино без сахара	*cappuccino without sugar*

The nouns **закуска, первое, второе,** and **десерт** refer to all four courses of a full meal: *appetizer, soup, entrée,* and *dessert.* If you want to say that you're having something *as an appetizer,* you need to use the preposition **на** + *accusative case:* **я буду салат на закуску** *(I will have salad as an appetizer).* **На первое, на второе,** and **на десерт** work the same way: **борщ со сметаной на первое** *(borscht with sour cream as a soup),* **курица на гриле на второе** *(grilled chicken for an entrée),* etc.

NUTS & BOLTS 1
EXPRESSING ABSTRACT QUANTITY

The quantitative word **несколько** *(a few of)* takes only the genitive plural case. This is so because it's used only with countable nouns, that is, with the nouns that can have the plural form. For example, you should say: **несколько вопросов** *(a few questions),* **несколько человек** *(a few people*–see Unit 5), **несколько порций** *(a few portions),* etc. All other quantitative words mentioned in Units 2, 3, and 7, such as **много** *(many/much),* **мало** *(little/not enough),* **сколько** *(how many/how much),* **немного** *(a little),* can be used with countable and uncountable nouns alike. So, you can say: **много молока** *(a lot of milk),* **много сахара** *(a lot of sugar),* but also **много вопросов** *(many questions).*

У нас есть несколько вопросов.

We have a few questions.

У нас есть много вопросов.

We have a lot of questions.

In addition, remember that **немного** means *a little,* whereas **мало** is *little.*

У нас есть немного денег.

We have a little bit of money.

У нас мало денег.

We have little money.

The first sentence conveys the positive view (we still have some), while the second conveys the negative one (we don't have enough).

PRACTICE 1

Say that you have some/a few of the following things. Use **несколько** wherever possible; when impossible, use **немного** instead.

1. человек   5. вода

2. вопрос   6. лёд

3. салат   7. бутылка

4. порция

NUTS & BOLTS 2

THE PREPOSITIONS без **AND** с

When you order or buy water in Russia, it's customary to say whether you'd like it sparkling or plain. *Sparkling water* is **вода с газом** (*lit., water with gas*) in Russian; *plain water* is **вода без газа** (*lit., water without gas*). The prepositions **с** (*with*) + *instrumental* and **без** (*without*) + *genitive* are commonly used in Russian in food and drink expressions. So, you may say: **с сахаром/без сахара** (*with/without sugar*), **со льдом/безо льда** (*with/without ice*), **с молоком/без молока** (*with/without milk*), **со сметаной/без сметаны** (*with/without sour cream*), **с майонезом/без майонеза** (*with/without mayonnaise*), **с лимоном/без лимона** (*with/without lemon*), etc.

PRACTICE 2

Give the Russian equivalents of the following sentences.

1. I will have borscht with sour cream for soup and salad with chicken for an entrée.

2. She drinks plain water with ice and lemon.

3. They have small portions.

4. I have a few questions.

5. We'll have dinner today without dessert.

6. Give me more ice, please. *(fml.)*

PHRASE LIST 2

заказать столик	*to make a reservation in a restaurant (lit., to place an order for a table)*
свободный столик	*available table in a restaurant (lit., free table)*
на семь часов	*for seven o'clock*
на субботу	*for Saturday*
на три человека	*for three people*
на троих	*for three people*
накрывать *(conj. I; -ай)—* накрыть *(conj. I; -ой)* стол	*to set the table*
к нашему приходу	*by the time of our arrival*
оплачивать *(conj. I; -ай)—* оплатить *(conj. II; -и)* счёт	*to pay the check (in a restaurant)*
давать—дать на чай	*to pay the tip, to tip*
чаевые	*tips*

NUTS & BOLTS 3
MORE RESTAURANT GRAMMAR

It's idiomatic to refer to a *table* in a restaurant by its diminutive form столик. This, of course, doesn't mean that the table is small. If you made a reservation in a restaurant, you should say **я заказал(а) столик в ресторане**. Reservations for a specific time or number of guests require the preposition **на** + *accusative* in Russian.

Я заказал(а) столик на субботу, на семь часов, на три человека.

I made a reservation for Saturday at seven for three people.

Remember that the Rule of Numbers takes over the accusative case (see Unit 3)!

Also, consider the following collective numerals commonly used in the accusative case for people: **двое** *(a party of two),* **трое** *(a party of three),* **четверо** *(a party of four).* These numerals change in the genitive case and become respectively: **на двоих, на троих, на четверых.** Notice that you don't need to add **человек** *(people)* to these numerals.

PRACTICE 3

Когда, во сколько и на сколько человек вы заказали столик в ресторане? *(When, for what time, and for how many people have you made a reservation in a restaurant?)* Answer the question using the prompts below. If needed, consult Unit 2 for days of the week. Write out the numerals.

1. Friday, 6:00, 4 people

2. Saturday, 7:30, 2 people

3. Tuesday, 1:00, 7 people

4. next Thursday, 7:00, 12 people

5. Sunday, 12:30, 3 people

NUTS & BOLTS 4

THE VERBS накрывать–накрыть **AND** оплачивать–оплатить
To set the table in Russian is **накрывать–накрыть на стол.** The imperfective **накрывать** is a standard Conjugation I verb, **ай**-stem, no mutations or stress shifts. The perfective **накрыть** is slightly irregular in the future tense: **накрою, накроешь, накроет.** The past tense is regular: **накрыл, накрыла, накрыли.** It's traditional to set the table in a family style in Russia. So, the middle of the table is usually fully covered with many dishes to choose from, especially appetizers, and you help yourself in your individual plate.

Tips are **чаевые** *(pl.)* in Russian. Literally, this means *tea money.* *To tip* is **дать на чай** *(lit., to give on the tea).*

Мы дали на чай двести рублей.
We tipped two hundred rubles.

Счёт is *a check* in the restaurant, as well as *a bill* or *an account in the bank.* It comes from the verb **считать** *(to count).* *To pay the check/bill* is **оплачивать/оплатить счёт.** The imperfective verb **оплачивать** is Conjugation I with an **ай**-stem and is completely regular. The perfective **оплатить** is Conjugation II with the **т/ч** mutation in the first person singular and the future tense stress shift: **оплачу, оплатишь, оплатят; оплатил, оплатила, оплатили.**

PRACTICE 4
Как сказать по-русски? Give the Russian equivalents of the following sentences.

1. How much did you tip him? *(informal)*

2. (They) set the table by the time of our arrival at seven. (see Unit 8 for subjectless sentences)

3. We paid our check and gave the tip.

4. (They) set the table for three.

5. We have one available table for you.

Tip!

The hardest part of taking any new language beyond a beginner level is acquiring new vocabulary. When trying to figure out the meaning of a new word in Russian, it helps to know how to break the word down. By breaking the word in question into its composite parts—prefix, root, suffix, and ending—you can start to see what each one of them means by itself. For example, the Russian verb **обсудить** consists of the following morphemes: **об-суд-и-ть.** The prefix **о(б)-** means *about* or *around;* the root **суд** means *trial, court, judgment;* the suffix **-и-** is the standard Conjugation II verbal suffix; and the ending **-ть** is the standard infinitive ending. Now you can see why the word **обсудить** means *to discuss.* Even when this technique doesn't let you guess the meaning of a word you don't know, it will help you learn it faster and remember it better. So, try to use etymology and morphology as a mnemonic device in your vocabulary building!

ANSWERS

PRACTICE 1: 1. несколько человек; **2.** несколько вопросов; **3.** немного салата; **4.** несколько порций; **5.** немного воды; **6.** немного льда; **7.** несколько бутылок

PRACTICE 2: 1. Я буду борщ со сметаной на первое и салат с курицей на второе. **2.** Она пьёт воду без газа, со льдом и с лимоном. **3.** У них маленькие порции. **4.** У меня несколько вопросов. **5.** Мы будем ужинать сегодня без десерта. **6.** Дайте мне, пожалуйста, побольше льда.

PRACTICE 3: 1. Я заказал(а) столик на пятницу, на шесть часов, на четыре человека/на четверых. **2.** Я заказал(а) столик на субботу, на семь часов тридцать минут, на два человека/на двоих. **3.** Я заказал(а) столик на вторник, на час, на семь человек. **4.** Я заказал(а) столик на следующий четверг, на семь часов, на двенадцать человек. **5.** Я заказал(а) столик на воскресенье, на двенадцать часов тридцать минут, на трёх человек/на троих.

PRACTICE 4: 1. Сколько ты ему дал(а) на чай? **2.** Стол накрыли к нашему приходу в семь часов. **3.** Мы оплатили счёт и дали на чай. **4.** Стол накрыли на троих. **5.** У нас есть для вас один свободный столик.

Lesson 35 (Sentences)

SENTENCE LIST 1

Что входит в салат «Греческий»?	*What's in (lit., what goes into) the Greek salad?*
Это салат из свежих помидоров, огурцов, лука, брынзы и оливок.	*It's a salad made of fresh tomatoes, cucumbers, onions, feta cheese, and olives.*
Какие закуски вы порекомендуете?	*What appetizers would you recommend?*
Я вам рекомендую попробовать стейк из говядины.	*I'd recommend you try the steak.*

Что вы будете/закажете на второе?	*What will you have/order for an entrée?*
С каким гарниром вы будете рыбу?	*What side dish will you have with fish?*
Я бы хотел(а) что-нибудь нежирное.	*I would like something lean.*
Я вегетарианец/ вегетарианка.	*I'm a vegetarian.*
Я не ем мяса *(or:* мясо).	*I don't eat meat.*
Что вы будете пить?/Вы будете что-нибудь пить?	*What will you drink?/Will you drink anything?*

Notes

The imperfective motion verb **входить** *(to enter)* also means *to be included*. Thus, the sentence **В салат «Греческий» входят свежие овощи и брынза** means *Fresh vegetables and feta cheese are the ingredients of the Greek salad (lit., they go into the Greek salad).* If you need to ask *What does the Greek salad consist of?*, you should say **Что входит в салат «Греческий»?**

Рекомендовать—порекомендовать are Conjugation I verbs. The suffix-**ова-** is a productive suffix in Russian. This means that it helps many foreign words make their way into Russian: **рекомендовать** *(to recommend),* **копировать** *(to copy),* **сканировать** *(to scan),* **организовать** *(to organize),* etc.

Пробовать—попробовать *(to try; to taste)* is another example of an **ова**-verb; compare it with the English *to probe.* In Russian, it means *to try* as in **я попробую заказать столик на вечер** *(I'll try to make a reservation for tonight)* or **попробуйте шашлык** *(try the shish kebab).*

Стейк из говядины means *steak made of beef (lit., out of beef).* Now, learn the following names for different types of meat. They will help you navigate through the menu in Russian.

говядина/из говядины	*beef*
телятина/из телятины	*veal*
баранина/из баранины	*lamb*
свинина/из свинины	*pork*
курица/из курицы	*chicken*

It is also common to see the adjectival form of *chicken,* **куриный**.

NUTS & BOLTS 1
THE SUBJUNCTIVE

The particle **бы** coupled with the past tense of the verb is used to express the subjunctive mood in Russian. The Russian subjunctive differs from the subjunctive mood in other languages, including English. In Russian, it expresses only unrealizable ideals in hindsight, similar to the English *would have,* as in *I would have done this.* It's important that there's no equivalent of the English *would* in Russian. When translated, the English *would* needs to be changed either to *would have* or to *will.* The only notable exception to this rule is the common Russian phrase **я хотел бы.** As opposed to the above rule, this expression doesn't mean *I would have liked* but rather *I would like,* whereas all other **бы** + *past tense* subjunctives mean *I would have* in Russian.

Я бы сказал(а) тебе.
I would have told you.

Он бы пошёл туда.
He would have gone there.

Мы бы заказали этот салат.
We would have ordered this salad.

Consider one more point for future reference: as opposed to English, the Russian clauses that express subjunctive condition and consequence in one sentence have exactly the same grammar. For example, instead of saying: *If I had known this, I would have told you the truth* (notice the grammatical disparity in both clauses in English—*I had known* and *I would have told*), the Russian clauses are identical: **Если бы я знал это, я бы сказал тебе правду (я бы знал = я бы сказал).**

PRACTICE 1
Say that the following people would like to have done the things below.

1. я—попробовать стейк из говядины

2. она—что-нибудь нежирное

3. мы—салат из свежих помидоров

4. мои друзья—заказать столик на вечер

5. он—оплатить счёт

PRACTICE 2
Fill in the blanks using the prompts in the parentheses. Pay attention to the choice of aspect and case!

1. Вы не можете _____ (to recommend) что-нибудь вегетарианское на второе?

2. Что _____ (goes into) в этот салат?

3. Это салат из _____ (fresh tomatoes), _____ (cucumbers), лука и брынзы.

4. Что _____ (would you like) на десерт? *(fml.)*

5. Я вам _____ (recommend) _____ (to try) рыбу с гарниром.

6. Я *(f.)* не _____ (vegetarian), но я не ем (pork).

SENTENCE LIST 2

Я бы хотел(а) заказать банкет на следующую субботу.	*I would like to make a banquet reservation for next Saturday.*
Сколько вас человек?	*How many people are in your party?*
Нас двенадцать человек.	*There are twelve of us.*
Вы что-нибудь будете из алкоголя?	*Will you be having alcoholic beverages?*
Принесите нам, пожалуйста, ещё хлеба/пива/вина.	*Bring us some more bread/beer/wine, please.*
Принесите, пожалуйста, бокал красного вина.	*Bring (me or someone else) a glass of red wine please.*
Принесите, пожалуйста, счёт.	*Bring (us) the check please.*
Принесите, пожалуйста, меню на английском языке.	*Bring us the menu in English please.*
Рассчитайте/посчитайте нас, пожалуйста.	*Can we have our check please?*
Извините, я тороплюсь.	*Excuse me, I'm in a rush.*
Во сколько закрывается ваш ресторан?	*What time are you (is your restaurant) closing?*

NOTES

Банкет *(banquet)* in Russian refers to any larger party in a restaurant. So, instead of **заказать столик** for a smaller party, you should **заказать банкет** for a larger one.

NUTS & BOLTS 2
THE GENITIVE PARTITIVE AND MORE ON THE GENITIVE

The verb **принести** *(to bring)* is a perfective motion verb. It consists of the prefix **при-** and the unidirectional verb **нести** (see Unit 2), which means *to carry while walking, to carry on foot.* Consequently, **принести** means *to bring on foot.* You should use this verb in the imperative form **(принесите, пожалуйста)** every time you need your server to bring anything to your table. Remember that Russians use imperatives in place of the English *would you please!* Now, learn the conjugation of the verb **принести: принесу, принесёшь, принесут; принёс, принесла, принесли.** Notice the irregular past tense!

If what you're asking for is an eatable/drinkable item, such as **хлеб** *(bread),* **масло** *(butter/oil),* **пиво** *(beer),* **вино** *(wine),* etc., you have an option of using either the accusative case or the so called genitive partitive (similar to the English *some bread*). So, you can say **принесите, пожалуйста, хлеб** or **принесите, пожалуйста, хлеба.** Both mean exactly the same thing in modern Russian, and you don't have to use the genitive partitive. However, when you ask for *more* **(ещё)** bread, wine, etc., it's customary to use **ещё** + *genitive.*

Принесите, пожалуйста, ещё хлеба.
Please bring some more bread.

Принесите, пожалуйста, ещё пива.
Please bring some more beer.

Принесите, пожалуйста, ещё вина.
Please bring some more wine.

Принесите, пожалуйста, счёт *(please bring the check)* is a perfectly acceptable way of asking for the check. However, most Russians prefer to soften this request by choosing one of the following colloquial expressions:

Посчитайте нас, пожалуйста.
Check, please.

Рассчитайте нас, пожалуйста.
Check, please.

When you're in a rush, you can say **извините, я тороплюсь** and ask to bring the check **побыстрее, пожалуйста** (*a little faster*—see

Unit 7). **Торопиться** is *to be in a hurry;* it's a Conjugation II verb with an **и**-stem, an **л**-mutation, and the future tense stress shift: **тороплюсь, торопишься, торопятся; торопился, торопилась, торопились.**

Извините, я тороплюсь. Принесите счёт побыстрее, пожалуйста.
Excuse me, I'm in a hurry. Please bring the check a little faster.

Notice the genitive case after the quantitative word **сколько:**

Сколько вас?
How many are you?

When you answer this question, you should follow the formula *pronoun in the genitive case + the number.*

Нас пять человек.
There are five of us.

Remember to use the Rule of Numbers and the irregular declension of **человек: один человек, два/три/четыре человека, пять человек!**

PRACTICE 3
Ask your server to bring the following items to your table. Remember to be on formal terms with the waiter or waitress (use plural imperatives); use the accusative for the desired items and the genitive for *more* of them!

1. белый хлеб *(more)*

2. бутылка красного вина

3. меню на английском языке

4. чёрная икра и водка *(more)*

5. бокал белого вина

PRACTICE 4
Give the Russian equivalents of the following sentences.

1. We'd like to make a reservation for a party of twelve.

2. What time are you closing? *(fml.)*

3. Excuse me, I'm in a rush. Can I have the check please?

4. Would you like any alcohol? *(fml.)*

5. -How many are you? -There are six of us.

Language link

After almost seventy years of the Soviet ban on private enterprise, many Russian cities are experiencing the renaissance of the old tradition. This is particularly noticeable in the food industry. Look at the website of **Пироги Штолле,** а **пирожки** chain in St. Petersburg, at *www.stolle.ru.* Their shops are a good example of this kind of revival. Read about the history of this place (an English version is also available) and check out the current menu in Russian!

ANSWERS
PRACTICE 1: 1. Я хотел бы попробовать стейк из говядины. **2.** Она хотела бы что-нибудь нежирное. **3.** Мы хотели бы салат из свежих помидоров. **4.** Мои друзья хотели бы заказать столик на вечер. **5.** Он хотел бы оплатить счёт.

PRACTICE 2: 1. порекомендовать; **2.** входит; **3.** свежих помидоров, огурцов; **4.** бы вы хотели; **5.** рекомендую попробовать; **6.** вегетарианка, свинины (ог: свинину)

PRACTICE 3: 1. Принесите, пожалуйста, ещё белого хлеба. **2.** Принесите, пожалуйста, бутылку красного вина. **3.** Принесите, пожалуйста, меню на английском языке. **4.** Принесите, пожалуйста, ещё чёрной икры и водки. **5.** Принесите, пожалуйста, бокал белого вина.

PRACTICE 4: 1. Мы бы хотели заказать банкет на двенадцать человек. **2.** Во сколько вы закрываетесь? **3.** Извините, я тороплюсь. Посчитайте меня, пожалуйста (принесите, пожалуйста, счёт). **4.** Вы будете что-нибудь из алкоголя? **5.** –Сколько вас? –Нас шесть человек.

Lesson 36 (Conversations)

CONVERSATION 1

An American visitor, Eileen Melon, stops for lunch in a café in Russia. She enters the restaurant and sits at a free table. The menu is already on the table. Eileen reads through it and makes up her mind. In a minute, a waiter comes up to her table to take her order.

Официант:	Здравствуйте. Вы уже выбрали?
Айлин:	Да, почти. Но у меня есть несколько вопросов. Что такое салат «Столичный»?
Официант:	Это салат из варёных овощей с куриным мясом и майонезом. В него входят варёное яйцо, картофель, морковь, зелёный горошек и солёные огурцы.
Айлин:	Я бы хотела что-нибудь без майонеза.
Официант:	Тогда закажите салат «Греческий». Он очень вкусный. Туда входят помидоры, огурцы, лук, оливки и брынза с оливковым маслом и уксусом.
Айлин:	Очень хорошо. Это большая порция?
Официант:	Нет, совсем маленькая, только на закуску.
Айлин:	Тогда я возьму на первое борщ со сметаной. А на второе я буду шашлык из курицы без гарнира.
Официант:	Что вы будете пить?
Айлин:	Минеральную воду без газа со льдом и с лимоном. Побольше льда, пожалуйста.

Официант:	Что-нибудь на десерт?
Айлин:	Только капуччино без сахара. Спасибо.

Waiter:	Hello. Have you chosen?
Eileen:	Yes, almost. But I have a few questions. What's the Stolichny salad?
Waiter:	It's made of cooked vegetables, chicken, and mayonnaise. It has boiled eggs, potatoes, carrots, green peas, and pickles.
Eileen:	I'd like something without mayo.
Waiter:	Then order the Greek salad. It's very tasty. It has tomatoes, cucumbers, onions, olives, and feta cheese with olive oil and vinegar dressing.
Eileen:	Very good. Is it a large portion?
Waiter:	Not at all, it's small. Just for an appetizer.
Eileen:	Then I'll have borscht with sour cream for a soup. And for an entrée, I'll have chicken shish kebab without a side-dish.
Waiter:	What will you drink?
Eileen:	Plain mineral water, with ice and lemon. Please, plenty of ice.
Waiter:	Anything for dessert?
Eileen:	Just cappuccino without sugar. Thank you.

NOTES

Notice Eileen's question **Что такое салат «Столичный»?** The relative pronoun **такое** doesn't have an English equivalent. It literally means *such*, but here it follows the interrogative **что** (this is why it's neuter). It's idiomatic to have it there, so use it every time you ask for a definition. For example, if you don't know what **троллейбус** is, you should ask **Что такое троллейбус?** If you don't know what **борщ** is, you should ask **Что такое борщ?**, etc.

The adjective **вкусный** means *tasty*. You should use it to describe food instead of the standard English *very good*. As an adjective (not an adverb), it agrees with the nouns it modifies: **вкусный салат** *(good/tasty salad)*, **вкусное мясо** *(good/tasty meat)*, **вкусная**

рыба (*good/tasty fish*), and **вкусные овощи** (*good/tasty vegetables*).
As an adverb, it refers to the entire meal ràther than a particular
dish: **Спасибо, было очень вкусно** (*thank you, (it) was very
good/tasty*).

NUTS & BOLTS 1
MORE ON POSSESSION
Let's review possession as we learned it in Unit 2. Consider the
sentence **У меня есть много вопросов.** (*I have many questions*)
The word **есть** in the *I have* sentences is often omitted when you
are using a word to modify what it is you possess.

У меня есть машина.

I have a car.

У меня большая машина.

I have a big car.

Now, let's return to the context in the conversation: the sentence
у меня много вопросов (without **есть**) would mean that it's already clear that Eileen has some question; she's stressing the fact
that she has a lot of them.

Let's learn more words you'd need in a restaurant. The first chart
below covers the common names for dishes, glasses, silverware,
and other things at your table setting.

тарелка	*plate*
чашка	*cup*
рюмка	*shot glass (on a stem)*
бокал	*wineglass*
стакан	*glass*

салфетка	*napkin*
нож	*knife*
вилка	*fork*
ложка	*spoon*
трубочка	*straw*
соломинка	*straw*
соль	*salt*
перец	*pepper*

Notice the different names for different types of glasses in Russian. **Рюмка** is a small shot glass on a stem, usually for vodka. Since Russians drink vodka exclusively as shots (never on ice and rarely in cocktails), **рюмка водки** is a rather common phrase in the Russian language. **Бокал** usually refers to a wine or champagne glass: **бокал вина** or **бокал шампанского**. **Стакан** is a somewhat inelegant word; it's used for water or beer and usually is avoided in the restaurant context. An empty *beer mug* is **пивная кружка;** when it's actually filled with beer, you refer to it as **кружка пива** *(a mug of beer).*

PRACTICE 1

Что у вас есть? *(What do you have?)* Ask what they have in the restaurant. Decide each time whether to use **есть** or not.

1. вы—суп—сегодня

2. какой суп—вы—сегодня

3. вы—пиво

4. вы—русское пиво

5. вы—капуччино

PRACTICE 2

Что Айлин заказала на обед в ресторане? *(What did Eileen order for lunch in the restaurant?)* Mention all of the dishes and drinks she ordered; be specific and say what they consisted of. Use the formulas: for an appetizer, for a soup, for an entrée, and for dessert.

CONVERSATION 2

Vera Kuzmina is talking with a manager in a restaurant. Next Saturday is her father's birthday, and she's making a reservation for twelve people. She's discussing the menu with the manager as well as other details of her reservation.

Вера: Я бы хотела заказать банкет на следующую субботу, часов на семь. Это возможно?

Менеджер: Сколько вас человек?

Вера: Нас двенадцать человек.

Менеджер: Да, возможно. У нас как раз есть три свободных столика на вечер. Давайте сразу обсудим меню.

Вера: Очень хорошо. Я бы хотела, чтобы вы накрыли стол с закуской к нашему приходу.

Менеджер: Что бы вы хотели на закуску?

Вера: Блины, копчёную рыбу, красную икру, салат из помидоров, побольше зелени и пирожки с мясом и капустой.

Менеджер: Что-нибудь из алкоголя?

Вера: Да, конечно. Бутылку водки, две бутылки сухого вина, красного и белого, сока всё равно какого и минеральной воды.

Менеджер: Очень хорошо. Я всё записал. А суп, второе и десерт гости закажут сами после закуски.

Вера: Договорились. Когда счёт будет готов, принесите его мне. Я его оплачу сама.

Менеджер: Замечательно. Ждём вас в субботу, в семь часов.

Vera:	I would like to make a reservation for a large party for next Saturday, for seven o'clock. Would it be possible?
Manager:	How large is your party? (How many are you?)
Vera:	There are twelve of us.
Manager:	Yes, it's possible. We just happen to have three available tables for the night. Let's discuss the menu right away.
Vera:	Very well. I would like you to set the table with appetizers by the time we arrive.
Manager:	What would you like for appetizers?
Vera:	Blini (pancakes), smoked fish, red caviar, tomato salad, a lot of greens, and pirozhki (pies) with meat and cabbage.
Manager:	Any alcohol?
Vera:	Yes, of course. A bottle of vodka, two bottles of wine, red and white, some juice (lit., doesn't matter what kind), and mineral water.
Manager:	Very well. I wrote everything down. As for soup, entrées, and dessert, the guests will order them themselves after the appetizers.
Vera:	Agreed. When the check is ready, bring it to me. I'll pay it myself.
Manager:	Excellent. We'll be waiting for you on Saturday at seven.

NOTES

This conversation gives you an idea of a standard party at a Russian restaurant. A long table is usually set by the time the guests arrive. Many appetizers are already on the table, served family style along with bottles with vodka, wine, and water. Guests sit down and help themselves with food and drinks. Then, they order other courses and drinks.

Notice the adverb **сразу** (right away). You can also use it with the emphatic particle **же: сразу же.** Use this adverb when you give directions to your server in a restaurant. Its alternative is **после** (after) + genitive. So, you can say **принесите, пожалуйста, суп** сразу же *(please bring the soup right away)*, or **принесите, пожалуйста, суп после закуски** *(please bring the soup after the appetizers)*.

NUTS & BOLTS 2
More on the Rule of Numbers

Notice the genitive plural ending of the adjective modifying the genitive singular noun: **три свободных столика** *(three available tables)*. This is the only instance of case disagreement in Russian, and you need to be aware of it. Here's the rule: although the nouns after the numbers 2, 3, and 4 (see the rule of numbers in Unit 3) are always in the genitive singular, the adjectives modifying them should be in the genitive plural. As a result, you have: **две новых книги** *(two new books)*, **три свободных столика** *(three available tables)*, and **четыре больших дома** *(four big houses)*.

It's also possible in modern Russian to use the nominative plural for the adjectives modifying feminine nouns in genitive singular after 2, 3, and 4. So, you could also say **две новые книги.** This happens because the genitive singular **книги** coincides with the nominative plural **книги.** What probably started as a simple mistake (misidentification of **две книги** as nominative plural and modifying it with a nominative plural adjective **новые)** has now become the acceptable norm.

PRACTICE 3

Сколько их? *(How many of them?)* Say how many the following things are. The numbers are in the parentheses. Remember to follow the rule of numbers for both nouns and adjectives.

1. красный помидор (2)
2. свободный столик (3)
3. вкусный пирожок (5)
4. большая порция (2)
5. маленькая рюмка водки (3)

NUTS & BOLTS 3
Making requests

When you want another person to do something you have in mind, you should use a special construction in Russian.

Я хочу, чтобы ты сделал это.

I want you to do this. (lit., I want that you do this.)

This clause uses the conjunction **чтобы** followed by the nominative personal pronoun for the person you're commanding, and the past tense of the verb. This is another example of the subjunctive mood in Russian.

Я хочу, чтобы вы накрыли стол к нашему приходу.

I want you to set the table by the time we arrive.

Use this construction **чтобы** + *noun in the nominative* + *verb in the past* every time you have one party imposing its wish upon another regardless of the actual tense in the principle clause.

PRACTICE 4

Как сказать по-русски? Give Russian equivalents to the following sentences. Remember to use the wishing subjunctive above!

1. I want you *(plural)* to bring a bottle of vodka.

2. She wanted me to order a salad.

3. They wanted us to make a reservation for a banquet on Saturday.

4. We want them to discuss the menu with us.

5. We wanted our waiter to bring more smoked fish.

Discovery activity

Что бы вы хотели попробовать в русском ресторане? *(What would you like to try in a Russian restaurant?)* Imagine your conversation with a waiter or waitress. Are there any Russian restaurants in your area? If there are, you could play it out in reality.

ANSWERS

PRACTICE 1: 1. У вас есть суп сегодня? **2.** Какой суп у вас сегодня? **3.** У вас есть пиво? **4.** У вас русское пиво? **5.** У вас есть капуччино?

PRACTICE 2: 1. На закуску Айлин заказала Греческий салат из помидоров, огурцов, лука, оливок и брынзы с оливковым маслом и уксусом. **2.** На первое Айлин заказала борщ со сметаной. **3.** На второе Айлин заказала шашлык из курицы без гарнира. **4.** На десерт Айлин заказала капуччино без сахара.

PRACTICE 3: 1. два красных помидора; **2.** три свободных столика; **3.** пять вкусных пирожков; **4.** две больших (большие) порции; **5.** три маленьких (маленькие) рюмки водки

PRACTICE 4: 1. Я хочу, чтобы вы принесли бутылку водки. **2.** Она хотела, чтобы я заказал салат. **3.** Они хотели, чтобы мы заказали банкет на субботу. **4.** Мы хотим, чтобы они обсудили меню с нами. **5.** Мы хотели, чтобы наш официант принёс побольше (ещё) копчёной рыбы.

UNIT 9 ESSENTIALS

У меня (есть) несколько вопросов.	*I have a few questions.*
салат из свежих овощей с курицей	*fresh vegetables and chicken salad*
Что входит в этот салат?	*What's in this salad?*
Я бы хотел(а) что-нибудь без майонеза.	*I'd like something without mayonnaise.*

Это большая порция?	*Is it a large portion?*
Что вы будете на закуску, на первое, на второе, на десерт?	*What will you have for an appetizer, soup, entrée, (and) dessert?*
Я буду минеральную воду со льдом и с лимоном.	*I'll have mineral water with ice and lemon.*
Я бы хотел(а) заказать столик на вечер.	*I'd like to make a reservation for tonight.*
У нас есть три свободных столика.	*We have three available tables.*
Сколько вас?	*How many people (are in your party)?*
Нас двенадцать человек.	*There are twelve of us.*
Я хотел(а) бы, чтобы вы накрыли стол к нашему приходу.	*I want you to set the table by the time of our arrival.*
пирожок/пирожки с мясом	*small meat pie(s)*
Принесите, пожалуйста, счёт.	*May I have the check please?*

UNIT 10
School, work, and leisure

In Unit 10, you'll learn how to carry on a simple conversation in Russian on the subject of school, work, and leisure. You'll expand your prior knowledge of these topics covered in Units 3 and 4. We'll tell you about the Russian educational system and how to approximate the generally incompatible Russian expressions to the American educational realia, and vice versa. You'll learn how to use Russian study verbs, subordinate sentences including the ones with the conjunction *whether*, the expressions for liking and loving, certain prepositions, more motion verbs, and other useful idiomatic expressions.

―――――――――― Lesson 37 (Words) ――――――――――

WORD LIST 1

факультет	*department (in a university)*
на факультете	*at the department*
курс/на курсе	*year of study (freshman, sophomore, etc.)*
курс по + *dat.*	*course, class in*
поступать *(imperf., conj. I; -ай)* **в/на**	*to apply to (a university)*
поступить *(perf., conj. II; -и; л-mutation)* **в/на**	*to be admitted to, enter (a university)*
преподавать + *acc.*	*to teach*
занятия по + *dat.*	*class in*
лекция по + *dat.*	*lecture in*
окончить *(conj. II; -и)* + *acc.*	*to graduate (from)*
вечеринка *(на* + *acc./prep.)*	*party (coll.) (at/to)*

NUTS & BOLTS 1
Talking about school

The Russian noun **факультет** generally means *university department* or an entire school, such as *Law School*. This is due to a major difference between Russian and American systems of education. You need to understand the specifics of the Russian educational system in order to find approximate equivalents of such untranslatable English words as *major* or *college*.

The Russian word for *university* is **университет**. A Russian university is basically equivalent to an American college or university with some differences. There is also an **институт** which has, if not a lower-ranking, then a smaller or more specialized connotation than **университет**, like **Институт культуры** or **Педагогический институт им. Герцена**. A Russian professional school is called **ПТУ** or **колледж** (borrowed from the British use of *college*). **Университет** or **институт** usually consists of *five years of study* (**пять курсов**), and, upon graduation, awards a *diploma* (**диплом**) in a particular professional field, such as history, economics, literature, biology, journalism, physics, chemistry, law, medicine, etc. The Russian **диплом** is considered more advanced than an American Bachelor degree, but somewhat less than a Master's degree (although sometimes it's equated with it). Since all Russian schools are specialized in a particular field, college applicants must decide what they want to do in life before they apply.

A large university in Russia, such as *Moscow State University* (**Московский государственный университет**), consists of a number of separate schools (**факультеты**) that have little academic interaction with one another. When a high school graduate applies to college, he or she doesn't apply to the university/college itself as he or she would in America, but ro a specific school within this university (**факультет**): the school of history, law, chemistry, etc. In addition, **факультеты** consist of smaller departments called **кафедры** that specialize in more narrow areas of one general field of study. For example, **физический**

факультет will have a **кафедра ядерной физики** *(the Nuclear Physics Department).* As a result, it's impossible to say *major in* in Russian, because this notion doesn't correspond to anything in the reality of Russian education. **Главный предмет** *(the main subject)* or **специализация** *(specialization)* would be the closest approximation of the English word *major.*

Now, let's learn the names of some of the main **факультеты** in Russian universities along with the names for the most common fields of study.

история	**исторический факультет**	*history*
экономика	**экономический факультет**	*economics*
филология	**филологический факультет**	*linguistics and literature*
философия	**философский факультет**	*philosophy*
юриспруденция	**юридический факультет**	*law*
география	**географический факультет**	*geography*
физика	**физический факультет**	*physics*
химия	**химический факультет**	*chemistry*
биология	**биологический факультет**	*biology*

психология	психологический факультет (факультет психологии)	*psychology*
журналистика	факультет журналистики	*journalism*

Remember that **факультет** as well as **кафедра** and **курс** *(year of study)* take the preposition **на.** So, you should say: **на экономическом факультете, на первом (втором, третьем, четвёртом, пятом) курсе.** But **университет** and **институт** take the preposition **в: в Московском университете** *(at Moscow University),* **в Колумбийском университете** *(at Columbia University),* etc.

Be careful to differentiate two meanings of the Russian noun **курс:** one is the year of study (**первый**—*freshman year,* **второй**—*sophomore year,* **третий**—*junior year,* **четвёртый**—*senior year,* and **пятый**—*the fifth year);* the other meaning of **курс** is a specific course/class at school. The latter takes the preposition **по** + *dative:* **курс по истории** *(a course in history),* **курс по физике** *(a course in physics),* **курс по русскому языку** *(a course in Russian),* etc.

Я учусь на экономическом факультете, на первом курсе.
I study in the economics department, in the first year.

Я учусь в Московском университете
I study at Moscow University.

Занятие (often in the plural form **занятия**) is the actual *class,* the session you go to.

У меня занятия утром.
I have classes in the morning.

Сегодня меня не было на занятии.
I wasn't in class today.

Лекция is a lecture, just like in English; and **семинар** is a seminar. Both take the prepositions **на** and **по**: **на лекции по истории** *(at a history lecture)*, **на семинаре по психологии** *(at a psychology seminar).*

When you apply to a school, you use the imperfective verb **поступать** (Conjugation I, **ай**-stem) **в/на** + *accusative*. The imperfective aspect implies *the process of applying* rather than the result.

Я поступаю в Московский университет на юридический факультет.
I'm applying to Moscow University for law school.

The perfective aspect of the same verb **поступить** (Conjugation II, **и**-stem, **л**-mutation, future stress shift) means *to be admitted.*

Я поступил в Московский университет на юридический факультет.
I was admitted to Moscow University in the law school.

PRACTICE 1
Как сказать по русски? What is the Russian for the following English terms? Use the Russian noun **курс** in the genitive case.

1. in freshman year
2. in sophomore year
3. in junior year
4. in senior year
5. in fifth year

PRACTICE 2
Answer the following questions using the prompts in the parentheses.

1. Куда она поступила? (Петербургский университет, юридический факультет)

2. Какой факультет они окончили? (биологический факультет)

3. Где он преподаёт? (Московский университет, философский факультет)

4. Куда ты поступал? (Нью-Йоркский университет, факультет психологии)

5. Какие курсы у тебя завтра? (история, русский язык)

6. На какую лекцию вы ходили вчера? (макроэкономика)

WORD LIST 2

бассейн	*swimming pool*
плавание *(n.)*	*swimming*
неважно	*not important*
баня	*bathhouse, sauna*
сауна	*sauna*
в свободное время	*in (one's) free time*
опера	*opera*
спектакль *(m.)* (**на +** *acc./prep.*)	*show, play (at)*
выставка (**на +** *acc./prep.*)	*exhibition (at)*
художественная школа	*art school*
(художественный) фильм	*motion picture, movie*
концерт (**на +** *acc./prep.*)	*concert (at)*
искусство	*art*
драматический театр	*drama theater*
живопись *(f.)*	*painting*

NUTS & BOLTS 2
TALKING ABOUT FREE TIME

The Russian word **спектакль** *(show, play)* usually refers to a show in a drama theater, not an *opera* (**опера**) or *ballet* (**балет**). When you go to the theater, you should use the motion verb **ходить** with the preposition **в** + *accusative:* **ходить в театр** *(go to the the-*

ater), **ходить в кино** *(go to the movies)*, **ходить в оперу** *(go to the opera-house)*. However, if, instead of the theater itself, you go to see a particular show, you should use the preposition **на** + *accusative:* **ходить на спектакль** *(see a specific play)*, **на концерт** *(concert)*, **на оперу** *(opera)*, **на выставку** *(exhibition)*, **на фильм** *(movie)*, etc. Remember that the verb **ходить** in the past tense stands for a round-trip.

Я ходил(а) на концерт.

I went to the concert (and came back).

The noun **искусство** denotes all types of arts. Notice that *art* as an adjective is **художественный** in Russian: **художественный музей** *(art museum)*, **художественная выставка** *(art exhibition)*, **художественная галерея** *(art gallery)*, **художественная школа** *(art school)*.

Живопись is a specific term for *painting*. It consists of two roots **жив-** *(to live)* and **пи(са-)** *(to write)*. The Russian verb **писать** is also used for *to paint*. So, you should say **писать картины** *(lit., write paintings)* rather than **рисовать** *(to draw)*. The latter is reserved for drawings with a pencil or chalk: **рисовать карандашом** *(to draw with a pencil)*. Consequently, a drawing is **рисунок** in Russian.

Я пишу картины.

I paint.

Я рисою (карандашом).

I draw.

Плавание *(swimming)* is a noun derived from the verb **плавать** *(to swim*—see Unit 5). Also notice the accusative case in the following expression:

Я плаваю в свободное время.

I swim in my free time.

PRACTICE 3

Куда вы ходили вчера? *(Where did you go yesterday?)* Answer this question using the prompts below.

1. concert
2. opera-house
3. an opera
4. a ballet

5. a play
6. a Russian movie
7. movies
8. art exhibition

PRACTICE 4

Give the Russian equivalents of the following phrases and sentences.

1. Russian art
2. He goes to art school.
3. She went to a swimming pool yesterday.
4. arts and theater
5. At a free time, I go to the drama theater.
6. We were in the art gallery.

Language link

Besides theater, arts, and sports, one of the favorite Russian pastimes is **ходить в баню** *(going to the bathhouse/sauna)*. **Русская баня** *(Russian sauna)* is similar to the Scandinavian or German one, except that the heat is more humid. People go there for three-four hours, sometimes even longer, with friends or alone. It's customary to eat and drink in **русская баня,** relax on the couch or in the pool, watch TV, or talk to friends in between your actual visits to the steam room, where you notoriously beat yourself or your partner with birch or oak-tree, **веники** (specially prepared branches with leaves, brooms). This is by no means a self-flagellation, even if it may look so at first glance. The branches are soft, and the beating simultaneously fans your body with hot air and massages it. Check out the website of one of the oldest bathhouses in Moscow, **Сандуновские бани,** at http://www.sanduny.ru.

ANSWERS

PRACTICE 1: 1. на первом курсе; **2.** на втором курсе; **3.** на третьем курсе; **4.** на четвёртом курсе; **5.** на пятом курсе

PRACTICE 2: 1. Она поступила в Петербургский университет, на юридический факультет. **2.** Они окончили биологический факультет. **3.** Он преподаёт в Московском университете, на философском факультете. **4.** Я поступал в Нью-Йоркский университет, на факультет психологии. **5.** У меня завтра курсы по истории и по русскому языку. **6.** Я ходил (мы ходили) на лекцию по макроэкономике.

PRACTICE 3: 1. Я вчера ходил(а) на концерт. **2.** Я вчера ходил(а) в оперу/оперный театр. **3.** Я вчера ходил(а) на оперу. **4.** Я вчера ходил(а) на балет. **5.** Я вчера ходил(а) на спектакль. **6.** Я вчера ходил(а) на русский (художественный) фильм. **7.** Я вчера ходил(а) в кино. **8.** Я вчера ходил(а) на художественную выставку.

PRACTICE 4: 1. русское искусство; **2.** Он ходит в художественную школу. **3.** Она вчера ходила в бассейн. **4.** искусство и театр; **5.** В свободное время я хожу в драматический театр. **6.** Мы были в художественной галерее.

―――――――――― Lesson 38 (Phrases) ――――――――――

PHRASE LIST 1

учиться на третьем курсе	*to be a junior (lit., to study as the third year student)*
слушать курсы по биологии	*to take courses in biology*

интересоваться физикой	to be interested in physics
заниматься русской историей	to study (focus on) Russian history
изучать химию	to study chemistry
учить русский язык	to study Russian
изучать русский язык	to study Russian
сдавать экзамен по + dat.	to take an exam in
сдать экзамен по + dat.	to pass an exam in
подготовиться/готовиться (conj. II; и; л-mutation) к + dat.	to study (prepare) for
особенно	especially
странно (adv.)	strange
странный (adj.)	strange
с самого начала	from the very start

NUTS & BOLTS 1
EXPRESSING TO STUDY IN RUSSIAN

You're already familiar with the verb **учиться** (see Unit 3). Now, you need to learn to differentiate among this and several other "study verbs" in Russian. As with the motion verbs, you can't simply translate them as *to study*. You need to specify each time what kind of studying the Russian verb implies in order to use the correct one.

1. **Учиться** is *to study* in the sense of *being formally registered as a student somewhere.*

   Я учусь в университете.
   I study at/go to the university.

   Ты учишься в школе.
   You study at/go to school.

Она учится на первом курсе.

She's a freshman.

Они учатся на историческом факультете.

They study in the history department.

2. **Изучать** + accusative is *to study* in the sense of *studying a scholarly discipline.*

Я изучаю математику.

I study math.

Ты изучаешь физику.

You study physics.

Они изучают лингвистику.

They study linguistics.

3. **Учить** + accusative is *to study a small piece of information, not profoundly.* You can **учить урок** *(study a lesson)* or **учить глаголы движения** *(study verbs of motion),* implying short-term activity. You should use this expression to say that you are studying a language.

Я учу русский язык.

I study the Russian language.

Ты учишь французский.

You study French.

Они учат немецкий.

They study German.

4. **Заниматься** (see Unit 4) is *to study* in the sense of *being physically engaged in the process of studying.* It usually takes the prepositional case denoting the place where one does the studying, and a time expression.

Я занимаюсь в кафе вечером.

I study in a café at night.

Ты занимаешься в библиотеке днём.

You study in a library in the afternoon.

5. **Заниматься** as *to research, to concentrate* your academic interest in a particular area of study. For example, you are a historian whose focus is the French revolution.

Я историк и запимаюсь Французской революцией.

I am a historian and I study the French revolution.

6. **Готовиться/подготовиться** means *studying for an exam, test, etc.,* and literally translates *to prepare for* in Russian.

Я готовлюсь к экзамену.

I study for an exam.

Ты готовишься к экзамену.

You study for a test.

Они готовятся к занятиям.

They study for their classes.

The perfective verb **подготовиться** means *to be ready/prepared for an exam, test, etc.*

Он подготовился к экзамену.

He got prepared/ready for the exam.

Она подготовилась к экзамену.

She got prepared/ready for the exam.

The six points above are rather schematic and allow for some overlapping in real practice. Nevertheless, they will help you organize the otherwise confusing study verbs in Russian.

When you *take courses* in Russian, you need to use the idiomatic expression **слушать курс(ы)** with the preposition **по** + *dative* (*lit., listen to a course/courses in*).

Я слушаю курс по литературе.

I am taking a course in literature.

Ты слушаешь курс по русскому языку.

You are taking a course in Russian.

Taking exams in Russian is **сдавать экзамены.** Notice the imperfective aspect of this verb. The perfective **сдать экзамен** is *to pass the exam.*

Он сдавал и сдал экзамен по математике.

He took and passed the exam in math.

PRACTICE 1
Fill in the blank with the appropriate study verb in Russian. Remember to make this verb agree with the rest of the grammar in the sentence.

1. Я _____ на третьем курсе Московского университета. *(study)*

2. Он _____ на физическом факультете. *(studied physics)*

3. Она вчера весь вечер _____ . *(studied for an exam in chemistry)*

4. Мы не _____ в школе. *(studied Russian)*

5. Они всегда _____ в этом кафе. *(study)*

6. Она очень хорошо _____. *(studied/got ready for this exam)*

PRACTICE 2
Give the Russian equivalents of the following sentences.

1. I take courses in Russian history.
2. I took the exam in math yesterday but didn't pass it.
3. He's focused in Russian literature from the very start.
4. This is a strange course. I won't be taking it.
5. Where did you study Russian? *(fml.)*
6. I need to study for (my) exam in Russian tonight.

PHRASE LIST 2

Чем вы занимались вчера вечером?	*What did you do last night?*
заниматься плаванием	*to do (practice) swimming, to swim*
заниматься живописью	*to do (practice) painting, to paint*
заниматься на тренажёрах	*to exercise on fitness machines/equipment*
заниматься бегом	*to do (practice) running*
бегать	*to run, to jog*
ходить в баню	*to go to the bathhouse/sauna*
почти каждую неделю	*almost every week*
почти каждый день	*almost every day*
рисовать карандашом	*to draw with a pencil*
писать акварелью	*to paint with watercolors*
писать маслом	*to paint with oil paints*
хотя	*although*
даже	*even*

NOTES
The expression **ходить в баню** has a multidirectional verb **ходить**. Therefore, it denotes a general activity. You should say:

я люблю ходить в баню *(I like going to the sauna)*; я часто хожу в баню *(I often go to the sauna)*; etc.

Рисовать карандашом or писать акварелью/маслом are the expressions that you can use for drawing and painting respectively. Notice the instrumental of means without preposition: карандашом *(with a pencil)*, акварелью *(with watercolors)*, and маслом *(with oil paints)*.

NUTS & BOLTS 2
MORE ON THE VERB заниматься
In addition to the basic meanings of *physical studying* and *having an academic focus* covered in Lesson 1 above, the verb заниматься also means *to be engaged in a hobby or a sport, to practice, or to go in for*.

Я занимаюсь плаванием.
I swim. I practice swimming. I go in for swimming.

One can also заниматься живописью *(painting)*, на тренажёрах *(on fitness machines)*, бегом *(running)*, etc. Notice the instrumental case for the activity you *practice* or *go in for*. It's used there by analogy with the expression заниматься спортом *(play sports/go in for sports)*, as explained in Unit 4.

The question Чем вы занимаетесь? is ambiguous. It means either *what do you go in for* or *what are you doing?* You determine the exact meaning of the question by the context. If asked Чем вы занимались вчера вечером? *(What did you do or what were you up to last night?)*, you usually answer with an imperfective verb.

Чем вы занимались вчера вечером?
What did you do last night? What were you up to last night?

Я смотрел(а) телевизор.
I watched TV.

Я гулял(а) по городу.

I walked around the city.

Я занималась/занималая в библиотеке.

I studied in the library.

PRACTICE 3

Translate the prompts in the parentheses using the verb **заниматься**.

1. Я хожу в бассейн каждую неделю. Я _____ . *(go in for swimming)*

2. Она любит искусство и _____ в художественной школе. *(practices painting)*

3. В спортклубе я обычно _____ . *(exercise on fitness machines)*

4. Когда я училась в университете, я _____ в университетской спортивной команде. *(did running)*

5. _____ вчера вечером? Я тебе звонил, но тебя не было дома. *(What did you do)*

NUTS & BOLTS 3

THE VERB бегать

Now, let's learn another motion verb **бегать** *(to run)*. This is a multidirectional motion verb. It belongs to Conjugation I with an **ай**-stem and stable stem stress: **бегаю, бегаешь, бегают; бегал, бегала, бегали.** As all multidirectional motion verbs, it denotes a general act of running.

Я люблю бегать.

I like running/to run.

It can also denote a recurrent action.

Я бегаю каждое утро.

I run/jog every morning.

Its unidirectional counterpart is **бежать.** It's a Conjugation II verb with an **a₂**-stem with a preceding husher, **могу**-type mutation (**г** instead of **ж** in the 1st singular and 3rd plural), and stable stress: **бегу, бежишь, бегут; бежал, бежала, бежали.** As most unidirectional verbs, it creates a background in the past and future for another action.

Когда я бежал(а) на станцию, я потерял(а) ключи.
When I was running/ran to the station, I lost my keys.

It also establishes background in the present tense when the action is happening as you speak.

Куда ты бежишь?
Where are you running?

PRACTICE 4
Как сказать по-русски? Give the Russian equivalents of the following sentences.

1. Although I draw, I don't paint with oils.

2. I play sports. I even run almost every day.

3. I've never been to the Russian bathhouse.

4. What do you do in the gym? *(infml.)*

5. They study/practice painting; they even paint with watercolors.

Culture note

Applying to college in Russia is a very different procedure from that in the U.S. Only high school graduates with a diploma in hand can apply. The application process entails taking four entrance exams **(вступительные экзамены),** usually consisting of three oral exams and one written composition, which are designed and administered by the admissions office (**приёмная комиссия**) of the specific school you apply to. These exams take place from June through July. Because you need to be physically present at the school of your choice for **вступительные экзамены,** it's very difficult to apply to more than one school. In the past, it was simply impossible. So, if your school rejected you, the only option left was to wait another year. This situation has changed. Now many schools accept the results of the entrance exams from other schools, thus offering a second chance to those who weren't admitted elsewhere.

ANSWERS

PRACTICE 1: 1. учусь; **2.** изучал физику; **3.** готовилась к экзамену по химии; **4.** учили русский; **5.** занимаются; **6.** подготовилась к этому экзамену

PRACTICE 2: 1. Я слушаю курсы по русской истории. **2.** Я сдавал экзамен по математике вчера, но не сдал его. **3.** Он занимается русской литературой с самого начала. **4.** Это странный курс. Я не буду его слушать. **5.** Где вы изучали/учили русский? **6.** Мне нужно готовиться к экзамену по русскому сегодня вечером.

PRACTICE 3: 1. занимаюсь плаванием; **2.** занимается живописью; **3.** занимаюсь на тренажёрах; **4.** занималась бегом/; **5.** Чем ты занимался

PRACTICE 4: 1. Хотя я рисую, я не пишу маслом. **2.** Я занимаюсь спортом. Я даже бегаю почти каждый день. **3.** Я никогда не был в русской бане. **4.** Чем ты занимаешься в спортивном клубе (зале)?/Что ты делаешь в спортзале? **5.** Они занимаются живописью; они даже рисуют акварелью.

SENTENCE LIST 1

На каком курсе ты учишься?	*In what year are you?*
Какие курсы ты слушаешь в этом семестре?	*What courses are you taking this semester?*
Мне очень нравится курс по истории.	*I really like the course in history.*
Я люблю историю.	*I like history.*
Какой у тебя/твой любимый предмет?	*What's your favorite subject?*
Чем ты интересуешься?	*What are you interested in?*
Я интересуюсь и физикой, и русской историей.	*I'm interested both in physics and Russian history.*
Я люблю иностранные языки.	*I like foreign languages.*
Я ещё не знаю, кем я хочу работать после окончания университета.	*I don't know yet what I want to do (work as) after graduating from the university.*
Ты придёшь к нам сегодня на вечеринку?	*Will you come today (tonight) to our party?*

NOTES

Russian doesn't have one universal name for *party*. **Вечеринка** is an acceptable conversational word for an informal get together. Other types of parties will have different names in Russian: **вечер** *(soirée, formal party)*, **тусовка** *(slang, hang-out)*, **день рожденья** *(birthday party)*, **банкет** *(large party in a restaurant, banquet)*, etc.

NUTS & BOLTS 1

A REVIEW OF VERBS EXPRESSING *TO LIKE*

Let's quickly review the difference between **любить**, **нравиться**, and **понравиться** covered in Unit 4.

1. Use **любить** with the people you love: **я люблю свого мужу** (*I love my husband*); with infinitives (what you like doing): **я люблю плавать** (*I like to swim/go swimming*); with things you eat or drink: **я люблю рыбу** (*I like fish*); with aesthetic choices: **я люблю Достоевского** (*I like Dostoevsky*).

2. Use **понравиться** when you have experienced in the past (or will experience in the future) anything new and liked it (or will like it): **я познакомилась с твоим братом, и он мне понравился** (*I met your brother and liked him*); **я попробовал(а) русский борщ, и он мне понравился** (*I tasted Russian borscht and liked it*); **посмотри этот фильм, он тебе понравится** (*watch this movie, you'll like it*).

3. Use **нравиться** when you're in the middle of an experience, and you're enjoying it in the present, past or (rarely) future: **мне нравится учиться в университете** (*I like studying at the university*) vs. **я люблю учиться** (*I like studying in general*).

If you say **я люблю мороженое** or **я люблю играть в теннис**, it means *I like* rather than *I love* these things in Russian. You can't intensify *liking* by replacing it with *loving* as you do in colloquial English. So, the only option left is to intensify *liking* with an adverb *very much*.

Я очень люблю мороженое.

I love ice cream.

Я очень люблю играть в теннис.

I love playing tennis.

Твой брат мне очень понравился.

I liked your brother very much.

Мне очень нравится здесь учиться.

I like studying here very much.

Other common intensifiers of *liking* in Russian are: **особенно** (*especially*), **действительно** (*really*), and **правда** (*truly*).

The verb **интересоваться** *(to be interested in something)* takes the instrumental case.

This is an **ова**-stem verb.

Я интересуюсь музыкой.
I'm interested in music.

Ты интересуешься кино.
You're interested in film.

Они интересуются театром.
They're interested in theater.

Он интересовался русской историей.
He was interested in Russian history.

Она интересовалась экономикой.
She was interested in economics.

The appropriate question to ask will start with **чем** *(with/in what)*.

Чем ты интересуешься?
What are you interested in?

The direct construction **Что тебя интересует?** *(What interests you?)* is less idiomatic.

Any question with an interrogative can easily be integrated into a sentence as a subordinate clause, where the interrogative simply becomes a conjunction.

Кем вы хотите работать?
What would you like to do?

Вы знаете, кем вы хотите работать?
Do you know what you'd like to do?

PRACTICE 1

Say that the people below like, liked, or will like the following things. Choose the appropriate Russian verb.

1. we—the movie last night

2. I—my new job *(present)*

3. she—Russian ballet *(present)*

4. you *(formal)*—this book *(future)*

5. they—Russian borscht yesterday in a restaurant

6. he—Russian borscht

7. we—swimming and running

PRACTICE 2

Как сказать по-русски? Give the Russian equivalents of the following sentences.

1. I don't know what time your party is.

2. I'm interested in foreign languages.

3. History is my favorite subject.

4. I don't know yet where I will stay/live in Moscow.

5. She was interested both in economics and history.

SENTENCE LIST 2

Я часто хожу в спортклуб после работы.	*I often go to the gym after work.*
В выходные я люблю ходить на выставки/в театр/на концерты/в кино/в клуб.	*On weekends, I like going to exhibitions/to the theater/to concerts/to the movies/to a club.*
Это очень удобно.	*This is very convenient.*
Для меня это неважно.	*It doesn't matter to me. (lit., It's not important for me.)*

Это очень полезно для здоровья.	This is very good for you (lit., useful for your health).
Ты не знаешь, есть ли там бассейн?	Do you (happen to) know, whether there's a swimming pool?
Там нет бассейна.	There's no swimming pool there.
В детстве я занимался/ занималась фотографией.	When I was I kid (lit., in childhood), photography was my hobby (I did photography).
Я буду рад(а) показать вам свои фотографии.	I'd be happy to show you my photographs.

NUTS & BOLTS 2

EXPRESSING *WHETHER OR NOT*

Look at the sentence **Ты не знаешь, есть ли там бассейн.** When the subordinate clause is a general question (not a question with an interrogative as in the sentence group 1 above), you need to make an inversion framed by the interrogative particle **ли** *(whether)* in order to turn it into a subordinate clause. This is how it works: in the first place, you put the word in question or **есть** *(is there* or *is there not);* the particle **ли** always goes second; and then follows the rest of the clause.

Let's consider one more example. If you need to say *I don't know whether he lives there,* you need first to determine which one out of the three words is in question: is it *he, lives,* or *there.* All three technically can be in question and emphasized.

Я не знаю, он ли живёт там.

I don't know whether he (or somebody else) lives there.

Я не знаю, живёт ли он там.

I don't know whether he lives (or works) there.

Я не знаю, там ли он живёт.

I don't know whether he lives there (or some place else).

Once you make up your mind, you put the word in question in the first position. Depending on your choice, the final result can be one of the three above. Most of the time, however, questions focus on the verb; consequently, it usually takes the first position.

PRACTICE 3

Integrate the following questions into the principle clause **я не знаю, . . .** (*I don't know whether . . .*). Choose the most logical word to be the focus of your question.

1. Он любит ходить на выставки?

2. Это удобно?

3. Там есть ресторан?

4. Это полезно для здоровья?

5. Она занималась в детстве музыкой?

6. Они часто ходят в театр?

NUTS & BOLTS 3

THE USE OF ЭТО + ADVERB

Notice the use of **это** + *adverb* in the sentences: **Это удобно** *(this is convenient);* **Это неважно** *(this is not important);* and **Это полезно** *(this is useful/healthy).* Learn to differentiate **это** from the pronouns **он, она, оно, они,** which substitute the specific nouns mentioned earlier and require adjectives rather than adverbs.

Я купил(а) бананы. Они полезные.
I bought bananas. They are healthy.

In this case, **они** replaces the specific noun **бананы**.

Я часто ем бананы. Это полезно.
I often eat bananas. This is healthy.

Here, **это** refers to the entire sentence rather than to one noun.

PRACTICE 4

Как сказать по-русски? Provide the Russian equivalents of the following sentences.

1. There's no gym there. It doesn't matter to me.

2. When I was a kid, I often went to concerts.

3. Vegetables are very good for (your) health.

4. I'll be glad to show you my photographs.

5. Do you know where they go after work? *(infml.)*

Tip!

The rule regarding the proper use of the *whether* construction in Russian is easier to understand than to remember. This is so because in English you use *whether* and *if* interchangeably. This, however, is not the case in Russian. *Whether* (**ли**) requires an inversion in the subordinate clause, whereas *if* is merely translated as **если** (+ the future tense when needed). In order to keep this distinction in mind, learn to differentiate *whether* and *if* in English and link one with **ли** and the other with **если.** For example, instead of saying *I don't know if there's a swimming pool,* say *I don't know whether there's a swimming pool.* This device will help you remember to do the inversion in Russian every time you say *whether* in English.

ANSWERS

PRACTICE 1: 1. Нам понравился фильм вчера вечером. **2.** Мне нравится моя новая работа. **3.** Она любит русский балет./Ей нравится русский балет. **4.** Вам понравится эта книга. **5.** Им понравился русский борщ вчера в ресторане. **6.** Он любит русский борщ./Ему нравится русский борщ. **7.** Мы любим плавать и бегать./Нам нравится плавать и бегать.

PRACTICE 2: 1. Я не знаю, во сколько Ваша вечеринка.
2. Я интересуюсь иностранными языками. 3. История–
мой любимый предмет. 4. Я ещё не знаю, где я буду жить в
Москве. 5. Она интересовалась и экономикой, и историей.

PRACTICE 3: 1. Я не знаю, любит ли он ходить на
выставки. 2. Я не знаю, удобно ли это. 3. Я не знаю, есть
ли там ресторан. 4. Я не знаю, полезно ли это для
здоровья. 5. Я не знаю, занималась ли она в детстве
музыкой. 6. Я не знаю, часто ли они ходят в театр.

PRACTICE 4: 1. Там нет спортклуба. Для меня это
неважно. 2. В детстве я часто ходил на концерты. 3. Овощи
очень полезны для здоровья. 4. Я буду рад показать тебе
мои фотографии. 5. Ты не знаешь, куда они идут/ходят
после работы?

─────── Lesson 40 (Conversations) ───────

CONVERSATION 1

An American exchange student in Russia, Justin Pratt, is speaking
with a Russian fellow student, Zhanna Gromova, at the university. They're discussing their current academic interests and plans
for the future.

Жанна:	**На каком курсе ты учишься?**
Джастин:	**У себя в Америке, я учился на третьем курсе, а здесь учусь на втором.**
Жанна:	**Тебе нравится учиться у нас?**
Джастин:	**Мне нравятся все курсы, которые я слушаю. Но особенно мне нравится курс по русской истории.**
Жанна:	**А в Америке ты тоже занимался русской историей?**
Джастин:	**Нет, в Америке я изучал физику и математику и только начал изучать русский язык.**

Жанна: Ты больше не хочешь быть физиком?

Джастин: Я интересуюсь и физикой, и русской историей. Но я ещё не решил, что выберу для будущей профессии.

Жанна: Это очень странно. Вот я, например, знала, что я хочу заниматься историей и преподавать с самого начала. Поэтому я поступала на исторический факультет.

Джастин: Когда я окончу университет, я пойду работать. А через год после этого я буду поступать в аспирантуру, чтобы учиться дальше. Тогда посмотрим.

Жанна: Ты придёшь сегодня к нам на вечеринку?

Джастин: Да, конечно. Там и увидимся.

Zhanna: *What year are you in?*

Justin: *At home, in America, I was a junior (lit., in the third year), but here I'm a sophomore (lit., in the second year).*

Zhanna: *Do you like studying here?*

Justin: *I like all of the courses I'm taking. But especially I enjoy the course in Russian history.*

Zhanna: *Did you also study Russian history in America?*

Justin: *No, in America, I studied physics and math, and just began to study Russian language.*

Zhanna: *So you no longer want to become a physicist?*

Justin: *I'm interested in both physics and Russian history. But I haven't decided yet, what I'll choose for my future profession.*

Zhanna: *This is very strange. Take me, for example. I knew that I wanted to study history and teach from the very start. This is why I applied to the History Department.*

Justin: *When I graduate, I am going to work. And a year after that, I'll apply to a grad school to study more. Then we'll see.*

Zhanna: *Are you coming to our party tonight?*

Justin: *Yes, of course. I'll see you there.*

Notice the use of **к нам** and **у нас** in this conversation (see also Unit 4). This is a very common way of saying *at our place*, whatever this place is. So, when Zhanna asks **Ты придёшь к нам на вечеринку?** *(Will you come to our party?)*, it literally means *to the party at our place* or *to us for a party*. The question **Тебе нравится у нас?** means anything from *Do you like it by us?* to *Do you like it here?* Of course, we know by the context that Zhanna is talking about their university.

Вот я, например, is an idiomatic and conversational way of saying *take me, for example*. Literally, it means *here's I, for example*. You can use this phrase with all nouns and pronouns: **вот мой отец, например,** *(take my father, for example)* or **вот она, например,** *(take her, for example)*, etc.

NUTS & BOLTS 1
SEQUENCE OF TENSES

Notice the tenses in the Russian sentence: **Я знал, что я хочу заниматься историей** *(I _knew_ that I _want_ to study history)*. What looks like a disagreement from the English perspective is in fact the norm in Russian. Russian has no sequence of tenses. Therefore, you can and should use the tense of the direct speech. The present or future tense can be easily embedded in the past tense context. In other words, you may say: *he _knew_ that he _is_* or *she _knew_ that she _will be_*.

Я знал(а), что он студент.

I knew that he was (lit., is) a student.

Я знал(а), что он будет в Москве летом.

I knew that he would (lit., will) be in Moscow in the summer.

PRACTICE 1

Integrate the following clauses into the past tense context. Remember not to follow the English sequence of tenses.

1. Я ей сказала, что *(I will go to the museum on Friday)*.

2. Он всегда знал, что *(he will become a doctor)*.

3. Он нам рассказал, что *(he will study in Moscow in the Physics Department)*.

4. Они написали нам, что *(they study Russian)*.

5. Она ответила, что *(she doesn't know)*.

NUTS & BOLTS 2

EXPRESSING *SO, ALL, SOME, MANY, NONE,* AND *EVERY*

The conjunction **поэтому** (see Unit 4) can be translated as *therefore, this is why,* or *so.* Be sure to use it instead of translating *so* literally as **так.** The latter is used only as an adverbial intensifier.

Это так хорошо.
This is so good.

Also, learn to differentiate **так** from the adjectival *so*—**такой, такая, такое, такие** in all cases.

Они такие хорошие.
They are so good.

Notice the phrase **все курсы.** First of all, remember the difference between **всё** (sg., *everything*) and **все** (pl., *all*). Then, remember that the Russian **все** stands for the two possible ways of saying in English *all + noun* and *all of + noun:* **все курсы** *(all courses, all of the courses),* **все студенты** *(all students, all of the students),* **все города** *(all cities, all of the cities),* etc. When you mention *a part of the group* rather than *the entire group,* you simply follow the similar English construction: **некоторые из студентов** *(some of the students),* **многие из студентов** *(many of the students),* **никто из студентов** *(none of the students),* **каждый из студентов** *(every one of the students),* etc.

PRACTICE 2

Как сказать по-русски? Give the Russian equivalents of the following English sentences.

1. All of the students will come to our party.

2. She knew that she wanted to study history. This is why she applied to the History Department.

3. Take, for example, my grandfather; he always said that it was important to study Russian.

4. This is such an interesting course!

5. I read all of the books on this subject. *(past)*

CONVERSATION 2

Zinaida Gurevich has recently started her new job at a bank in Moscow. She's going out to lunch with one of her new coworkers, Leonid Lunin. To get to know each other a little better, they talk about their extramural interests and hobbies.

Леонид:	Вы знаете, напротив нашей работы есть хороший спортивный клуб. Я часто хожу туда после работы заниматься спортом. Это очень удобно.
Зина:	Вы не знаете, есть ли там бассейн?
Леонид:	Нет, бассейна нет, но для меня это не важно. Я там занимаюсь на тренажёрах, бегаю и хожу в баню или в сауну.
Зина:	А я обычно плаваю. Я в детстве занималась плаванием и с тех пор продолжаю ходить в бассейн два-три раза в неделю.
Леонид:	Плавать—очень полезно. А чем ещё вы занимаетесь в свободное время?
Зина:	Я больше никаким спортом не занимаюсь. Только люблю гулять по городу и много ходить пешком. Но я очень люблю театр.
Леонид:	Оперу или балет?

Зина: Нет, драматический театр. Хотя музыку я тоже люблю и даже играю на пианино. Но почти каждую неделю, в выходные, я хожу в театр на какой-нибудь спектакль.

Леонид: А я больше люблю ходить на выставки. Я в детстве занимался живописью и даже ходил в художественную школу. Я и сейчас немного рисую и пишу акварелью.

Зина: Очень интересно! Я бы хотела посмотреть!

Леонид: Приходите ко мне в гости, я буду рад показать их вам.

Зина: С удовольствием!

Leonid: Do you know that there's a good gym across from our work. I often go there after work to work out. It's very convenient.

Zina: Would you know if there's a swimming pool?

Leonid: No, there's no swimming pool, but it doesn't matter to me. I work out on exercise machines, run/jog, and go to the sauna.

Zina: And I usually swim. I went in for swimming when I was a kid, ever since, I've continued going to the pool two to three times a week.

Leonid: Swimming is good for you. What else do you do with your free time?

Zina: I don't do/play any other sports. I just like wandering around the city and walking a lot (on foot). But I like theater very much.

Leonid: Opera or ballet?

Zina: Actually, drama theater. Although I like music too and even play the piano. But almost every week, on weekends, I go to the theater to see a play.

Leonid: I like going to exhibitions better. When I was a kid, I studied/practiced painting and even went to an art school. Even now, I draw a bit and paint with watercolors.

Zina: Oh, how interesting! I'd like to see (them).

> Leonid: *Come to see me (at home). I'd be glad to show them to you.*
>
> Zina: *With pleasure!*

NOTES

Notice that the Russian motion verb **ходить** is similar to the English *to go* in the sense of *attending* and *frequenting*. So, like in English, you should say in Russian: **я хожу в спортивный зал** *(I go to the gym)*; **я хожу в баню** *(I go to the sauna)*; **я хожу в какой-нибудь театр** *(I go to a theater)*.

The indefinite particle **-нибудь** in the last phrase is added to the adjectival interrogative **какой**. Together they mean *some* or *some kind of*. The first part **какой** is used there because it modifies the noun **театр**; the second part **-нибудь** is used regardless that this is a statement (see Unit 5), because it *doesn't matter at all what theater I go to*.

Notice the genitive of negation (see Unit 6) in the sentence: **Там нет бассейна** *(there's no swimming pool there)*.

The verb **продолжать** *(conj. I; ай)*—**продолжить** *(conj. II; и)* means *to continue* (see also Unit 6). It can either take the infinitive: **продолжать ходить в бассейн** *(continue to go to the swimming pool)*, or a noun: **продолжить разговор** *(continue a conversation)*. The idiomatic phrase **продолжайте, пожалуйста** means *go on please* or *continue please*.

The preposition **напротив** *(across from)* takes the genitive case in Russian. So, you should say: **напротив входа в метро** *(across from the metro entrance)*, **напротив работы** *(across from work)*, **напротив музея** *(across from the museum)*, etc.

NUTS & BOLTS 3
EXPRESSING *SINCE* AND *NO LONGER*
The expression **с тех пор** *(since then)* consists of the preposition **с**, *the genitive plural of the noun* **пора** *(time, season)*, and *the genitive*

plural of the adjective **та** *(that)*. So, it literally means *from those times*. You can also use the noun **пора** adverbially, as in English, when you say *it's time to do something*.

Мне пора идти домой.
It's time for me to go home.

Нам пора спать.
It's time for us to go to bed.

No longer or *no more* is **больше не** in Russian.

Я больше не играю на пианино.
I no longer play the piano.

Они больше не живут в Москве.
They no longer live in Moscow.

In the sentence **Я больше никаким спортом не занимаюсь** *(I don't play/do any other [any more] kinds of sports)*, **больше не** means essentially the same thing, except that it limits the kinds of sports you play rather than the duration of the action proper.

PRACTICE 3
Say that the people below no longer do the following things.

1. моя дочь—ходить в художественную школу

2. она—заниматься живописью

3. мы—ходить в бассейн

4. он—писать акварелью

5. я—любить оперу

NUTS & BOLTS 4
THE VERB хотеть AND PERFECTIVE INFINITIVES
Notice the perfective aspect of the infinitive **посмотреть** *(to look, take a look)* in the following sentence.

Я бы хотел(а) посмотреть.

I would like to take a look.

As a rule of thumb, the verb **хотеть** always takes perfective infinitives. This is so because whatever you want is a new thing, and newness (change of state) usually requires perfective verbs in Russian (see Unit 6). The exceptions from this rule are obvious: every time you have an indication that what you want is a recurrent action, that is, when the following infinitive is accompanied by one of the adverbs that denote recurrence, then the infinitive should clearly be imperfective.

Я хочу вам помочь.

I want to help you.

Я хочу вам помогать каждую пятницу.

I want to help you every Friday.

Я хочу вам помогать всегда.

I want to help you always.

Я хочу вам помогать всё лето.

I want to help you for the whole summer.

In other words, you should consider perfective as the default aspect after the verb **хотеть** and imperfective as an exception—the one that is more difficult to miss.

PRACTICE 4

Say that you'd like to do the following things using **я хотел(а) бы.** Choose the correct form of the infinitives below. The imperfective infinitives are given first.

1. покупать/купить билеты на концерт

2. идти/пойти на новую выставку

3. фотографировать/сфотографировать Красную площадь

4. фотографировать/сфотографировать весь день во время экскурсии

5. смотреть/посмотреть новый фильм

6. продолжать/продолжить заниматься плаванием два-три раза в неделю

PRACTICE 5
Как сказать по-русски? Give the Russian equivalents of the following sentences.

1. The theater is located across from the museum.

2. I'd like to buy two tickets to the opera.

3. I started learning Russian in college (university), and I've continued studying it ever since.

4. I no longer play sports.

5. Let's go to some kind of exhibition!

Discovery activity

Где вы учились? Какие курсы вы слушали? Какие курсы были ваши любимые? Кем и где вы работаете? Чем вы любите заниматься в свободное время? Расскажите обо всём этом по-русски. Imagine that you are being interviewed in Russia. Say as much as you can about where and what you studied, where you work, and what you like to do at your leisure.

ANSWERS
PRACTICE 1: 1. Я ей сказала, что я пойду в музей в пятницу. **2.** Он всегда знал, что он станет врачом. **3.** Он нам рассказал, что он будет учиться в Москве на физическом факультете. **4.** Они написали нам, что они учат русский. **5.** Она ответила, что она не знает.

PRACTICE 2: 1. Все студенты придут к нам на вечеринку (на нашу вечеринку). **2.** Она знала, что она хотела изучать историю. Поэтому она поступала на исторический факультет. **3.** Вот, например, мой дедушка, он всегда говорил, что важно учить/изучать русский язык. **4.** Это такой интересный курс! **5.** Я прочитал(а) все книги об этом предмете.

PRACTICE 3: 1. Моя дочь больше не ходит в художественную школу. **2.** Она больше не занимается живописью. **3.** Мы больше не ходим в бассейн. **4.** Он больше не пишет акварелью. **5.** Я больше не люблю оперу.

PRACTICE 4: 1. Я хотел(а) бы купить билеты на концерт. **2.** Я хотел(а) бы пойти на новую выставку. **3.** Я хотел(а) бы сфотографировать Красную площадь. **4.** Я хотел(а) бы фотографировать весь день во время экскурсии. **5.** Я хотел(а) бы посмотреть новый фильм. **6.** Я хотел(а) бы продолжать заниматься плаванием два-три раза в неделю.

PRACTICE 5: 1. Театр находится напротив музея. **2.** Я бы хотел(а)/хочу купить два билета на оперу. **3.** Я начал(а) изучать русский в колледже (университете), с тех пор я продолжаю его изучать. **4.** Я больше не занимаюсь спортом. **5.** Давай(те) пойдём на какую-нибудь выставку!

UNIT 10 ESSENTIALS

Я учусь на третьем курсе.	*I study in (the) third year.*
Я учусь на химическом факультете.	*I study in the Chemistry Department/School.*
Я ещё в детстве знал, что хочу стать химиком.	*Since I was a kid, I knew that I wanted to become a chemist.*
Я слушаю курс по физике.	*I'm taking a course in physics.*
Мне нравятся все курсы, которые я слушаю.	*I like all of the courses I'm taking.*
Я интересуюсь математикой.	*I'm interested in math.*
Я учу русский язык.	*I study Russian.*

Я изучаю экономику.	*I study economics.*
Я раньше занимался/ занималась русской историей.	*I used to study (focus on) Russian history.*
Я занимаюсь плаванием два-три раза в неделю.	*I swim (go in for swimming) two-three times a week.*
Я больше не занимаюсь никаким спортом.	*I no longer play any other sports.*
Вы не знаете, есть ли там бассейн?	*Would you know, whether there's a pool?*
Я поступал(а) и поступил(а) в Московский университет.	*I applied to Moscow University and was admitted.*
Я больше люблю ходить на выставки.	*I like going to exhibitions better.*
Я бы хотел(а) посмотреть ваши фотографии.	*I'd like to see your photographs.*

Станция метро «Маяковская» (линия 3)		
Выход в город к Московскому вокзалу ←	Переход на станцию «Пл. Восстания» (линию 1) в центре зала, вниз по эскалатору К поездам до станций: «Девяткино», «Гражданский проспект», «Академическая», «Политехническая», «Пл. Мужества», «Лесная», «Пл. Ленина» (Финляндский вокзал), «Чернышевская», «Пл. Восстания», «Лиговский пр.», «Пушкинская», «Технологический институт», «Балтийская» (Балтийский вокзал), «Нарвская», «Кировский Завод», «Автово», «Пр. Ветеранов»	Выход в город на Невский пр. и ул. Восстания →

Mayakovskaya Metro Station

Exit to the city toward the Moscow train station ←	Transfer to the Vosstaniya Square station (Line 1), in the center of the hall, down the escalator Toward the stations: Devyatkino, Grazhdansky Avenue, Akademicheskaya, Politechnicheskaya, Muzhestva Sq., Lesnaya, Lenin Sq. (Finlyandsky train station), Chernishevskaya, Vosstania Sq., Ligovsky Ave., Pushkinskaya, Technological Institute, Baltiskaya (Baltiskaya train station), Narvskaya, Kirovsky factory, Avtovo, Veteranov Ave.	Exit to the city to Nevsky Prospect (Avenue) and Vosstania Street →

VOCABULARY

станция	station
линия	line
выход	exit
переход	transfer
вокзал	train station
поезд	train
пл. (площадь)	square

пр. (проспект)	*avenue*
ул. (улица)	*street*
завод	*factory*

Please answer the following questions—in English—based on the above text.

1. What is the name of this metro station?
2. Where should you go if you need to exit this metro station?
3. Where should you go if you need to be on Nevsky Prospect?
4. Where should you go if you need to be at the Moscow train station?
5. Where should you go if you need to make a transfer to Line 1?
6. Where do you need to go if you need to be on Ligovsky Avenue?
7. How can you reach the Finlyandsky train station?

ANSWERS

1. Mayakovskaya; 2. exit the station either on the left or right; 3. exit the station on the right only; 4. exit the station on the left only; 5. make a transfer in the middle of the station, down the escalator; 6. make a transfer onto Line 1 (in the middle of the station, down the escalator) up to the station «Лиговский пр.»; 7. make a transfer onto Line 1 (in the middle of the station, down the escalator) up to the station «Пл. Ленина» (Финляндский вокзал)

———————— Russian in Action 2 ————————

Бизнес-ланч в нашем ресторане—только 290 руб.

Бизнес-ланч меню ежедневно с 12–00 до 15–00, кроме субботы и воскресенья

<u>Закуски (одна на выбор)</u>

Салат «Греческий»

Салат из свежих помидоров и огурцов со сметаной

Салат «Столичный»

Салат из крабов

<u>Супы (один на выбор)</u>

Борщ холодный

Суп грибной

Щи домашние

Уха (рыбный суп)

<u>Основные блюда (одно на выбор)</u>

Шашлык из свинины

Стейк из лосося с гарниром

Блины с красной икрой или сёмгой

<u>Десерты (один на выбор)</u>

Яблочный штрудель

Мороженое в ассортименте

<u>Напитки</u>

Кофе: американо, эспрессо или каппуччино

Чай: чёрный или зелёный

Минеральная вода: с газом или без газа

Business lunch in our restaurant—only 290 rubles

Business lunch menu daily from 12:00 to 3:00 p.m. except Saturdays and Sundays

Appetizers (choose one)

Greek salad

Fresh salad with tomatoes, cucumbers, and sour cream

Stolichnyi salad

Crab salad

Soups (choose one)

Cold borscht (beet soup)

Mushroom soup

Homemade shchi (cabbage soup)

Oukha (fish soup)

Entrées (choose one)

Pork shish kebab

Salmon steak with a side

Crepes with salmon roe or lox

Desserts (choose one)

Apple strudel

Assorted ice creams

Beverages (choose one)

Coffee: americano, espresso, or cappuccino

Tea: black or green

Mineral water: plain or carbonated

VOCABULARY

бизнес-ланч	_business lunch_
салат «Греческий»	_Greek salad_
салат «Столичный»	_"Capital" salad (potato salad)_
сметана	_sour cream_
краб	_crab_
свежий	_fresh_
грибной _(adj.)_	_mushroom_
гриб _(noun)_	_mushroom_
шашлык	_shish kebab_
стейк	_steak_
сёмга, лосось	_salmon (two kinds of), lox_
с гарниром	_with a side dish_
яблочный штрудель	_apple strudel_
мороженое	_ice cream_
в ассортименте	_assorted_
руб. (рубля/рублей)	_ruble(s)_
кроме	_except_
ежедневно	_daily_

Try to look just at the Russian menu and answer the following questions in English.

1. When is this menu available?

2. What should you order if you'd like tomatoes and sour cream?

3. What would you order if you'd like a cold soup?

4. What would you order if you'd like some meat (but not fish) for an entrée?

5. What desserts are available?

6. What coffee drinks are available?

7. Do they have green tea?

ANSWERS

1. It's available daily from 12:00 to 3:00 p.m. except Saturdays and Sundays. 2. свежий салат из помидоров и огурцов со сметаной *(fresh salad with tomatoes, cucumbers, and sour cream);* 3. холодный борщ *(cold borscht);* 4. шашлык из свинины *(pork shish kebab);* 5. apple strudel and assorted ice creams; 6. americano, espresso, and cappuccino; 7. Yes, they do.

——————— Russian in Action 3 ———————

Прогноз погоды на неделю с 9 по 15 июля

понедельник	днём +20–23 °C, ночью +15–16 °C, переменная облачность с прояснениями, возможен кратковременный дождь, влажность воздуха до 60%
вторник	днём +22–24 °C, ночью +16–17 °C, солнечно, без осадков, сильный ветер во второй половине дня
среда	днём +19–21 °C, ночью +13–15 °C, облачно с прояснениями, ветер порывистый, вероятность дождя 60%

четверг	днём +18–20 °С, ночью +11–13 °С, пасмурно, местами с прояснениями, вероятность дождя 30%
пятница	днём +21–23 °С, ночью +16°С, солнечно, без осадков
суббота	днём до +25 °С, ночью +14–17 °С, переменная облачность, без осадков
воскресенье	днём +21–22 °С, ночью +14–15 °С, переменная облачность, кратковременный дождь, возможно с грозой, влажность воздуха до 70%

Seven-Day Forecast, July 9–15

Monday	*in the afternoon +20–23 °C, at night +15–16 °C, partly sunny with clearings, possible showers, humidity up to 60%*
Tuesday	*in the afternoon +22–24 °C, at night +16–17 °C, sunny, no precipitation, strong winds in the second part of the day*
Wednesday	*in the afternoon +19–21 °C, at night +13–15 °C, cloudy with clearings, gusty winds, probability of rain 60%*
Thursday	*in the afternoon +18–20 °C, at night +11–13 °C, overcast with some clearings, probability of rain 30%*
Friday	*in the afternoon +21–23 °C, at night +16°C, sunny, no precipitation*
Saturday	*in the afternoon up to +25 °C, at night +14–17 °C, partly sunny, no precipitation*

Sunday	in the afternoon +21–22 °C, at night +14–15 °C, partly sunny, showers, possible thunderstorm, humidity up to 70%

VOCABULARY

осадки	*precipitation*
кратковременный дождь	*passing showers*
гроза	*thunderstorm*
солнечно	*sunny*
пасмурно	*overcast*
переменная облачность	*partly sunny*
облачно	*cloudy*
ветер порывистый/ сильный	*gusty/strong winds*
влажность воздуха	*humidity*
вероятность	*probability*
с прояснениями	*with clearings*
возможно	*possible*
до + *genitive*	*up to*

Answer the following questions in English based on the weather report above.

1. When is there rain in this forecast?

2. When is the warmest day of this week?

3. When is the coldest night of this week?

4. What are the cloudless days in this forecast?

5. When is there wind in this forecast?

6. What is the forecast for Friday?

ANSWERS

1.Monday, Wednesday, Thursday, and Sunday; 2. Saturday; 3. Thursday night; 4. Tuesday and Friday; 5. Tuesday and Wednesday; 6. +21–23 °C in the afternoon, +16 °C at night, sunny, no precipitation

---
Russian in Action 4

Аренда рабочего места в нашем интернет-кафе ежедневно с 7.00 до 24.00

1 час	140–00 руб.
1 час для студентов	90–00 руб.
1 час для постоянных клиентов	90–00 руб.

Внимание: на каждый следующий час—20–00 руб. скидка

Подключение к Интернету через WiFi

1 час	70–00 руб.
2 часа	120–00 руб.
5 часов	300–00 руб.

Внимание: действие пакета до 10-ти дней

Тарифы flat rate

1 день	400–00 руб.
1 неделя	2000–00 руб.
1 месяц	7000–00 руб.
1 неделя утром—с 7.00 до 12.00	900–00 руб.
1 неделя днём и вечером—с 12.00 до 24.00	1200–00 руб.
проверка почты—1 неделя по 30 минут в день	280–00 руб.
проверка почты для студентов—1 неделя по 30 мин. в день	200–00 руб.

Прочие услуги Интернет-кафе

сканирование	1 стр.—30–00 руб.
чёрно-белая печать/ копирование	1 стр.—5–00 руб. 1 стр. для студентов—3–00 руб.
печать цветная	1 стр.—50–00 руб.
запись информации	на наш CD—120–00 руб. на наш DVD—150–00 руб.
отправка факса (1 стр.)	по городу—20–00 руб. по России—45–00 руб. заграницу—90–00 руб.
приём факса (1 стр.)	20–00 руб.

Renting a computer with internet access in our internet café daily from 7:00 a.m. to 12:00 a.m.

1 hour	*140.00 rubles*
1 hour for students	*90.00 rubles*
1 hour for regular customers	*90.00 rubles*

Attention: there is a 20 ruble discount for every additional hour

Internet access via WiFi

1 hour	*70.00 rubles*
2 hours	*120.00 rubles*
5 hours	*300.00 rubles*

Attention: the packages are valid for up to 10 days

Flat rate tariffs

1 day	*400.00 rubles*
1 week	*2000.00 rubles*
1 month	*7000.00 rubles*
1 week from 7:00 a.m. to 12 p.m.	*900.00 rubles*
1 week from 12 p.m. to 12 a.m.	*1200.00 rubles*
checking e-mail—1 week, 30 min. per day	*280.00 rubles*

checking e-mail for students—1 week, 30 min. per day	*200.00 rubles*

Other internet café services

scanning	*1 page—30.00 rubles*
black-and-white printing/copying	*1 page—5.00 rubles* *1 page for students—3.00 rubles*
printing in color	*1 page—50.00 rubles*
burning	*our CD—120.00 rubles* *our DVD—150.00 rubles*
sending fax (1 page)	*in the city—20.00 rubles* *in Russia—45.00 rubles* *abroad—90.00 rubles*
receiving fax (1 page)	*20.00 rubles*

VOCABULARY

аренда рабочего места	*renting internet access (lit., renting a working space)*
ежедневно	*daily*
для постоянных клиентов	*for regular customers*
внимание	*attention*
на каждый следующий час	*for each additional hour*
скидка	*discount*
действие	*valid (lit., action)*
пакет	*package (lit., packet)*
до 10-ти дней	*up to 10 days*

проверка почты	*checking e-mail*
по 30 мин. (минут) в день	*30 minutes per day*
прочие услуги	*other services*
сканирование	*scanning*
черно-белая печать	*black-and-white printing*
копирование	*copying*
цветной	*in color (lit., colored)*
запись информации	*recording information, burning*
факс	*fax*
отправка	*sending*
приём	*receiving*
1 стр. (страница)	*1 p. (page)*
1 мин. (минута)	*1 min. (minute)*
1 руб. (рубль)	*1 ruble*
по городу	*in the city*
по России	*in Russia*
заграницу	*abroad (direction)*

Please answer the following questions in English.

1. How much does one hour of internet access with a student discount cost?

2. What is the discount per each additional hour?

3. How much do two hours of WiFi cost?

4. How many days is the five-hour WiFi package good for?

5. How much does the package for one month of unlimited access cost?

6. What is the best package if you're a student staying in Russia for one week and you need to briefly check your e-mail on a daily basis?

7. How much would it cost you to transfer your digital pictures from your camera to a CD provided by the café?

8. How much would it cost you to print out one page in color?

9. How much would it cost you to send a one-page fax from this café to the U.S.?

ANSWERS
1. 90 rubles; **2.** 20 rubles; **3.** 120 rubles; **4.** for 10 days; **5.** 7,000 rubles; **6.** one week of 30-min.-per-day e-mail checking is 200 rubles for students/проверка почты для студентов—1 неделя по 30 мин. в день—200–00 руб.; **7.** 120 rubles; **8.** 50 rubles; **9.** 90 rubles

--------------------- Letter and e-mail writing ---------------------

A. A NOTE ON LETTER WRITING
Both in formal and informal writing, the addressee's name, title, and postal address usually appear only on the envelope. In formal letters, an institution's name and address often appear at the top of the document, while the date is found at the bottom of the page. Since the demise of the Soviet Union, the form of address in formal writing has changed. Instead of writing to a *comrade* (**товарищ**), Russians now write to *Mr.* or *Ms.* (**господин, госпожа**). The abbreviated forms are **г-н** (or simply **г.**) for *Mr.* and **г-жа** for *Ms.* In formal writing the use of a title is common, and if one wants to write to editorial offices of newspapers or journals, the phrase *Dear editorial board* (**Уважаемая редакция**) is commonly used.

The abbreviated form of the date differs from the one used in the United States. December 20, 2008, for example, is written as **20–12–08** or as **20/XII/08**. Address writing is often different as well, though this is constantly in flux as Russians switch to an international style of address writing. Traditionally, however, Russians began with the city on the first line, write the street and house number, then apartment number, on the second, and on the third line, the name of the addressee (in dative case). This has almost been replaced completely with the American or international style.

B. BUSINESS LETTERS

Всероссийское
издательство
«Наука»
Отдел по
международным
связям
г. Москва 157332
ул. Петрова, д. 8

Уважаемый г. Степанов!
Мы получили Ваш заказ на доставку последних номеров журнала «Континент». К сожалению, в связи с повышением почтовых тарифов, мы не смогли отправить заказ вовремя. Поставка журналов ожидается в первых числах ноября.

С уважением,
Г. И. Аполлонов
директор отдела по международным связям

12 октября 2008[1] г.
г. Москва

---

[1] The date may also follow the addressee's address.

All-Russian Publishing
House "Nauka"
Section on Foreign
Affairs
Moskva 157332
Petrova St. 8

Dear Mr. Stepanov,
We have received your order to deliver the latest issues of the magazine
Kontinent. Unfortunately, due to the increases in postal tariffs, we
could not send you your order on time. The delivery of the issues is
expected in early November.

Sincerely,
G. I. Apollonov
Director of the Section
on
Foreign Affairs

October 12, 2008
Moscow

Совместное
предприятие «Роза»
г. Москва 122771
ул. Васнецова, д. 2

Уважаемый г. Кожинов!
Отвечаем на Ваш запрос о возможности установить
торговые связи с Германией. К сожалению, в настоящее
время мы не в состоянии помочь Вам в этом деле. Наше
предприятие не уполномочено действовать в качестве
посредника между западными и русскими фирмами.

С уважением,
Н. И. Сошников
директор

13/XI/08
г. Москва

Joint Venture "Rose"
Moskva 122771
Vasnetsova St. 2

Dear Mr. Kozhinov,
This is in response to your inquiry about the possibility of establishing
trade contacts with Germany. Unfortunately, we are unable to help you
with this issue. Our business is not authorized to act as a mediator
between Western and Russian firms.

Sincerely,
N. I. Soshnikov
Director

November 13, 2008
Moscow

C. INFORMAL LETTERS

27–10–08

Дорогой Иван!

Наконец, приехал в Псков. С билетами было трудно, но в конце концов Ирина достала, и даже на скорый поезд. В общем, могу взяться за работу. Директор нашёл неплохую квартиру. Наверное, действительно хотят, чтобы мне было удобно. Жалко, что не успели поговорить в Москве, но в ноябре собираюсь приехать и, конечно, позвоню.

Скучаю по московским друзьям.

Не забывай. Пиши!

Сергей

10–27–08

Dear Ivan,

I have finally arrived in Pskov. There was difficulty with the tickets, but, in the end, Irina managed to get them and even for an express train. So, I can get down to work. The director found a decent apartment (for me). It seems they really want to make me comfortable. Too bad we didn't have time to talk in Moscow, but I plan to come in November and will call you, of course.

I miss my Moscow friends.

Don't forget me. Write!

Sergei

Дорогая Наташа!

Давно уже не получаю от тебя писем и очень беспокоюсь о родителях. Как здоровье отца? Собирается мама уходить на пенсию или опять откладывает? Позвони мне на работу, домашний телефон ещё не подключили.

Девочки растут, Марина пошла в первый класс. Таня даёт ей советы.

Все у нас хорошо. Миша передаёт привет. Надеюсь увидеть всех вас на праздники.

Целую,
ваша Галя

11–17–08

Dear Natasha,

I have not received letters from you in a while, and I worry a lot about our parents. How is Father's health? Is Mom going to retire, or is she delaying again? Call me at work: our home phone has not yet been connected.

The girls are growing. Marina started first grade. Tania gives her advice.

Everything is fine with us. Misha sends regards. I hope to see all of you for the holidays.

Kisses,
Your Galia

D. FORM OF THE ENVELOPE

The American format of the envelope is almost all you'll see now in Russia, with the sender's name *(gen.)* and address in the upper left corner, and the addressee's name *(dat.)* and address in the lower right corner.

Г. И. Синицына
ул. Королёва, д.15, кв. 33
г. Новосибирск 308970

Семеновой Наталье Ивановне
ул. Кураева, д.1, кв.75
г. Ставрополь
324560

G. I. Sinitsina
Koroleva 15, apt.33
Novosibirsk 308970

Semenova Natalia Ivanovna
Kuraeva 1, apt.75
Stavropol
324560

E. E-MAILS

When Russians write e-mails or create websites, they follow the American format.

Дата:	среда, 9 августа 2008
От кого:	Сидоровская Юлия \<sarabumba@mail.ru\>
Кому:	Грибовой Наталье \<natasha1972@wplus.spb.ru\>
Тема:	Ответ на письмо от 29.07.08

Привет, Наташа!

Получила твоё письмо, прочитала его, поменяв кодировку, но, к сожалению, не смогла открыть вложенный файл. Компьютер выдал сообщение, что в нём вирус. Но зато мне удалось открыть ссылку на сайт, которую ты прислала. На этом сайте я нашла всю необходимую информацию. Я также подписалась на рассылку и теперь получаю новости каждый день. Это было не сложно: я зарегистрировалась на сайте, ввела логин и пароль, и оставила свой электронный адрес.

Пиши на мой домашний адрес. Жду ответа.

Юля

Date: *Wednesday, August 20, 2008*
From: *Sidorovskaya Yulia <sarabumba@mail.ru>*
To: *Gribovoy Natali <natasha1972@wplus.spb.ru>*
Subject: *Answer to the letter from 07/29/08*

Dear Natasha,

(I) received you letter, (and) read it having changed the encoding, but
unfortunately, couldn't open the attached file. The message popped up
that it had a virus. However, I could open the link that you had sent. I
found all of the necessary information on that site. I also signed up for
the mailing list, and now I get the news every day. It wasn't hard: I
registered on the site, entered my login and password, and typed in (lit.,
left) my e-mail address.

(Please) write to my personal (e-mail) address. Waiting for your reply,

Yulia

SUPPLEMENTAL VOCABULARY

1. PEOPLE

person	человек *(m.)*
people	люди *(pl.)*
man	человек *(m.)*, мужчина *(m.)*
woman	женщина *(f.)*
adult	взрослый *(m.)*
child	ребёнок *(m.)*
children	дети *(pl.)*
boy	мальчик *(m.)*
girl	девочка *(f.)*
teenager	подросток *(m.)*
teenagers	подростки *(pl.)*
tall/short	высокий/низкий
old/young	старый/молодой
fat/thin	толстый/худой
friendly/unfriendly	дружелюбный/недружелюбный
happy, merry/sad	счастливый, весёлый/грустный
beautiful/ugly	красивый, прекрасный/уродливый
sick/healthy	больной/здоровый
strong/weak	сильный/слабый
famous	знаменитый
intelligent	умный
talented	талантливый

2. FAMILY AND RELATIONSHIPS

mother	мать *(f.)*, матери *(gen., sg.)*
father	отец *(m.)*, отца *(gen., sg.)*
son(s)	сын *(m.)*, сыновья *(pl.)*, сыновей *(gen., pl.)*
daughter	дочь *(f.)*, дочери *(gen., sg.)*

sister(s)	сестра *(f.)*, сёстры *(pl.)*, сестёр *(gen., pl.)*
baby (babies)	ребёнок *(m.)*, дети *(pl.)*, младенец *(m.)*, младенца *(gen., sg.)*
brother(s)	брат *(m.)*, братья *(pl.)*, братьев *(gen., pl.)*
husband(s)	муж *(m.)*, мужья *(pl.)*, мужей *(gen., pl.)*
wife (wives)	жена *(f.)*, жёны *(pl.)*
aunt	тётя *(f.)*
uncle	дядя *(m.)*
grandmother	бабушка *(f.)*
grandfather	дедушка *(m.)*
cousin	двоюродный брат *(m.)*, двоюродная сестра *(f.)*
mother-in-law	тёща *(f.)*, свекровь *(f.)*
father-in-law	тесть *(m.)*, свёкор *(m.)*
stepmother	мачеха *(f.)*, приёмная мать
stepfather	отчим *(m.)*, приёмный отец
stepson	пасынок *(m.)*, приёмный сын
stepdaughter	падчерица *(f.)*, приёмная дочь
boyfriend	друг *(m.)*, бойфренд *(coll.)*
girlfriend	подруга *(f.)*, девочка, гёрлфренд *(coll.)*
fiancé(e)	невеста *(f.)*, жених *(m.)*
friend(s)	друг *(m.)*, друзья *(pl.)*, друзей *(gen., pl.)*
relative	родственник *(m.)*
to know	знать
to meet (a person)	встречать—встретить[1]
to love	любить—полюбить

[1]When a verb is translated, both imperfective and perfective forms (in this order) are given.

to marry (someone)	**выходить—выйти замуж за (кого?), жениться** *(imper./perf.)* **на (ком?)**
to divorce (someone)	**разводиться—развестись с (кем?)**
to get a divorce	**получать—получить развод** *(m.)*
to inherit	**унаследовать** *(imper./perf.)*

3. WEATHER

It's raining.	**Идёт дождь.**
It's snowing.	**Идёт снег.**
It's hailing.	**Идёт град.**
It's windy.	**Дует ветер., Ветрено.**
It's hot.	**Жарко.**
It's cold.	**Холодно.**
It's sunny.	**Светит солнце., Солнечно.**
It's cloudy.	**Облачно.**
It's beautiful.	**Чудесно., Прекрасно.**
storm	**шторм** *(m.)* **(на море)**
thunderstorm	**гроза** *(f.)*
wind	**ветер** *(m.)*
sun	**солнце** *(n.)*
thunder	**гром** *(m.)*
lightning	**молния** *(f.)*
hurricane	**ураган** *(m.)*
temperature	**температура** *(f.)*
degree	**градус** *(m.)*
rain	**дождь** *(m.)*
snow	**снег** *(m.)*
cloud	**облако** *(n.)*
fog	**туман** *(m.)*
smog	**смог** *(m.)*
umbrella	**зонт** *(m.)*

4. AROUND TOWN

city (cities), town	город (m.), города (pl.)
village	деревня (f.)
car	машина (f.)
bus	автобус (m.)
train	поезд (m.), поезда (pl.)
taxi	такси (n.)
subway/metro	метро (n., indecl.)
traffic	движение (n.)
building	здание (n.)
apartment building	жилое здание (n.)
library	библиотека (f.)
restaurant	ресторан (m.)
store	магазин (m.)
street	улица (f.)
park	парк (m.)
train station	вокзал (m.), станция (f.)
airport	аэропорт (m.)
airplane	самолет (m.)
intersection	перекрёсток (m.)
lamppost, streetlight	фонарный столб (m.), фонарь (m.)
traffic light	светофор (m.)
bank	банк (m.)
church	церковь (f.), церкви (pl.), церквей (gen., pl.)
temple	храм (m.)
synagogue	синагога (f.)
mosque	мечеть (f.)
sidewalk	тротуар (m.)
bakery	булочная (f.), пекарня (f.)
butcher shop	мясной магазин (m.)

café/coffee shop	кафе *(n.)*, кофейня *(f.)*
drugstore/pharmacy	аптека *(f.)*
supermarket	универсам *(m.)*, супермаркет *(m.)*
market	рынок *(m.)*
at the market	на рынке
shoe store	обувной магазин *(m.)*
clothing store	магазин одежды
electronics store	магазин бытовой техники
bookstore	книжный магазин
department store	универмаг *(m.)*
mayor	мэр *(m.)*
city hall/municipal building	мэрия *(f.)*, городской совет *(m.)*
to buy	покупать—купить
to go shopping	ходить—сходить за покупками
near/far	близко/далеко
urban	городской
suburban	пригородный
rural	сельский

5. AT SCHOOL

school	школа *(f.)*
university	университет *(m.)*
classroom	класс *(m.)*, аудитория *(f.)*
course	курс *(m.)*
teacher (male/female)	учитель *(m.)*, учителя *(pl.)*
professor (male/female)	профессор *(m.)*, профессора *(pl.)*
student (male)	студент *(m.)*
student (female)	студентка *(f.)*
subject	предмет *(m.)*
notebook	тетрадь *(f.)*
textbook	учебник *(m.)*
math	математика *(f.)*

history	**история** *(f.)*
chemistry	**химия** *(f.)*
biology	**биология** *(f.)*
literature	**литература** *(f.)*
language	**язык** *(m.)*
art	**искусство** *(n.)*
music	**музыка** *(f.)*
gym	**физкультура** *(f.)*
recess	**перемена** *(f.)*
test	**письменный экзамен** *(m.)*
grade	**класс** *(m.)*
report card	**дневник** *(m.)*
diploma	**диплом** *(m.)*
degree	**учёная степень** *(f.)*
difficult/easy	**сложно/легко**
to study	**учиться**
to learn	**изучать—изучить**
to pass	**сдавать—сдать**
to fail	**проваливать—провалить (что)**
to fail an exam	**проваливаться—провалиться на экзамене**

6. TRAVEL AND TOURISM

tourist (male)	**турист** *(m.)*
tourist (female)	**туристка** *(f.)*
hotel	**отель** *(m.)*, **гостиница** *(f.)*
youth hostel	**молодёжная гостиница** *(f.)*
reception desk	**регистрация** *(f.)*
to check in	**зарегистрироваться** *(imperf./perf.)*
to check out	**выписываться—выписаться**
reservation	**бронь** *(f.)*, **заказ** *(m.)*
passport	**паспорт** *(m.)*

tour bus	туристический автобус *(m.)*
guided tour	экскурсия *(f.)*
on a guided tour	на экскурсии
camera	фотоаппарат *(m.)*
information center	информационныйцентр *(m.)*
map	карта *(f.)*
brochure	проспект *(m.)*, брошюра *(f.)*
monument	памятник *(m.)*
to go sightseeing	осматривать—осмотреть достопримечательности *(pl.)*
to take a picture	фотографировать—сфотографировать
Can you take our picture?	Вы не могли бы нас сфотографировать?

7. AT HOME

house	дом *(m.)*, дома *(pl.)*
apartment	квартира *(f.)*
room	комната *(f.)*
living room	гостиная *(f.)*
dining room	столовая *(f.)*
kitchen	кухня *(f.)*
bedroom	спальня *(f.)*
bathroom	ванная комната *(f.)*
hall	коридор *(m.)*
closet	шкаф *(m.)*
window	окно *(n.)*
door	дверь *(f.)*
table	стол *(m.)*
chair	стул *(m.)*, стулья *(pl.)*, стульев *(gen., pl.)*
sofa	софа *(f.)*
couch	диван *(m.)*

curtains	занавески *(pl.)*
carpet	ковёр *(m.)*
television	телевидение *(n.)*
TV set	телевизор *(m.)*
CD player	CD проигрыватель *(m.)*, CD (си-ди) плеер *(m.)*
lamp	лампа *(f.)*
DVD player	DVD проигрыватель *(m.)*, DVD (ди-ви-ди) плеер *(m.)*
sound system	музыкальный центр *(m.)*
painting, picture	картина *(f.)*
shelf	полка *(f.)*
stairs	лестница *(f.)*
ceiling	потолок *(m.)*, потолки *(nom., pl.)*
wall	стена *(f.)*
floor	пол *(m.)*
big/small	большой/маленький
new/old	новый/старый
wood	дерево *(n.)*
wooden	деревянный
plastic	пластмасса *(f.)*
made of plastic	пластмассовый

8. IN THE KITCHEN

refrigerator	холодильник *(m.)*
(kitchen) sink	(кухонная) раковина *(f.)*
kitchen	кухня *(f.)*
kitchen table	кухонный стол *(m.)*
kitchen counter	столешница *(f.)*
stove	плита *(f.)*
oven	дуовка *(f.)*
microwave	микроволновая печь *(f.)*, СВЧ (эс-вэ-че) печь

cupboard	буфет *(m.)*
drawer	ящик *(m.)*
plate	тарелка *(f.)*
cup	чашка *(f.)*
bowl	миска *(f.)*
glass	стакан *(f.)*
spoon	ложка *(f.)*
knife	нож *(m.)*
can	консервная банка *(f.)*
box	коробка *(f.)*
bottle	бутылка *(f.)*
carton	коробка *(f.)*, пакет *(m.)*
coffeemaker	кофеварка *(f.)*
teakettle	чайник *(m.)*
blender	миксер *(m.)*
iron	утюг *(m.)*
ironing board	гладильная доска *(f.)*
broom(s)	веник, веники, метла *(f.)*, мётлы *(pl.)*
dishwasher	посудомоечная машина *(f.)*
washing machine	стиральная машина *(f.)*
dryer	сушильная машина *(f.)*
to cook	готовить—приготовить
to do the dishes	мыть—вымыть посуду *(f.)*
to do the laundry	стирать—постирать
dishwashing detergent	моющее средство (порошок [*m.*]) для посудомоечной машины
laundry detergent(s)	стиральный порошок *(m.)*, порошки *(pl.)*, моющее средство *(n.)*
bleach	отбеливатель *(m.)*
clean/dirty	чистый/грязный

9. IN THE BATHROOM

toilet	туалет *(m.)*
sink (washbasin)	раковина *(f.)*
bath tub	ванна *(f.)*
shower	душ *(m.)*
mirror	зеркало *(n.)*
towel	полотенце *(n.)*
toilet paper	туалетная бумага *(f.)*
shampoo	шампунь *(m.)*
soap	мыло *(n.)*
shower gel	гель *(m.)* для душа
shaving cream	крем *(m.)* для бритья
razor	бритва *(f.)*
to wash oneself	мыться—помыться, вымыться
to take a shower	принимать душ
to take a bath	принимать ванну
to shave	бриться—побриться
cologne	одеколон *(m.)*
perfume	духи *(pl.)*
deodorant	дезодорант *(m.)*
bandage	пластырь *(m.)*
powder	пудра *(f.)*

10. FOOD

dinner (early evening meal, supper)	ужин *(m.)*
lunch (early afternoon meal)	обед *(m.)*, ланч *(m.)*
breakfast	завтрак *(m.)*
meat	мясо *(n.)*
chicken	курица *(f.)*
beef	говядина *(f.)*
pork	свинина *(f.)*

fish	рыба *(f.)*
shrimp	креветки *(pl.)*
lobster	омар *(m.)*
bread	хлеб *(m.)*
egg(s)	яйцо *(n.)*, яйца *(pl.)*
cheese	сыр *(m.)*
rice	рис *(m.)*
vegetable	овощ *(m.)*
lettuce	салат-латук *(m.)*
tomato	помидор *(m.)*
carrot	морковь *(f. sg.)*
cucumber(s)	огурец *(m.)*, огурцы *(pl.)*
pepper	перец *(m.)*
fruit	фрукт *(m.)*
apple	яблоко *(n.)*
orange	апельсин *(m.)*
banana	банан *(m.)*
pear(s)	груша *(f.)*, груши *(pl.)*
grapes	виноград *(m. sg.)*
drink(s)	напиток *(m.)*, напитки *(pl.)*
water	вода *(f. sg.)*
milk	молоко *(n. sg.)*
juice	сок *(m.)*
coffee	кофе *(m., indecl.)*
tea	чай *(m.)*
wine	вино *(n.)*
beer	пиво *(n.)*
soft drink, soda	безалкогольный напиток *(m.)*, газировка *(f.)*, газированная вода
salt	соль *(f.)*
sugar	сахар *(m.)*

honey	мёд *(m.)*
hot/cold	**горячий/холодный**
sweet/sour	**сладкий/кислый**

11. THE HUMAN BODY

head	**голова** *(f.)*
face	**лицо** *(n.)*
forehead(s)	**лоб** *(m.)*, **лбы** *(pl.)*
eye(s)	**глаз** *(m.)*, **глаза** *(nom., pl.)*
eyebrow	**бровь** *(f.)*
eyelash	**ресница** *(f.)*
ear(s)	**ухо** *(n.)*, **уши** *(pl.)*
nose	**нос** *(m.)*
mouth(s)	**рот** *(m.)*, **рты** *(pl.)*
tooth	**зуб** *(m.)*
tongue	**язык** *(m.)*
cheek	**щека** *(f.)*
chin(s)	**подбородок** *(m.)*, **подбородки** *(pl.)*
hair	**волосы** *(pl.)*
neck	**шея** *(f.)*
chest	**грудь** *(f.)*
breast	**грудь** *(f.)*
shoulder(s)	**плечо** *(n.)*, **плечи** *(pl.)*
arm	**рука** *(f.)*
elbow(s)	**локоть** *(m.)*, **локти** *(pl.)*
wrist	**запястье** *(n.)*
hand	**рука** *(f.)*
stomach, abdomen	**желудок** *(m.)*, **брюшная полость** *(f. fml.)*, **живот** *(m.)*
leg	**нога** *(f.)*
knee(s)	**колено** *(n.)*, **колени** *(pl.)*
ankle	**щиколотка** *(f.)*

foot	ступня (f.), нога (f.)
finger(s)	палец (m.), пальцы (pl.)
toe	палец на ноге
skin	кожа (f.)
blood	кровь (f.)
brain	мозг (m.)
heart	сердце (n.)
lungs	лёгкие (pl.)
bone	кость (f.)
muscle	мышца (f.)
tendon	сухожилие (n.)

12. COMPUTERS AND THE INTERNET

computer	компьютер (m.)
keyboard	клавиатура (f.)
monitor	монитор (m.)
screen	экран (m.)
printer	принтер (m.)
mouse	мышка (f.)
modem	модем (m.)
memory	память (f.)
CD-ROM	компакт-диск (m.)
CD-ROM drive	дисковод (m.)
file	файл (m.)
document	документ (m.)
cable (DSL)	кабель (m.) DSL (ди-эс-эл), кабель отдельного подключения
internet	интернет (m.)
website	веб сайт (m.)
web page	веб страница (m.)
e-mail	электронная почта (f.)

e-mail message	сообщение *(n.)*
chat room	чат *(m.)*
web log (blog)	блог *(m.)*
attachment	вложенный файл *(m.)*
to send an e-mail	посылать—послать сообщение *(n.)*
to send a file	посылать—послать файл *(m.)*
to forward	пересылать—переслать
to reply	отвечать—ответить
to delete	удалять—удалить
to save a document	сохранять—сохранить документ *(m.)*
to open a file	открывать—открыть файл *(m.)*
to close a file	закрывать—закрыть файл
to attach a file	вкладывать—вложить, присоединять—присоединить файл

13. ENTERTAINMENT

movie, film	фильм *(m.)*, кино *(n., indecl.)*
to go to the movies	ходить—пойти в кино
to see a movie	смотреть—посмотреть фильм *(m.)*
theater	театр *(m.)*
to see a play	посмотрсть спектакль *(m.)*
opera	опера *(f.)*
concert	концерт *(m.)*
at a concert	на концерте
club	клуб *(m.)*
circus	цирк *(m.)*
ticket	билет *(m.)*
museum(s)	музей *(m.)*, музеи *(pl.)*
gallery	галерея *(f.)*

painting	живопись *(f., sg.)*
sculpture	скульптура *(f.)*
television program	телевизионная программа *(f.)*
to watch television	смотреть—посмотреть телевизор *(m.)*
comedy	комедия *(f.)*
documentary	документальный фильм *(m.)*
drama	художественный фильм *(m.)*
book	книга *(f.)*
magazine	журнал *(m.)*
to read a book	читать—прочитать книгу
to read a magazine	читать—прочитать журнал
to listen to music	слушать—послушать музыку
song	песня *(f.)*
band	группа *(f.)*
the news	новости *(pl.)*
talk show	ток-шоу *(n., indecl.)*
to flip channels	переключать—переключить каналы
to have fun	получать—получить удовольствие *(n.)*
to be bored	скучать *(imperf.)*
funny	забавный, смешной
interesting	интересный
exciting	волнующий
scary	страшный
party	вечеринка *(f.)*
restaurant	ресторан *(m.)*, кафе *(n., indecl.)*
to go to a party	ходить—пойти на вечеринку
to have a party	устраивать—устроить вечеринку
to dance	танцевать—потанцевать

14. SPORTS AND RECREATION

soccer	футбол *(m.)*
basketball	баскетбол *(m.)*
baseball	бейсбол *(m.)*
football	американский футбол
hockey	хоккей *(m.)*
tennis	теннис *(m.)*
gymnastics	гимнастика *(f.)*
figure skating	фигурное катание *(n.)*
swimming	плавание *(n.)*
volleyball	волейбол *(m.)*
running	бег *(m.)*
jogging	бег трусцой
game	игра *(f.)*
team	команда *(f.)*
stadium	стадион *(m.)*
coach	тренер *(m.)*
player	игрок *(m.)*
champion	чемпион *(m.)*
ball	мяч *(m.)*
(to go) hiking	ходить в поход
(to go) camping	ходить (в поход) с палаткой
to play (a sport)	заниматься спортом
to play (a game)	играть—сыграть игру
to win	выигрывать—выиграть
to lose	проигрывать—проиграть
to draw/tie	играть—сыграть вничью/ничьюя
cards	карты *(pl.)*
billiards	бильярд *(m.)*
chess	шахматы *(pl.)*
checkers	шашки *(pl.)*

backgammon	**нарды** *(pl.)*
bingo	**лото** *(n., indecl.)*
crossword puzzle	**кроссворд** *(m.)*

15. CLOTHING

shirt	**рубашка** *(f.)*
pants	**брюки** *(pl.),* **штаны** *(pl., coll.)*
jeans	**джинсы** *(pl.)*
T-shirt	**футболка** *(f.)*
shoe(s)	**туфля** *(f.),* **туфли** *(pl.)*
men's shoe(s)	**ботинок** *(m.),* **ботинки** *(pl.)*
boot(s)	**сапог** *(m.),* **сапоги** *(pl.)*
sock(s)	**носок** *(m.),* **носки** *(pl.)*
belt(s)	**ремень** *(m.),* **ремни** *(pl.)*
sneakers	**кроссовки** *(pl.)*
tennis shoes	**теннисные туфли** *(pl.)*
dress	**платье** *(n.)*
skirt	**юбка** *(f.)*
blouse	**блузка** *(f.)*
suit	**костюм** *(m.)*
sweater(s)	**свитер** *(m.),* **свитера** *(pl.)*
hat	**шляпа** *(f.)*
glove(s)	**перчатка** *(f.),* **перчатки** *(pl.)*
scarf	**шарф** *(m.)*
jacket	**пиджак** *(m.)*
coat	**пальто** *(n., indecl.)*
earring(s)	**серьга** *(f.),* **серьги** *(pl.)*
bracelet	**браслет** *(m.)*
necklace(s)	**ожерелье** *(n.),* **ожерелья** *(pl.)*
eyeglasses	**очки** *(pl.)*
sunglasses	**тёмные очки** *(pl.),* **солнцезащитные очки** *(pl.)*

watch	часы *(pl.)*
ring	кольцо *(n.)*
underpants	трусы *(pl.)*
undershirt	майка *(f.)*
bathing trunks	плавки *(pl.)*
bathing suit	купальник *(m.)*
pajamas	пижама *(f.)*
cotton	хлопок *(m.)*
leather	кожа *(f.)*
silk	шелк *(m.)*
size	размер *(m.)*
to wear	носить

16. AT THE OFFICE

office	офис *(m.)*
desk	стол *(m.)*
computer	компьютер *(m.)*
telephone	телефоп *(m.)*
fax machine	факс *(m.)*
bookshelf	книжная полка *(f.)*
file cabinet	ящик *(m.)* для картотеки, картотека *(f.)*
file	папка *(f.)*
boss (male/female)	начальник *(m.)*
colleague (male/female)	коллега *(m.)*
worker (male)	работник *(m.)*
worker (female)	работница *(f.)*
employee (male)	сотрудник *(m.)*
employee (female)	сотрудница *(f.)*
staff	штат *(m.)*
company	фирма *(f.)*, компания *(f.)*
business(es)	дело *(n.)*, дела *(pl.)*, бизнес *(m.)*

factory	фабрика (*f.*), завод (*m.–plant*)
meeting room	комната (*f.*) для совещаний, переговоров
meeting	совещание (*n.*), переговоры (*pl.*)
appointment	приём (*m.*), встреча (*f.*)
salary	зарплата (*f.*)
job	работа (*f.*), профессия (*f.*), задание (*n.*)
busy	занятый
to work	работать
to earn	зарабатывать–заработать

17. JOBS

police officer (male/female)	милиционер (*m.*)
lawyer (male/female)	адвокат (*m.*)
doctor (male/female)	врач (*m.*)
engineer (male/female)	инженер (*m.*)
businessman	бизнесмен (*m.*)
businesswoman	бизнесмен (*m.*), бизнесвумен (*f.*, *less commonly used*)
salesman	продавец (*m.*)
saleswoman	продавец (*m.*), продавщица (*f.*)
teacher (male)	учитель (*m.*)
teacher (female)	учитель (*m.*), учительница (*f.*)
professor (male/female)	профессор (*m.*), профессора (*pl.*)
banker (male/female)	банкир (*m.*)
architect (male/female)	архитектор (*m.*)
veterinarian (male/female)	ветеринар (*m.*)
dentist (male/female)	стоматолог (*m.*), зубной врач (*m.*)
stay-at-home mom	домохозяйка (*f.*)
carpenter (male/female)	плотник (*m.*)
construction worker (male/female)	строитель (*m.*)

taxi driver (male/female)	таксист (m.)
artist (male)	художник (m.)
artist (female)	художник (m.), художница (f.)
writer (male)	писатель (m.)
writer (female)	писатель (m.), писательница (f.)
poet (male)	поэт (m.)
poet (female)	поэт (m.), поэтесса (f.)
plumber (male/female)	водопроводчик, слесарь-сантехник
electrician (male/female)	электрик (m.)
journalist (male)	журналист (m.)
journalist (female)	журналист (m.), журналистка (f.)
actor	актёр (m.)
actress	актриса (f.)
musician (male/female)	музыкант (m.)
farmer (male/female)	фермер (m.)
secretary (male)	секрстарь (m.)
secretary (female)	секретарь (m.), секретарша (f.) (coll.)
assistant (male)	ассистент (m.)
assistant (female)	ассистентка (f.)
unemployed (male)	безработный
unemployed (female)	безработная
retired (male)	пенсионер (m.)
retired (female)	пенсиоперка (f., coll.)
full-time	полная занятость (f.), на ставку
part-time work	почасовая работа (f.)
part-time worker	почасовик (m.)
steady job	постоянная работа (f.)
summer job	работа на лето (f.), летняя работа (f.)

18. NATURE

tree(s)	дерево *(n.)*, деревья *(pl.)*, деревьев *(gen., pl.)*
flower(s)	цветок *(m.)*, цветы *(pl.)*, цветов *(gen., pl.)*
forest(s)	лес *(m.)*, леса *(pl.)*
mountain	гора *(f.)*
field(s)	поле *(n.)*, поля *(pl.)*, полей *(gen., pl.)*
river	река *(f.)*
lake(s)	озеро *(n.)*, озёра *(pl.)*, озёр *(gen., pl.)*
ocean	океан *(m.)*
sea(s)	море *(n.)*, моря *(pl.)*, морей *(gen., pl.)*
beach	пляж *(m.)*
desert	пустыня *(f.)*
rock	скала *(f.)*
stone	камень *(m.)*
sand(s)	песок *(m.)*, пески *(pl.)*
sky (skies)	небо *(n.)*, небеса *(pl.)*
sun	солнце *(n.)*
moon	луна *(f.)*
star	звезда *(f.)*
water	вода *(f.)*
land	земля *(f.)*
plant	растение *(n.)*
hill	гора *(f.)*, холм *(m.)*
pond	пруд *(m.)*

The following is a list of Russian language websites and other informational websites that students of Russian may find interesting and useful.

www.livinglanguage.com	Living Language's site offers online courses, descriptions of supplemental learning material, resources for teachers and librarians, and much more
www.lingvo.ru/lingvo	Lingvo Online, a comprehensive online Russian-English dictionary
www.google.ru	The Russian version of Google
www.rsnet.ru	The official government website of the Russian Federation
www.mos.ru	The official website of the city of Moscow
www.piter.ru	The official website of the city of St. Petersburg
www.vlc.ru	The official website of the city of Vladivostok
www.rian.ru	State-run Russian news agency **РИА Новости**
www.pravda.ru	The Russian newspaper **Правда**

www.onlinenewspapers. com/russia.htm	A comprehensive listing of other Russian language newspapers online
www.1tv.ru	Russian television channel **Первый канал**
www.ruvr.ru	Russian radio station **РГРК «Голос России»,** featuring programs on politics and current events
www.rusradio.ru	Russian radio station **Русское Радио,** featuring popular music and other entertainment programming
www.cia.gov/library/ publications/the-world-factbook/index.html	Basic statistical information on Russia and other Russian-speaking countries

Summary of Russian Grammar

1. THE RUSSIAN ALPHABET

Russian letter	Script		Name
Аа	*А*	*а*	*ah*
Бб	*Б*	*б*	*beh*
Вв	*В*	*в*	*veh*
Гг	*Г*	*г*	*geh*
Дд	*Д*	*д*	*deh*
Ее	*Е*	*е*	*yeh*
Ёё	*Ё*	*ё*	*yoh*
Жж	*Ж*	*ж*	*zheh*
Зз	*З*	*з*	*zeh*
Ии	*И*	*и*	*ee*
Йй	*Й*	*й*	*ee kratkoye*
Кк	*К*	*к*	*kah*
Лл	*Л*	*л*	*ell*
Мм	*М*	*м*	*em*
Нн	*Н*	*н*	*en*
Оо	*О*	*о*	*oh*
Пп	*П*	*п*	*peh*

Rússian letter	Script	Name
Рр	*Р* *р*	err
Сс	*С* *с*	ess
Тт	*Т* *m*	teh
Уу	*У* *у*	ooh
Фф	*Ф* *ф*	eff
Хх	*Х* *х*	khah
Цц	*Ц* *ц*	tseh
Чч	*Ч* *ч*	cheh
Шш	*Ш* *ш*	shah
Щщ	*Щ* *щ*	shchah
ы	*ы* *ы*	ih
ь	*ь* *ь*	soft sign
ъ	*ъ* *ъ*	hard sign
Ээ	*Э* *э*	eh
Юю	*Ю* *ю*	yoo
Яя	*Я* *я*	yah

2. PRONUNCIATION

VOWELS

The letter **a,** when stressed, is pronounced like the English *ah;* when unstressed before a stressed syllable, **a** is pronounced *ah,* but shorter, and in most other positions is given a neuter sound.

The letter **o,** when stressed, is pronounced *oh;* when unstressed in first place before the stressed syllable or used initially, **o** is pronounced *ah,* and in all other positions has a neuter [ə] sound.

The letter **y** is pronounced both stressed and unstressed like the English *ooh.*

The letter **ы** is pronounced somewhat like the *iy* sound in *buoy.*

The letter **э** is pronounced like the *eh* in *echo.*

Five vowels—**e, ё, и, ю,** and **я**—have a glide (the sound similar to the final sound in the English word *may)* in front of them. The function of these vowels is the palatalization of the preceding consonant, to which they lose the above mentioned glide. However, when they follow a vowel or a soft or hard sign, or when they appear in the initial position of a word, they are pronounced as in the alphabet, i.e., with the initial glide.

The letter **и** always palatalizes the preceding consonant and is pronounced like the *ee* in *beet,* except when it follows the letters **ж, ц,** and **ш** (which are never palatalized) or when it follows a preposition ending in a consonant, such as **в;** then it is pronounced like the Russian sound **ы.**

The letter **й** is never stressed. It is pronounced like the final sound in *boy.*

The letter **e** always palatalizes the consonant that precedes it, except when the consonant is **ж, ц,** or **ш.** When stressed, it is pronounced like the *yeh* in *yet;* in unstressed positions it is pronounced like the *e* in *bet.* Initially, it is pronounced with the glide: when stressed, like *yeh;* unstressed, like *yeeh.*

The letter **ё** always palatalizes the preceding consonant, and is always stressed. It is pronounced *yoh* as in *yawn* (spoken with a rounded east coast accent).

The letter **я** always palatalizes the preceding consonant; when stressed, it is pronounced *yah,* and when unstressed, it is pronounced like a shortened *ee.* Initially, it retains its glide; when stressed, it is pronounced *yah,* and when unstressed, *yeeh.*

The letter **ю** always palatalizes the preceding consonant. It is pronounced *ooh* in the body of the word; initially it retains its glide and is pronounced *yooh.*

The letter **ь** is called the soft sign; it palatalizes the preceding consonant, allowing the following vowel to retain its glide.

The letter **ъ** is called the hard sign. It indicates that the preceding consonant remains hard and that the following vowel retains its glide.

Consonants

As in many languages, most Russian consonants may be voiced or voiceless, and form several pairs.

Russian	English	
б в г д ж з	*b v g d zh z*	voiced
п ф к т ш с	*p f k t sh s*	voiceless

When two consonants are pronounced together, they must both be either voiced or voiceless. In Russian, the second one always remains as it is, and the first one changes accordingly.

всё, все, вчера	**в** *(v)* pronounced as *f*
сделать, сдать	**с** *(s)* pronounced as *z*

The preposition **в** (in) is very often pronounced *f*:

В школе is pronounced *f shkoh-leh.*

All consonants—apart from **л, м, н, р, ц, ч,** and **щ**—are voiceless at the end of a word. Nearly all consonants can also be hard or soft (i.e., palatalized or nonpalatalized) when followed by the letter **ё, и, ю, я** or **ь.** The consonants **ж, ц,** and **ш** are always hard; the consonants **ч, щ,** and **й,** are always soft.

One more note on pronunciation: the letter **г,** when appearing in endings between the vowels **е** and **о,** is pronounced *v,* as in the word **ничего.**

3. GENDER

All Russian nouns, pronouns, adjectives, and ordinal numerals, as well as cardinal numerals and even several verb forms have gender: masculine, feminine, or neuter. In the plural, there is only one form for all genders.

	Masculine	Feminine	Neuter	Plural
Noun, pronoun, past tense verb endings	hard consonant, **ь**	**а/я**	**о/е**	**а/я, ы/и**
Adjective, ordinal numeral, participle ending	**ой/ый/ий**	**ая/яя**	**ое/ее**	**ые/ие**

Pronouns, adjectives, and ordinal numerals always agree in gender and number with the nouns they modify or represent.

4. CASES

a. With few exceptions, all nouns, pronouns, and adjectives decline. Each declension has six cases.

Nominative	**Кто? Что?**	*Who? What?*
Genitive	**Кого? Чего?** **От кого? От чего?** **У кого? У чего?** **Без кого? Без чего?**	*Whom? What?* *From whom? From what?* *At or by whom/what?* *Without whom/what?*
Dative	**Кому? Чему?** **К кому? К чему?**	*To whom? To what?* *Toward whom/what?*
Accusative	**Кого? Что?** **Куда?**	*Whom? What?* *Where (direction toward)?*
Instrumental	**Кем? Чем?** **С кем? С чем?**	*By whom? By what?* *With whom? With what?*
Prepositional or Locative	**О ком? О чём?** **В ком? В чём?** **Где?**	*About whom/what?* *In whom? In what?* *Where (location)?*

b. Overall characteristics of the cases and most used prepositions:

1. The nominative case supplies the subject of the sentence.

2. The genitive case is the case of possession and negation. It is also used with many prepositions, the most common of which are:

без	*without*
для	*for*
до	*up to*
из	*out of*
около	*near*
от	*from*
после	*after*
у	*at* or *by*

3. The dative case is used in the meaning of *to whom*. Prepositions governing the dative case are:

к	*to*
по	*along*

4. The accusative is the direct object case. Prepositions used with this case include:

в	*to, into*
за	*behind (direction)*
на	*to, into, on (direction)*

5. The instrumental case indicates the manner of action or instrument with which the action is performed. Prepositions governing the instrumental case include:

между	*between*
перед	*in front of*
над	*over*
под	*under (location)*
за	*behind (location)*

6. The prepositional or locative case indicates location and is also used when speaking about something or someone. The prepositions most frequently used with this case are:

в	*in*
на	*on*
о	*about*
при	*in the presence of*

5. DECLENSION OF NOUNS

Masculine singular			
	Hard		Soft	
	Animate	Inanimate	Animate	Inanimate
	student	*question*	*inhabitant*	*shed*
Nom.	студент	вопрос	житель	сарай
Gen.	студента	вопроса	жителя	сарая
Dat.	студенту	вопросу	жителю	сараю

Masculine singular				
	Hard		Soft	
	Animate	Inanimate	Animate	Inanimate
	student	*question*	*inhabitant*	*shed*
Acc.	студента	вопрос	жителя	сарай
Inst.	студентом	вопросом	жителем	сараем
Prep.	о студенте	о вопросе	о жителе	о сарае

Masculine plural				
Nom.	студенты	вопросы	жители	сараи
Gen.	студентов	вопросов	жителей	сараев
Dat.	студентам	вопросам	жителям	сараям
Acc.	студентов	вопросы	жителей	сараи
Inst.	студентами	вопросами	жителями	сараями
Prep.	о студентах	о вопросах	о жителях	о сараях

NOTE

The accusative case of animate masculine nouns is the same as the genitive, while the accusative of inanimate masculine nouns is the same as the nominative.

Feminine singular			
	Hard	Soft	
	room	*earth*	*family*
Nom.	комната	земля	семья
Gen.	комнаты	земли	семьи
Dat.	комнате	земле	семье
Acc.	комнату	землю	семью
Inst.	комнатой(-ою)[1]	землёй(-ёю)	семьёй(-ёю)
Prep.	о комнате	о земле	о семье

[1] This variant is poetic or dialectal.

Feminine plural			
Nom.	комнаты	земли	семьи
Gen.	комнат	земель	семей
Dat.	комнатам	землям	семьям
Acc.	комнаты	земли	семьи
Inst.	комнатами	землями	семьями
Prep.	о комнатах	о землях	о семьях

Neuter singular			
	Hard	Soft	
	window	*sea*	*wish*
Nom.	окно	море	желание
Gen.	окна	моря	желания
Dat.	окну	морю	желанию
Acc.	окно	море	желание
Inst.	окном	морем	желанием
Prep.	об[2] окне	о море	о желании

[2] б is added to the preposition here for the sake of euphony.

Neuter plural			
Nom.	окна	моря	желания
Gen.	окон	морей	желаний
Dat.	окнам	морям	желаниям
Acc.	окна	моря	желания
Inst.	окнами	морями	желаниями
Prep.	об[3] окнах	о морях	о желаниях

[3] This variant is poetic or dialectal.

A. Some irregular declensions

Singular				
	Masculine	Feminine		Neuter
	road	*mother*	*daughter*	*name*
Nom.	путь	мать	дочь	имя
Gen.	пути	матери	дочери	имени
Dat.	пути	матери	дочери	имени
Acc.	путь	мать	дочь	имя
Inst.	путём	матерью	дочерью	именем
Prep.	о пути	о матери	о дочери	об имени

Plural					
Nom.	пути	матери	дочери	имена	дети
Gen.	путей	матерей	дочерей	имён	детей
Dat.	путям	матерям	дочерям	именам	детям
Acc.	пути	матерей[4]	дочерей	имена	детей[4]
Inst.	путями	матерями	дочерями	именами	детьми
Prep.	о путях	о матерях	о дочерях	об именах	о детях

[4] The accusative plural of animate neuter nouns and most feminine nouns is the same as the genitive plural.

6. DECLENSION OF ADJECTIVES

	Singular					
	Masc.	Fem.	Neut.	Masc.	Fem.	Neut.
	ый	ая	ое	ой	ая	ое
Nom.	новый	новая	новое	сухой	сухая	сухое
Gen.	нового	новой	нового	сухого	сухой	сухого
Dat.	новому	новой	новому	сухому	сухой	сухому
Acc.	same as nom. or gen.	новую	новое	same as nom. or gen.	сухую	сухое
Inst.	новым	новой (-ою)	новым	сухим	сухой (-ою)	сухим
Prep.	о новом	о новой	о новом	о сухом	о сухой	о сухом

	Plural	
Nom.	новые	сухие
Gen.	новых	сухих
Dat.	новым	сухим
Acc.	same as nom. or gen.	same as nom. or gen.

Plural		
Inst.	новыми	сухими
Prep.	о новых	о сухих

	Singular			Plural
	Masc.	Fem.	Neut.	
Nom.	синий	синяя	синее	синие
Gen.	синего	синей	синего	синих
Dat.	синему	синей	синему	синим
Acc.	same as nom. or gen.	синюю	синее	same as nom. or gen.
Inst.	синим	синей(-ею)	синим	синими
Prep.	о синем	о синей	о синем	о синих

7. DECLENSION OF PRONOUNS

	Singular				
	1st person	2nd person	3rd person		
			Masc.	Neut.	Fem.
Nom.	я	ты	он	оно	она
Gen.	меня	тебя	его	его	её

Singular					
	1st person	2nd person	3rd person		
			Masc.	Neut.	Fem.
Dat.	мне	тебе	ему	ему	ей
Acc.	меня	тебя	его	его	её
Inst.	мной (-ою)	тобой (-ою)	им	им	ей (ею)
Prep.	обо мне	о тебе	о нём	о нём	о ней

Plural			Reflexive
	1st person	2nd person	3rd person	Reflexive pronoun *(sing. or pl.)*
Nom.	мы	вы	они	—
Gen.	нас	вас	их	себя
Dat.	нам	вам	им	себе
Acc.	нас	вас	их	себя
Inst.	нами	вами	ими	собой (-ою)
Prep.	о нас	о вас	о них	о себе

My	Singular			Plural
	Masc.	Fem.	Neut.	All genders
Nom.	мой	моя	моё	мои
Gen.	моего	моей	моего	моих
Dat.	моему	моей	моему	моим
Acc.	same as nom. or gen.	мой	моё	same as nom. or gen.
Inst.	моим	моей(-ею)	моим	моими
Prep.	о моём	о моей	о моём	о моих

Твой *(sing., your),* **свой** *(one's own, their own)* are declined in the same way.

For the third-person possessive, the genitive case of the personal pronouns is used. It always agrees with the gender and number of the possessor.

Nominative	Genitive	English
он	его	*his*
она	её	*her*
оно	его	*its*
они	их	*their*

Our		Singular		Plural
	Masc.	Fem.	Neut.	All genders
Nom.	наш	наша	наше	наши
Gen.	нашего	нашей	нашего	наших
Dat.	нашему	нашей	нашему	нашим
Acc.	same as nom. or or gen.	нашу	наше	same as nom. or gen.
Inst.	нашим	нашей (-ею)	нашим	нашими
Prep.	о нашем	о нашей	о нашем	о наших

Ваш *(pl. or polite, your)* is declined in the same way.

All		Singular		Plural
	Masc.	Fem.	Neut.	All genders
Nom.	весь	вся	всё	все
Gen.	всего	всей	всего	всех
Dat.	всему	всей	всему	всем
Acc.	same as nom. or gen.	всю	всё	same as nom. or gen.

All	Singular			Plural
	Masc.	Fem.	Neut.	All genders
Inst.	всем	всей(-ею)	всем	всеми
Prep.	обо всём	обо всей	обо всём	обо всех

This/these	Singular			Plural
	Masc.	Fem.	Neut.	All genders
Nom.	этот	эта	это	эти
Gen.	этого	этой	этого	этих
Dat.	этому	этой	этому	этим
Acc.	same as nom. or gen.	эту	это	same as nom. or gen.
Inst.	этим	этой	этим	эт-ими
Prep.	об этом	об этой	об этом	об этих

That/ those	Singular			Plural
	Masc.	Fem.	Neut.	All genders
Nom.	тот	та	то	те
Gen.	того	той	того	тех

That/those	Singular			Plural
	Masc.	Fem.	Neut.	All genders
Dat.	тому	той	тому	тем
Acc.	same as nom. or gen.	ту	то	same as nom. or gen.
Inst.	тем	той	тем	теми
Prep.	о том	о той	о том	о тех

Oneself/themselves	Singular			Plural
	Masc.	Fem.	Neut.	All genders
Nom.	сам	сама	само	сами
Gen.	самого	самой	самого	самих
Dat.	самому	самой	самому	самим
Acc.	same as nom. or gen.	саму	само	same as nom. or gen.
Inst.	самим	самой	самим	самими
Prep.	о самом	о самой	о самом	о самих

Whose	Singular			Plural
	Masc.	Fem.	Neut.	All genders
Nom.	чей	чья	чьё	чьи
Gen.	чьего	чьей	чьего	чьих
Dat.	чьему	чьей	чьему	чьим
Acc.	same as nom. or gen.	чью	чьё	same as nom. or gen.
Inst.	чьим	чьей	чьим	чьими
Prep.	о чьём	о чьей	о чьём	о чьих

8. COMPARATIVE OF ADJECTIVES

To form the comparative of an adjective, drop the gender ending and add **-ee** for all genders and the plural. The adjective does not decline in the comparative.

красивый	*pretty*
красивее	*prettier*
тёплый	*warm*
теплее	*warmer*
весёлый	*merry*
веселее	*merrier*

Irregular comparative forms:

хороший	*good*
лучше	*better*
большой	*big*
больше	*bigger*
маленький	*small*
меньше	*smaller*
широкий	*wide*
шире	*wider*
узкий	*narrow*
уже	*narrower*
плохой	*bad*
хуже	*worse*
высокий	*tall*
выше	*taller*
тихий	*quiet*
тише	*quieter*
дорогой	*dear, expensive*
дороже	*dearer, more expensive*
простой	*simple*
проще	*simpler*

толстый	*fat*
толще	*fatter*

9. SUPERLATIVE OF ADJECTIVES

The superlative of adjectives has two forms. The simpler form—the one we will discuss here—makes use of the word **самый, самая, самое, самые** *(the most)*.

самый большой	*the biggest*
самая красивая	*the prettiest*
самый умный	*the most clever*

The word **самый** declines with the adjective:

в самом большом доме
in the largest house

Он пришёл с самой красивой женщиной.
He came with the prettiest woman.

10. CASES USED WITH THE CARDINAL NUMERALS ОДИН *(M.)*, ОДНА *(F.)*, ОДНО *(N.)*, ОДНИ *(PL.)* AND ДВА *(M.)*, ДВЕ *(F.)*, ДВА *(N.)*.

A. When the number is used in the nominative (or, in a few instances, the accusative) case:

after **один, одна, одно**—use the nominative singular;

after **одни**—use the nominative plural;

after **два, две, три, четыре** (in the nominative/accusative)—use the genitive singular;

after **пять, шесть, семь,** etc. (in the nominative/accusative)—use the genitive plural.

B. When the number is compound, the case of the noun depends on the last digit:

двадцать один карандаш *(nominative singular)*
twenty-one pencils

двадцать два карандаша *(genitive singular)*
twenty-two pencils

двадцать пять карандашей *(genitive plural)*
twenty-five pencils

11. DECLENSION OF CARDINAL NUMERALS
All cardinal numerals decline, agreeing in case with the noun they modify (with the exception of the nominative and the accusative cases, discussed above).

Я остался без одной копейки. *(genitive singular)*
I was left without one kopeck.

Он был там один месяц без двух дней. *(genitive plural)*
He was there one month less two days.

Мы пришли к пяти часам. *(dative plural)*
We arrived about five o'clock.

Они говорят о семи книгах. *(prepositional plural)*
They are talking about seven books.

Declension of numerals

One/only	Singular			Plural
	Masc.	Fem.	Neut.	All genders
Nom.	один	одна	одно	одни
Gen.	одного	одной	одного	одних
Dat.	одному	одной	одному	одним
Acc.	same as nom. or gen.	одну	одно	same as nom. or gen.
Inst.	одним	одной(-ою)	одним	одними
Prep.	об одном	об одной	об одном	об одних

	two	three	four	five
Nom.	два/две	три	четыре	пять
Gen.	двух	трёх	четырёх	пяти
Dat.	двум	трём	четырём	пяти
Acc.	same as nom. or gen.	same as nom. or gen.	same as nom. or gen.	пять
Inst.	двумя	тремя	четырьмя	пятью
Prep.	о двух	о трёх	о четырёх	о пяти

NOTE:
All numbers from 6 to 20 follow the same declension pattern as 5.

12. ORDINAL NUMERALS

All ordinal numerals are like adjectives, and decline in the same way as adjectives.

Masc.	Fem.	Neut.	Plural (all genders)
первый	первая	первое	первые
второй	вторая	второе	вторые

When they are compound, only the last digit changes its form, and only that digit is declined.

двадцатый век	*twentieth century*
Это было тридцать первого декабря.	*That was on December 31.*
третий раз	*third time*
Вторая мировая война закончилась в тысяча девятьсот сорок пятом году.	*World War II ended in 1945 (lit., one thousand, nine hundred, forty-fifth year).*
в пятом году *(prep., sing.)* or пятый год	*in the fifth year*

13. DOUBLE NEGATIVES

With words such as:

ничего	nothing
никто	nobody
никогда	never
никуда	nowhere

a second negative must be used:

Я ничего	не	хочу, знаю.
I nothing	*not (don't)*	*want, know.*
Никто	**не**	**видит, говорит.**
Nobody	*not (don't)*	*see, speak.*
Он никогда	**не**	**был в Москве.**
He never	*not (don't)*	*was in Moscow.*
Мы никогда	**не**	**говорим порусски.**
We never	*not (don't)*	*speak Russian.*

A negative adverb or pronoun must use a negative with the verb it modifies.

14. VERBS

Russian verbs are either regular or irregular. Regular verbs fall into two primary categories: Conjugation I and Conjugation II. There are three types of verbal stems that belong to Conjugation II: e-verbs (e.g., видеть), и-verbs (e.g., говорить), and a_2-verbs with preceding hushers (e.g., слышать). All other Russian stems are Conjugation I (работать, жить). There are also several irregular verbs (есть, хотеть). Russian verbs are also classed as either perfective or imperfective.

A. Typical conjugations of imperfective verbs

Conjugation I
читать *(to read)*

Present	
я читаю	мы читаем
ты читаешь	вы читаете
он читает	они читают

Past
читал *(m.)*, читала *(f.)*, читало *(n.)*, читали *(pl.)*

Future	
я буду читать	мы будем читать
ты будешь читать	вы будете читать
он будет читать	они будут читать

Conditional
читал бы, читала бы, читало бы, читали бы

Imperative
читай, читайте

Participles

Active	
Present	**читающий**
Past	**читавший**

Passive	
Present	**читаемый**

Present gerund	**читая**

Conjugation II
говорить *(to speak)*

Present	
я говорю	**мы говорим**
ты говоришь	**вы говорите**
он говорит	**они говорят**

Past
говорил *(m.)*, **говорила** *(f.)*, **говорило** *(n.)*, **говорили** *(pl.)*

Future

я буду говорить	мы будем говорить
ты будешь говорить	вы будете говорить
он будет говорить	они будут говорить

Conditional

говорил бы, говорила бы, говорило бы, говорили бы

Imperative

говори, говорите

Participles

Active

Present	говорящий
Past	говоривший

Present gerund	говоря

B. Mixed conjugation

Present tense
хотеть *(to want)*

я хочу	мы хотим
ты хочешь	вы хотите
он хочет	они хотят

NOTE:

This verb in the singular has first conjugation endings with the **т** changing to **ч**. In the plural it has second conjugation endings. The past tense is regular.

C. REFLEXIVE VERBS

Verbs ending with **-ся** or **-сь** are reflexive (**-ся** usually follows a consonant, and **-сь** a vowel). These verbs follow the general form of conjugation, retaining the endings **-ся** after consonants and **-сь** after vowels.

заниматься *(to study)*

я занимаюсь	мы занимаемся
ты занимаешься	вы занимаетесь
он занимается	они занимаются

D. THE VERB быть *(to be)*

The verb **быть** *(to be)* is usually omitted in the present tense, but is used in the past tense:

был *(m.)*
была *(f.)*
было *(n.)*
были *(pl.)*

and in the future tense:

я буду	мы будем
ты будешь	вы будете
он будет	они будут

It is also used as an auxiliary verb in the imperfective future.

E. Conjugation of some stem mutating verbs in the present tense

вести *(to lead)* (д-type)

я веду	мы ведём
ты ведёшь	вы ведёте
он ведёт	они ведут

жить *(to live)* (в-type)

я живу	мы живём
ты живёшь	вы живёте
он живёт	они живут

звать *(to call)* (non-syllabic а-type)

я зову	мы зовём
ты зовёшь	вы зовёте
он зовёт	они зовут

нести *(to carry)* (с-type)

я несу	мы несём
ты несёшь	вы несёте
он несёт	они несут

F. Conjugations of some irregular verbs in the present tense

брать *(to take)*

я беру	мы берём
ты берёшь	вы берёте
он берёт	они берут

давать *(to give)*

я даю	мы даём
ты даёшь	вы даёте
он даёт	они дают

есть *(to eat)*

я ем	мы едим
ты ешь	вы едите
он ест	они едят

G. Conjugations of irregular perfective verbs (perfective future)

дать *(to give)*

я дам	мы дадим
ты дашь	вы дадите
он даст	они дадут

H. Perfective and imperfective aspects of a verb

Russian verbs can be perfective or imperfective. Imperfective verbs express continuous or repeated and non-consequential actions. They have three tenses: past, present, and future. Perfective verbs indicate completion of action, beginning of action, or both, and have only two tenses: past and future.

Some perfective verbs are formed by adding the prefixes **с-, на-, вы-, в-, по-,** etc. to imperfective verbs. When a prefix is added to a verb, not only is the perfective formed, but very often the meaning of the verb is changed at the same time.

Imperfective	Perfective
писать *(to write)*	**написать** *(to write down, to finish writing)*
	переписать *(to copy)*

When the meaning of the verb changes, the new verb **переписать** *(to copy)* that has been formed must have its own imperfective. To form the imperfective of such new forms, the suffixes **-ыв-, -ив,** or **-ав** are added.

Imperfective	Perfective	Imperfective
писать *(to write)*	**переписать** *(to copy)*	**переписывать**
читать *(to read)*	**прочитать** *(to finish reading or to read through)*	**прочитывать**
	перечитать *(to read over)*	**перечитывать**

Imperfective	Perfective	Imperfective
знать (to know)	**узнать** (to find out or to recognize)	**узнавать**
давать (to give)	**дать** **отдать** (to give out or away) **передать** (to pass) **задать** (to assign) **сдать** (to deal cards)	**отдавать** **передавать** **задавать** **сдавать**

Some perfective verbs have different roots.

Imperfective	Perfective	Imperfective
говорить (to speak)	**заговорить** (to begin talking)	**заговаривать**
сказать (to tell)	**рассказать** (to tell a story) **заказать** (to order something to be made or done) **приказать** (to order, to command)	**рассказывать** **заказывать** **приказывать**

Prefixes can be added to either **говорить** or **сказать,** and each addition makes a new verb, e.g.:

за-говорить	to begin talking
за-казать	to order something
от-говорить (от-говаривать)	to talk someone out of something
рассказать	to tell a story

The past tense of the perfective verb is formed in the same way as the past tense of the imperfective verb.

I. Future tense

The future tense has two forms: imperfective future and perfective future. As it has already been pointed out, the imperfective future is formed by using the auxiliary verb **быть** with the infinitive of the imperfective verb.

я буду		*I will*	
ты будешь		*you will*	
он будет	**говорить, читать, понимать,** etc.	*he will*	*speak, read, understand, etc.*
мы будем		*we will*	
вы будете		*you will*	
они будут		*they will*	

The perfective future is formed without the use of the auxiliary verb **быть.**

Present		Perfective future	
я пишу	*I write*	**я напишу**	*I will write*
ты говоришь	*you speak*	**ты скажешь**	*you will say*
он идёт	*he goes*	**он придёт**	*he will come*

Present		Perfective future	
мы читаем	*we read*	**мы прочитаем**	*we will read (it)*
вы смотрите	*you look*	**вы посмотрите**	*you will look*
они едут	*they go (by vehicle)*	**они приедут**	*they will come (by vehicle)*

Note
The perfective verb is conjugated in the same way as the imperfective verb.

J. Verbs of motion
Verbs of motion have many variations of meaning. A different verb is used to express movement by a conveyance than the one used to express movement by foot.

Each of these verbs (i.e., indicating movement by foot or movement by conveyance) has two forms: one describes a single action in one direction, and the other, a repeated action. All of these forms are imperfective. The perfective is formed by adding a prefix to a single action verb. But bear in mind that the addition of the prefix changes the meaning of the verb. The same prefix added to the repeated action verb forms the imperfective of a new verb.

Imper-fective	Repeated action		Single action	Perfective
	ходить	to go on foot	идти	
	ездить	to go by vehicle	ехать	
выходить		to go out on foot		выйти
выезжать		to go out by vehicle		выехать
приходить		to come on foot/arrive		прийти
приезжать		to come by vehicle/arrive		приехать
заходить		to drop in/visit on foot		зайти
заезжать		to drop in/visit by vehicle		заехать
	носить	to carry on foot	нести	
	возить	to carry by vehicle	везти	
приносить		to bring on foot		принести
привозить		to bring by vehicle		привезти

идти *(to go on foot)*

(single action in one direction)

Present tense	Past tense
я иду	шёл *(m.)*
ты идёшь	шла *(f.)*
он идёт	шло *(n.)*
мы идём	шли *(pl.)*
вы идёте	
они идут	

ходить *(to go on foot)*

(repeated action)

Present tense	Past tense
я хожу	regular
ты ходишь	
он ходит	
мы ходим	
вы ходите	
они ходят	

ехать *(to go by vehicle)*

(single action in one direction)

Present tense	Past tense
я еду	regular
ты едешь	
он едет	
мы едем	
вы едете	
они едут	

ездить *(to go by vehicle)*

(repeated action)

Present tense	Past tense
я езжу	regular
ты ездишь	
он ездит	
мы ездим	
вы ездите	
они ездят	

нести *(to carry on foot)*

(single action in one direction)

Present tense	Past tense
я несу	нёс *(m.)*
ты несёшь	несла *(f.)*
он несёт	несло *(n.)*
мы несём	несли *(pl.)*
вы несёте	
они несут	

носить *(to carry on foot)*

(repeated action)

Present tense	Past tense
я ношу	regular
ты носишь	
он носит	
мы носим	
вы носите	
они носят	

везти *(to carry by vehicle)*

(single action in one direction)

Present tense	Past tense
я везу	вёз *(m.)*
ты везёшь	всзла *(f.)*
он везёт	везло *(n.)*
мы везём	везли *(pl.)*
вы везёте	
они везут	

возить *(to carry by vehicle)*

(repeated action)

Present tense	Past tense
я вожу	regular
ты возишь	
он возит	
мы возим	
вы возите	
они возят	

K. Subjunctive and conditional moods

The subjunctive and conditional in many languages constitute one of the most difficult grammatical constructions. However, in Russian they are the easiest. To form the subjunctive or conditional, the past tense of the verb is used together with the particle **бы**.

если бы	*if*
если бы я знал	*if I knew, if I had known*
я пошёл бы	*I would have gone, I would go*
Я позвонил бы, если бы у меня был ваш номер.	*I would have called you, if I had your telephone number.*

L. Imperatives

To form the Russian imperative:

1. Conjugate the verb in the present. If you can hear the sound /й/ (not see the letter!) in the conjugation, stop right there—you'll have your imperative.

Present stem	Imperative
чита[й-у]	**читай(те)**
организу[й-у]	**организуй(те)**
боле[й-у]	**болей**

2. If there's no /й/, then go the 1st person singular and see if the ending is stressed. If it is, replace this ending with the stressed **-и**. This is your imperative.

First person	Imperative
говорю́	**говори́(те)**
пишу́	**пиши́(те)**
иду́	**иди́те**

3. If the 1st person singular form doesn't have end stress, truncate the verb by replacing the unstressed ending with the soft sign. This is your imperative.

First person	Imperative
бу́ду	**будь(те)**
ста́ну	**стань(те)**
отве́чу	**отве́ть(те)**

4. If the 1st person singular ending is unstressed but there's a cluster of two consonants, you can't truncate it. So you add the unstressed **-и**.

First person	Imperative
по́мню	**по́мни(те)**
зако́нчу	**зако́нчи(те)**

5. Some imperatives are slightly irregular.

First person	Imperative
бью (би-у́)	**бе́й(те)**
пью (пи-у́)	**пе́й(те)**

6. Some are completely irregular.

Irregular verb	Imperative
дать	**да́й(те)**
есть	**е́шь(те)**

Note: Remember that imperatives are the seventh member of the present tense paradigm, which means that the mutation rules apply as usual: Conjugation I verbs keep their mutation throughout the paradigm including the imperative form; Conjugation II verbs don't. E.g., **пиши(те)** (I), **режь(те)** (I) v. **ответь(те)** (II), **люби(те)** (II).

When forming imperatives, the reflexive verb retains its ending **-ся** after a consonant or **-й,** and **-сь** after a vowel.

мыться *(to wash oneself)*	**моешься**	**мойся**	**мойтесь**
заниматься *(to study)*	**занимаешься**	**занимайся**	**занимайтесь**

In giving an order indirectly to a third person, the forms **пусть** and **пускай** *(coll.)* are used with the third-person singular.

Пусть он читает.	*Let him read.*	*He should read.*
Пускай она говорит.	*Let her speak.*	*She should speak.*

M. PARTICIPLES AND GERUNDS

Participles and gerunds are very important parts of the Russian language, so it is necessary to know how to recognize them and to understand them. However, it should be made clear that they are not used very often in simple conversation, but rather in literature and scientific writing.

Participles are verb-adjectives; gerunds are verb-adverbs. Participles are adjectives made out of verbs. The difference between an adjective and a participle is that a participle retains the verbal qualities of tense, aspect, and voice. In every other respect they are adjectives. They have three genders: masculine, feminine, and neuter. They decline the same as adjectives and agree with the words they modify in gender, case, and number.

	Present	Past
говорить *(to speak)*	**говорящий, -ая, -ее, -ие**	**говоривший, -ая, -ее, -ие**

Prepositional plural

Мы говорим о говорящих по-английски учениках.

We are talking about students who speak English (lit., speaking English students).

Gerunds are verb-adverbs and as such do not change, but can be imperfective and perfective. The imperfectives are characterized by a simultaneous action in any tense. The perfectives are used when there are two actions, one following the other; when the first action is completed, the second one starts.

Imperfective

читать	**Читая, он улыбался.** *While reading, he was smiling.* (two simultaneous actions)

Perfective

прочитать	**Прочитав газету, он встал и ушёл.** *Having finished reading the paper, he got up and went away.* (one action following the other)